THE CAMBRIDGE COMP

A leading thinker of the European Enlightenment, Voltaire is also a central figure in France's collective cultural memory. The popularity of *Candide* has made him perhaps best known as a writer of tales. Yet these represent only a fraction of his entire œuvre. Voltaire created a style of authorship that made him the most famous writer in Europe and turned his name into a brand for a certain style of writing and thinking. This Companion covers his plays, fiction, pamphlets, correspondence and biblical criticism, as well as his historical, political and philosophical thought, to give a wide-ranging view of his writings. The most comprehensive book on Voltaire available in English, it makes accessible the most recent research in France as well as the English-speaking world, in a series of original essays and a guide to sources for further study. The essays demonstrate why Voltaire remains an essential point of reference in defining the modern intellectual today.

NICHOLAS CRONK is Professor of French Literature and Director of the Voltaire Foundation in the University of Oxford.

THE CAMBRIDGE
COMPANION TO
VOLTAIRE

EDITED BY
NICHOLAS CRONK
Voltaire Foundation and St Edmund Hall, Oxford

CAMBRIDGE
UNIVERSITY PRESS

CAMBRIDGE UNIVERSITY PRESS
Cambridge, New York, Melbourne, Madrid, Cape Town, Singapore, São Paulo, Delhi

Cambridge University Press
The Edinburgh Building, Cambridge CB2 8RU, UK

Published in the United States of America by Cambridge University Press, New York

www.cambridge.org
Information on this title: www.cambridge.org/9780521614955

© Cambridge University Press 2009

First published 2009

Printed in the United Kingdom at the University Press, Cambridge

A catalogue record for this publication is available from the British Library

Library of Congress Cataloguing in Publication data
The Cambridge companion to Voltaire / [edited by] Nicholas Cronk.
p. cm.
Includes bibliographical references and index.
ISBN 978-0-521-84973-9 (hardback)
ISBN 978-0-521-61495-5 (pbk.)
1. Voltaire, 1694-1778–Criticism and interpretation. I. Cronk, Nicholas. II. Title.
PQ2122.C36 2008
848'.509–dc22   2008031153

ISBN 978-0-521-84973-9 hardback
ISBN 978-0-521-61495-5 paperback

CONTENTS

CONTENTS

ILLUSTRATIONS

CONTRIBUTORS

DAVID BEESON, Strasbourg

MIGUEL BENÍTEZ, University of Seville

DANIEL BREWER, University of Minnesota

NICHOLAS CRONK, University of Oxford

OLIVIER FERRET, University of Lyon 2

GRAHAM GARGETT, University of Ulster (Coleraine)

RUSSELL GOULBOURNE, University of Leeds

GIANNI IOTTI, University of Pisa

JOHN LEIGH, University of Cambridge

CHRISTIANE MERVAUD, University of Rouen

JOHN RENWICK, University of Edinburgh

PHILIP STEWART, Duke University

GEOFFREY TURNOVSKY, University of Washington

CATHERINE VOLPILHAC-AUGER, ENS Lettres et sciences humaines, Lyon

ACKNOWLEDGEMENTS

I wish to thank my friends and colleagues at the Voltaire Foundation, for stimulating my thinking about Voltaire and for much practical help. I am particularly grateful to Russell Goulbourne, who translated two of the essays in this volume; and to Madeline Barber, who read the proofs. For her work on the index, I wish to thank Julia Goddard. And finally, I owe special thanks to Jean-Claude Bonnet for the generous loan of a remarkable photograph.

CHRONOLOGY

1694: Birth of François-Marie Arouet, in or near Paris.

1704–11: Attends Jesuit college of Louis-le-Grand.

1711–15: Studies the law, and writes poetry.

1713: First journey abroad, to The Hague.

1715: Death of Louis XIV. France governed by the regency of the Duc d'Orléans until 1723.

1716: Exiled to Sully-sur-Loire; accused of writing a satire about the Regent.

1717: Imprisoned in the Bastille on account of another satire.

1718: Begins using the name Voltaire, an anagram of 'Arouet l[e] j[eune]' – Arouet the younger – where 'i' and 'j', 'u' and 'v' are interchangeable. His tragedy, *Œdipe*, staged successfully at the Comédie-Française.

1721: Composition of poem best known under the title *Épître à Uranie*, expressing views hostile to Christianity.

1723: Epic poem *La Ligue* published (later revised as *La Henriade*).

1725: Louis XV marries, and Voltaire briefly enjoys favour at court.

1726: After a quarrel with the Chevalier de Rohan-Chabot, he is beaten by the nobleman's servants. His fury causes him to be put in the Bastille. Released after a month, on condition that he leave Paris; he departs for England, arriving in London in May.

1727: English press reports that the 'famous French poet' has been presented to George I. He meets politicians as well as writers, and is in London at the time of Sir Isaac Newton's state funeral. Spends winter months lodging in Maiden Lane, just north of the Strand. In December, publishes a small book in English, *An Essay upon the Civil Wars of France, and also upon the Epick Poetry of the European Nations.*

1728: *March* Publication in London of *La Henriade*, dedicated to Queen Caroline. Leaves England hurriedly in November, and spends winter in Dieppe.

1729: Arrives in Paris, where he will stay until 1733.

1731: Publication of first history, *Histoire de Charles XII.*

1732: His tragedy *Zaïre* enjoys triumphant success.

1733: *Letters Concerning the English Nation* (a translation of an early version of the *Lettres philosophiques*, without the twenty-fifth letter on Pascal) published in London. *Le Temple du goût* appears in France.

1734: *Lettres philosophiques* published in France with a false imprint. The work is condemned by the Parlement de Paris, and Voltaire goes into hiding. He settles at Cirey, home of his mistress and companion Émilie Du Châtelet, a philosopher and scientist in her own right, with whom he will share an intense period of literary and scientific activity.

1735: Allowed to return to Paris, but continues to live mainly at Cirey.

1736: Begins correspondence with Frederick of Prussia (later Frederick II); it will continue until 1778. His poem *Le Mondain* provokes a scandal, and he flees to Holland.

1738: Publication of *Éléments de la philosophie de Newton*; and of the *Discours en vers sur l'homme* (1738–39).

1741: First performance of *Mahomet*, a play about religious fanaticism.

1743: Elected a fellow of the Royal Society in London.

1745: Beginning of love affair with his niece, Marie-Louise Denis, recently widowed. Appointed Royal Historiographer by Louis XV, enjoys another brief period of favour at court.

In celebration of a royal victory, he writes a poem, *La Bataille de Fontenoy*, and an opera libretto, *La Princesse de Navarre*, set to music by Jean-Philippe Rameau.

1746: Elected to the Académie Française (after a failed attempt in 1743, when he lost against Marivaux). Appointed *gentilhomme ordinaire de la chambre*.

1747: *Zadig* (under its first title, *Memnon*) appears, the first publication of a philosophical fiction. Voltaire and Mme Du Châtelet obliged to flee Paris.

1748: Flees to court of Stanislas (Louis XV's father-in-law) in Lunéville, near Nancy.

1749: Death of Mme Du Châtelet. Voltaire returns to Paris.

1750: Shares his home with his widowed niece, Mme Denis, who will remain his mistress and companion for the rest of his life. Accepts Frederick's invitation to join him in Berlin.

1751: Publication of *Le Siècle de Louis XIV*.

1752: Quarrels with Maupertuis, president of the Academy of Berlin, and writes a bitter satire against him, the *Diatribe du docteur Akakia*.

1753: *March* Rift with Frederick deepens, and Voltaire leaves Berlin.

June He and Mme Denis are forcibly detained at Frankfurt, on Frederick's orders. Voltaire settles in Colmar.

1754: Unwelcome at the courts of Paris and Berlin, he looks for a home in the area of Geneva or Lausanne.

1755: Purchases Les Délices at Geneva, his principal home for the next three years (and now the Institut et musée Voltaire). *La Pucelle* appears in a pirated edition.

1756: Publishes *Essai sur les mœurs*, a universal history, and *Poème sur le désastre de Lisbonne*, a philosophical treatment of evil, inspired by the Lisbon earthquake of the previous autumn. D'Alembert visits Les Délices.

1757: Acts as unofficial diplomatic intermediary between France and Prussia after the outbreak of the Seven Years War in 1756.

1758:   Visits the Elector Palatine at Schwetzingen, near Mannheim.

1759:   *January/February Candide* is published.

            February He purchases Ferney, in France, but near Geneva and the border: this will be his home for the rest of his life.

1761:   He constructs a church close to his chateau, with the inscription 'Deo erexit Voltaire' ('Voltaire erected this to God').

1762:   Begins campaign to rehabilitate Jean Calas, a Protestant merchant from Toulouse executed on doubtful evidence for the murder of his son.

1763:   Publication of *Traité sur la tolérance*.

1764:   *Dictionnaire philosophique portatif* is published.

1765:   Calas is rehabilitated.

1766:   The young Chevalier de La Barre is executed in Amiens, for mutilating a crucifix. *Le Philosophe ignorant* is published.

1767:   *L'Ingénu* is published.

1768:   Mme Denis separates from Voltaire for a period of twenty months, returning in 1769. Voltaire takes Easter communion (and again in 1769).

1770:   *Questions sur l'Encyclopédie*, published in nine volumes, until 1772.

1774:   Louis XV dies, and is succeeded by Louis XVI. Publication of *Le Taureau blanc*.

1778:   Returns to Paris in February, for the first time since 1750. His friends visit; he sits for the sculptor Houdon; he attends a meeting of the Académie Française; and is present at the Comédie-Française for a triumphal performance of his tragedy *Irène*. Taken ill, he dies on 30 May. He cannot be buried in consecrated ground, and his body is smuggled out of Paris by night, and interred at Scellières, in Champagne. His library is bought by Catherine II, and is shipped from Ferney to St Petersburg, where it remains today, in the National Library of Russia.

1784–9:   A complete edition of Voltaire's writings published in seventy volumes (the so-called Kehl edition), under the direction of the playwright Pierre de Beaumarchais.

1791:   In July, in a great Revolutionary ceremony, Voltaire's remains are brought back to Paris and placed in the Panthéon. Inscribed on the catafalque are the words: 'He taught us to be free.'

ABBREVIATIONS

D	*Correspondence and Related Documents*, OCV, vols 85–135 [D followed by a number refers to the number of the letter in this edition; these references are incorporated in the text]
EM	*Essai sur les mœurs*, 2 vols, ed. R. Pomeau (Paris: Garnier, 1963)
Letters	*Letters Concerning the English Nation*, ed. N. Cronk (Oxford: Oxford University Press, 1994)
LP	*Lettres philosophiques*, ed. G. Lanson, revised A.-M. Rousseau (Paris: Didier, 1964)
Mél.	*Mélanges*, Pléiade, ed. J. Van den Heuvel (Paris: Gallimard, 1961)
Moland	*Œuvres complètes de Voltaire*, ed. L. Moland (Paris: Garnier, 1877–85)
OCV	*Œuvres complètes de Voltaire* (Oxford: Voltaire Foundation, 1968–)
OH	*Œuvres historiques*, Pléiade, ed. R. Pomeau (Paris: Gallimard, 1957)
RC	*Romans et contes*, Pléiade, ed. F. Deloffre et J. Van den Heuvel (Paris: Gallimard, 1979)
SVEC	*Studies on Voltaire and the Eighteenth Century*
VST	*Voltaire en son temps*, R. Pomeau and others, new edn, 2 vols (Paris: Fayard; Oxford: Voltaire Foundation, 1995)

NICHOLAS CRONK

Introduction

The French seventeenth century is commonly referred to as 'the age of Louis XIV' – indeed it was Voltaire who popularised the expression. But the eighteenth century is rarely described as the age of Louis XV: it is, by common consent, 'the age of Voltaire'. Commenting on this anomaly, in a speech to mark the centenary of Voltaire's death in 1878, Victor Hugo declared that until Voltaire's time, centuries always bore the names of heads of state; but, he went on, 'Voltaire is more than a head of state, he is a head of ideas' ('Voltaire est plus qu'un chef d'états, c'est un chef d'idées').[1] The essays in this volume will explore how one writer came to occupy such a dominant position in his century, and to exercise such continuing influence.

No eighteenth-century writer was depicted more often than Voltaire; and no image of him has greater iconic status than the bust sculpted by Jean-Antoine Houdon (fig. 1). In fact, there is not one bust but a whole assortment of them, in various materials and presentations; the number of surviving portrait busts makes clear that Voltaire was Houdon's best-selling subject.[2] Mme Denis, Voltaire's niece and mistress, even commissioned a full-length version, the large seated statue in marble which now dominates the first-floor foyer of the Comédie-Française. Voltaire's head, wearing no wig, is turned to the right, his eyes in a piercing glance, his lips drawn tightly in a smile. So potent and so omnipresent was this image that writers in the nineteenth century not only debated Voltaire's ideas, they argued about his smile. The Romantic poet Alfred de Musset famously described Voltaire's 'hideous smile'.[3] Joseph de Maistre evidently had the phrase in mind when he spoke of Voltaire's 'ghastly grin' ('rictus épouvantable'), a phrase which Gustave Flaubert quotes when he mocks the received bourgeois wisdom concerning the writer whom he admired: 'Voltaire: Superficial knowledge. Famous for his ghastly grin' ('Science superficielle. Célèbre par son rictus épouvantable').[4] Victor Hugo tried to set the record straight: 'This smile is wisdom. This smile, I repeat, is Voltaire' ('Ce sourire, c'est la sagesse. Ce sourire, je le répète, c'est Voltaire').[5] Despite the ambiguity of its smile, or perhaps because of

Fig. 1 Jean-Antoine Houdon, bust of Voltaire (private collection)

it, Houdon's bust has come to symbolise Voltaire, and indeed 'the age of Voltaire'.

The most immediate reason for Voltaire's dominance of his century is simply that he wrote far more than anyone else. There has been no comprehensive edition of his writings since the 1880s, and the project to publish the first ever full critical edition of his complete works, currently being undertaken by the Voltaire Foundation in Oxford, will result in an edition of some two hundred volumes. Steeped in classical as well as more recent European literature, Voltaire was a master of virtually all literary genres. His writings include poetry in many different styles (epic, mock epic, ode, epistle, satire and much occasional verse), theatre (tragedy, comedy, even opera librettos for the composer Jean-Philippe Rameau), history, short prose works in a variety of forms (tales, dialogues, satires, pamphlets); and for good measure, a scientific treatise. And in addition to all that, he has the most extensive correspondence of any writer of the period. The only genre he did not practise was the sentimental novel – and that he parodies in his satirical fictions. If we know Voltaire as one of the greatest prose writers in the French language, his contemporaries regarded him as the greatest poet of the age. It is worth recalling that his philosophical response to the horrific Lisbon earthquake was first formulated in verse (the *Épître sur le désastre de Lisbonne*) well before it found expression in prose (*Candide*).

The act of writing in so many different genres constituted an insurance policy with posterity. The reputations of some writers come in and out of favour as certain forms or styles are in or out of fashion. If Voltaire has never gone out of fashion, or out of print, that is in part because each generation, each country, each reader, can choose from this vast œuvre what appeals most. In the eighteenth century, Voltaire was widely acclaimed as an epic poet and tragedian, on the basis of works which are now scarcely read or performed. *Zaïre*, the last of Voltaire's tragedies to survive in the repertoire of the Comédie-Française, has not been performed there since 1936. In the twentieth century, Voltaire's reputation was based more squarely on the *Lettres philosophiques* (following Lanson's pioneering edition of 1909) and on the satirical tales, such as *Zadig*, *Candide*, *L'Ingénu*, which we have come to call *contes philosophiques* (a label which Voltaire himself did not use).[6] In the second half of the twentieth century, there was a marked revival of interest in Voltaire as a historian, with paperback editions appearing of such works as *Le Siècle de Louis XIV* and the *Essai sur les mœurs*; and the publication by Theodore Besterman of a fifty-odd-volume edition of Voltaire's correspondence was a landmark, both because it provided much new information about Voltaire's life, and because the correspondence emerged, perhaps for the first time, as a literary masterpiece in its own right. And what of Voltaire in the twenty-first century? There remain texts, some of them important ones, which still await their first ever critical edition (for example, the *Questions sur l'Encyclopédie*), and in years to come, the appearance of new volumes of the Oxford edition will continue to focus attention on texts which have hitherto been ignored or seemed inaccessible.

Modern interest in ideas of the public sphere and public opinion lend a new importance to Voltaire's voluminous production of brochures and pamphlets, long thought ephemeral works, but which now seem to reveal an original and even unexpectedly modern aspect of Voltaire's writing. A successful production in Paris in 2007 of one of his comedies, *L'Écossaise*, suggests that the theatrical repertoire has not yet yielded all its secrets.[7] It is perhaps Voltaire's poetry that seems most intractable to modern taste; yet the appearance of an affordable edition of *La Pucelle* (a very rude mock-burlesque epic about Joan of Arc) might well challenge even that prejudice.

The sheer range and quantity of Voltaire's writing can, paradoxically, do him a disservice. There is the suggestion that Voltaire is a Jack-of-all-trades – clever certainly, but perhaps superficial. And so we fall into the condescension of a Roland Barthes, who in a well-known essay concludes that 'Voltaire was a happy writer, but doubtless the last'.[8] This notion of an innocent thankfully spared the horrors of the twentieth and twenty-first centuries does not do justice to the complexity of the man, or of his writings.

A writer famous for one great work is easier to grasp than a writer who seems bewilderingly active on so many fronts. True, no single one of Voltaire's writings on political theory is as celebrated as Montesquieu's *De l'esprit des lois* or Jean-Jacques Rousseau's *Contrat social*; on the other hand, his voluminous political writings – and activities – had an immediate and practical impact which arguably the works of Montesquieu and Rousseau did not. His fiction might be judged timid alongside experimental works such as Rousseau's *La Nouvelle Héloïse* or Denis Diderot's *Jacques le fataliste*; but on closer inspection, *Candide* emerges as an innovative fiction which in some ways anticipates the technical daring of *Jacques*. Voltaire's polemical writings contain nothing as monumental as the *Encyclopédie* of Diderot and D'Alembert (to which he contributed only a few articles, mainly on literary topics); yet in his late 70s he produced a seven-volume compendious work, the *Questions sur l'Encyclopédie* (1770–2), an instant best-seller which has been unaccountably neglected by critics.

Even if Voltaire's celebrity does not depend on a single great work, *Candide* remains the first point of contact with Voltaire for many readers. This satirical work was a best-seller from the moment it was published in 1759, and so it remains today. Its sheer anarchic absurdity seems to translate into all languages and appeal to all readers (including those who know nothing of the philosophical debate which is supposedly the work's subject): in a happy phrase, Italo Calvino describes the work as 'an essay in velocity'.[9] Perhaps no other book of the eighteenth century has been so often illustrated: Paul Klee wrote in his journal that it was reading *Candide* that inspired him to become an illustrator.[10] A novel of 1958 by the Danish writer Hans Jürgen Lembourn (translated into English as *The Best of All Worlds, or What Voltaire Never Knew*, 1960) resituates Voltaire's work in the modern world; while a French film *Candide* (1960), starring Pierre Brasseur and Louis de Funès, updates the action to the Second World War.[11] Leonard Bernstein's comic operetta *Candide*, premiered in 1956, continues to hold the stage: it is hard to think of another eighteenth-century fiction that would have so successfully survived the translation to film and musical.[12] A production of Bernstein's work scheduled for La Scala, Milan, in 2006 had to be cancelled, amid accusations of censorship, largely on account of a scene in which various war-hungry leaders including Tony Blair and George W. Bush performed a drunken dance dressed only in their ties and underpants: the director Robert Carsen was possibly over-zealous in modernising Voltaire's anti-war satire, but there is no denying the satire's continuing power to shock and offend.

Uniquely among the *philosophes*, Voltaire rapidly emerged as a prominent European, rather than merely French, writer. When in London in the 1720s, he deliberately cultivated his English readership, and he grew to become the most famous living writer in Europe. His *Poème sur le désastre de Lisbonne* was soon read across the continent, translated into all the major European languages; before the century was over there had been three separate translations of the poem into Polish alone. In the late 1750s, the young and confident Edward Gibbon, then 20 or 21 years of age, paid a call on the great man in Lausanne: 'Before I was recalled from Switzerland, I had the satisfaction of seeing the most extraordinary man of the age; a poet, an historian, a philosopher, who has filled thirty quartos, of prose and verse, with his various productions, often excellent, and always entertaining. Need I add the name of Voltaire?'[13]

In the course of the 1760s Voltaire would become even more celebrated, for it was his activities during this period which turned the famous writer into the famous campaigner, so creating the image of the prophet of tolerance which has endured to this day. During this decade Voltaire undertook a number of high-profile campaigns against judicial and ecclesiastical intolerance, most famous among them the Calas affair. Jean Calas, a Protestant merchant in Toulouse, was executed in 1762 for the murder of his son who allegedly had expressed a desire to convert to Catholicism; after a campaign lasting three years, the verdict was quashed and Calas's innocence declared. Voltaire's activities on behalf of the Calas family led to a string of works targeting intolerance, the *Traité sur la tolérance*, the *Dictionnaire philosophique* and many other pamphlets besides. The writer had become a political activist. The character 'Moi' in Diderot's satire *Le Neveu de Rameau* is probably speaking for Diderot when he declares that 'there are certain things

I would give everything I own to have done. *Mahomet* [Voltaire's tragedy dealing with religious intolerance] is a sublime work; but I would rather have rehabilitated the memory of Calas.'[14]

Already in his lifetime the name of Voltaire became synonymous with a set of values: dislike of bigotry and superstition, belief in reason and toleration, and in freedom of speech. The authorities in France had in fact very limited success in censoring what Voltaire wrote, but he liked to portray himself as the victim of censorship. In November 1763, Voltaire wrote from Ferney to David Hume, recently arrived in Paris: 'We are generally speaking, half philosophers as we are half free. We dare neither see truth in its full light; nor unveil openly the little glimpses we discover . . . The abetters of superstition clip our wings and hinder us from soaring.'[15] Voltaire's passionate rhetoric always impresses, even when, as here, he is writing in English.

Voltaire even coined what we would now call a campaign slogan, *Écrasez l'Infâme*, which translates roughly as 'Crush the despicable', where 'l'Infâme' stands for superstition, intolerance or irrational behaviour of any kind. Voltaire has an eye and an ear for the telling phrase. *Candide* has given us several immediately recognisable expressions: 'pour encourager les autres', and, of course, 'il faut cultiver notre jardin'. You don't need to be French to recognise 'If God had not existed, it would have been necessary to invent him'; though the original French, 'Si Dieu n'existait pas, il faudrait l'inventer', is all the more memorable for being cast in the form of an alexandrine (the twelve-syllable line of high verse): Voltaire knew that he was on to a winner when he first used the line in a poem of 1769, and thereafter he was ingenious in finding ways to repeat it at every opportunity.[16] When we say that God is (not) on the side of the big battalions, we may not even know we are quoting Voltaire, but we are.[17]

This talent for the telling phrase is of course central to Voltaire's achievement, for he always insisted on the need for writing to be effective as well as enjoyable. As he recorded in one of his notebooks, 'A book must be like a sociable man, made for the needs of men' ('Un livre doit être comme un homme sociable, fait pour les besoins des hommes').[18] It is not sufficient simply to please, and Voltaire famously contrasted his own practice with that of Jean-Jacques Rousseau: 'Jean-Jacques writes for writing's sake and I write to act' ('Jean Jacques n'écrit que pour écrire et moy j'écris pour agir', D14117).

If Voltaire's life is remarkable enough, his after-life is extraordinary. He symbolises the Enlightenment's rigorous separation of religion and politics which remains the defining (if increasingly contested) element of modern secular culture.[19] As a focus for a certain set of values, Voltaire has become a cultural icon: his continuing, often conflictual, presence is what Daniel

Brewer calls in this volume 'the Voltaire effect'. In nineteenth-century France, Voltaire defined the political divide: on the 'left', radicals acclaimed the deist Voltaire as an atheist, while on the 'right', Catholics denounced him as the Antichrist. Gustave Flaubert makes the point succinctly in *Madame Bovary*: Emma dies with a Catholic priest to one side of her bed, and the self-proclaimed Voltairean pharmacist Homais to the other. (Neither, of course, is of any use to her: the irony is also Voltairean.) Victor Hugo declared that 'Voltaire's reputation, diminished as a poet, has grown as an apostle' ('Voltaire, diminué comme poète, a monté comme apôtre').[20] As a writer-campaigner, Voltaire stands as the first of a succession of 'engaged' French writers, which includes Victor Hugo himself writing against capital punishment, Émile Zola defending Dreyfus, and Jean-Paul Sartre protesting against the war in Vietnam. Voltaire remains an emblematic figure in French politics: when in early 2007 the French presidential candidate Nicolas Sarkozy came to London to address young French entrepreneurs working in England, he assured them, perhaps to their surprise, that they were following in the footsteps of Voltaire.

Atheists, humanists, Christians, Freemasons have all claimed the great man as one of their own. Voltaire's status as cultural icon places him in the frontline whenever any individual or interest group is in need of a hero – or a fall guy. In an era of identity politics, this leaves him vulnerable to appropriation on all fronts, witness a recent article on ecofeminism and *Candide*.[21] A proposed reading of the tragedy *Mahomet* in Geneva in 2006 led to protests, both from the local Islamic community that their religion was under attack, and from the director who in an open letter in *Le Monde* declared himself the victim of censorship.[22] In 1942, in German-occupied Paris, a disreputable pamphlet acclaimed Voltaire as a patriot on account of his dislike of Jews,[23] and even today the anachronistic claim that he was anti-Semitic resurfaces periodically.[24] Even more extravagantly, Voltaire has been denounced for his alleged complicity in the slave trade, an accusation which has continued to be repeated even though it has long been known to be false.[25] More complex and more interesting is the question of Voltaire's 'anthropology', and his views about race deserve more study. Arguing against his contemporary the Comte de Buffon, Voltaire insists on the irreducible differences between races. True, Candide is moved to tears by the pitiful spectacle of the negro from Surinam; but this is not because he is a slave, it is because he has been harshly treated by his master.[26] This eighteenth-century humanitarian is no twenty-first-century liberal.

Given his European reputation, Voltaire has been a point of cultural reference outside France as much as within. When the English satirist James Gillray chose to depict the infant Jacobinism (revolutionary democracy) receiving his education at the knee of Voltaire, he naturally imagined the French philosopher in the form of Houdon's seated figure (fig. 2). William Blake's early poem 'Mock on, mock on, Voltaire, Rousseau' (c.1804) expresses forcefully the Romantic-cum-Christian rejection of what he perceived as narrow Enlightenment rationalism:

> Mock on, mock on, Voltaire, Rousseau!
> Mock on, mock on – 'Tis all in vain!
> You throw the sand against the wind,
> And the wind blows it back again.
>
> And every sand becomes a gem
> Reflected in the beams divine;
> Blown back they blind the mocking eye,
> But still in Israel's paths they shine.
>
> The atoms of Democritus
> And Newton's particles of light
> Are sands upon the Red Sea shore,
> Where Israel's tents do shine so bright.[27]

Predictably, an anonymous poet replied on Voltaire's behalf:

> Hope on, hope on, Boswell and Blake
> Hope on and pray: 'tis all in vain.
> You think perhaps the dust that blows
> Will someday come to life again?

In the twentieth century, there was perhaps less concern with Voltaire as an antagonist (or not) of the Catholic Church, and more interest in him as the emblem of reason, in an age which seemed ever less confident of its Enlightenment inheritance. The 1933 Warner Bros film *Voltaire*, starring George Arliss in the lead role and directed by John Adolphi, opens with a title announcing that Voltaire 'attacked intolerance and injustice' and 'educated the masses to think and act'. The crafty Voltaire skirmishes with the king, but when the crowds gather to cheer the author, the king orders his writings to be burned. Warned by Voltaire that revolution will come, the king tells him: 'Make us laugh – give us your wit, but keep your wisdom.' With Europe on the brink of war, the poet W. H. Auden evoked the patriarch of Ferney as an emblem for the writer's fight against persecution and stupidity. His poem 'Voltaire at Ferney' is dated February 1939:

> Yet, like a sentinel, he could not sleep. The night was full of wrong,
> Earthquakes and executions. Soon he would be dead,

Fig. 2 James Gillray, *Voltaire Instructing the Infant Jacobinism*, oil on paper, c.1798
(New York Public Library)

And still all over Europe stood the horrible nurses
Itching to boil their children. Only his verses
Perhaps could stop them: He must go on working. Overhead
The uncomplaining stars composed their lucid song.[28]

Perhaps with Auden in mind, the contemporary poet Peter Porter has written a poem probing Voltaire's cultivation of the garden as an exercise in influencing opinion:

> Therefore what I choose to cultivate,
> Like an attendant servant's smile,
> Is the allotment of debate.[29]

An altogether more disturbing image is Salvador Dalí's painting *The Slave Market with Disappearing Bust of Voltaire* (1940). The surreal depiction of the Houdon bust set in a landscape creates an emblematic juxtaposition of reason and unreason – an effect reinforced by a visual trick in which the bust of Voltaire ironically contains within its features two Catholic nuns.[30]

Voltaire's targets – stupidity, war, fanaticism, dogmatism – are perennial, and so we (must) continue to read him. Leonard Bernstein recalled that, when he was creating his operetta *Candide* in the mid-1950s, 'everything that America stood for seemed to be on the verge of being ground under the heel of Senator Joseph McCarthy'. When *Candide* now plays in New York, London or Paris, the audiences probably no longer think of 1950s McCarthyism, but other persecutions, other wars, other acts of bigotry are in their minds. With the recent rise of terrorism, as a fact, and as an object of media attention, hardly a week passes without the appearance in the British press of an article quoting Voltaire's 'I disapprove of what you say, but I will defend to the death your right to say it.'[31] This rallying cry of tolerant multiculturalism is so well known in the English-speaking world that it seems pedantic to point out that the expression was coined by an Englishwoman in 1906.[32] No matter: the idea is Voltairean, and since he omitted to formulate the expression himself, it was necessary to invent it.

Beyond Voltaire's continuing presence in our political consciousness, he remains firmly established in our cultural landscape. Any number of writers have been inspired by him. The heroine of George Bernard Shaw's comedy *Candida* (1895) is clearly named with Voltaire in mind, and Shaw's essays and prefaces are packed with allusions to Voltaire, whose views on established religion he warmly endorsed. His comic parable *The Adventures of the Black Girl in Her Search for God* (1932), banned in the Irish Free State, takes *Candide* as its model – and includes Voltaire in its cast of characters.[33] When Shaw bequeathed his own bust to the Shakespeare Memorial National Theatre, he specified that it should be placed 'in the foyer as the bust of Voltaire by Houdon is placed in the foyer of the Comédie-Française'.[34] Lytton Strachey, a prominent member of the Bloomsbury group, devoted several essays to Voltaire and hung a portrait of him by Jean Huber over his desk, where it dominated his study.[35] More recently, the novelist Leonardo Sciascia has written against oppression and obscurantism in his native Sicily, and Voltaire's crusading rationalism, as well as the form and ironic style of his tales, is all-pervasive in his works. In *Death of an Inquisitor* (*Morte dell'Inquisitore*, 1964), Sciascia quotes in a footnote from Voltaire's article 'Inquisition' in the *Dictionnaire philosophique*, to reinforce a historical point about the Inquisition;[36] while in *Candido* (1977), he uses the form of the Voltairean *conte* to tell the tale of a young boy born in Sicily at the time of the Liberation who makes his way in a world torn between two rival systems of thought, Christianity and Marxism, and ending up dissatisfied with both. In many novels – recently, for example, Denitza Bantcheva's *La Traversée des Alpes* (2006) – Voltaire remains a major reference for both authors and their characters.

Novelists sometimes go further and (re-)create Voltaire as a fictional character: there are at least five instances of this phenomenon in novels published since 2000. The Swedish writer Kjell Espmark wrote in 2000 the tale *Voltaires resa* (*Voltaire's Journey*), imagining a rejuvenated Voltaire arriving unexpectedly in the modern world. The Argentinian writer Pablo de Santis published in 2001 *El calígrafo de Voltaire* (*Voltaire's Calligrapher*), an adventure story with a strong element of the fantastic in which Voltaire employs the young protagonist to enquire into the Calas affair. In *A Visit from Voltaire* (2003), a comic novel by the American novelist Dinah Lee Küng, Voltaire visits and befriends an American mother-of-three living in Switzerland, and, in the tradition of the best self-help books, teaches her how to live a happy and full life. The prolific Russian novelist Vassily Axionov published in 2004 *Volteriani i volteriantsi* (*Voltaireans and Voltairists*), a picaresque tale in which Voltaire and Catherine the Great, who in reality only ever corresponded, finally get to meet. And in 2007, the French novelist Jacques-Pierre Amette published *Un Été chez Voltaire* (*A Summer with Voltaire*), an imaginative recreation of the summer of 1761 at Ferney, Voltaire's residence for the last twenty years of his life, when two Italian actresses came to rehearse one of Voltaire's plays. In diverse languages and cultures, when a writer searches for an emblematic eighteenth-century or enlightened figure, it is the protean Voltaire who comes most readily to mind.

We began with the iconic Houdon bust, the image made grotesque by Gillray in the nineteenth century, and made strange by Dalí in the twentieth. It has always intrigued artists: Cézanne made a drawing after the bust (c.1885), and the sculptor Rodin made a careful study of the copy of the bust in the Louvre:

> What a marvel! It is the personification of malice. The slightly oblique gaze seems to be on the look-out for an adversary. The pointed nose is like a fox's: it seems to be twisted to sniff out abuse and absurdities on all sides; you can see it twitching. And the mouth: what a masterpiece! It is framed by two furrows of

Fig. 3 Trainee teachers at an *école normale*, c.1928 (private collection)

irony. It is chewing over some sarcasm or other. A cunning old gossipy woman, that's the impression given by this Voltaire, so sparky, so sickly, so un-masculine.

(Quelle merveille! . . . C'est la personnification de la malice. Les regards légèrement obliques semblent guetter quelque adversaire. Le nez pointu ressemble à celui d'un renard: il paraît se tirebouchonner pour flairer, de côté et d'autre, les abus et les ridicules; on le voit palpiter. Et la bouche: quel chef-d'œuvre! Elle est encadrée par deux sillons d'ironie. Elle a l'air de mâchonner je ne sais quel sarcasme. Une vieille commère très rusée, voilà l'impression produite par ce Voltaire à la fois si vif, si malingre et si peu masculin.)[37]

What, finally, are we to make of this haunting photograph of two young men engaged in cleaning the Houdon bust of Voltaire (fig. 3)? The setting is an *école normale*, one of the teacher-training colleges established in France in the Third Republic to produce the army of primary school teachers (*instituteurs*) who would take literacy to the masses. The date, almost certainly, is 1928, the 150th anniversary of Voltaire's death, and an event celebrated in this training college with a ceremonial dusting of the great man's bust. It is hard to think of a more potent embodiment of Voltaire's status as secular symbol of Republican France, and more broadly, as an emblem of French civilisation. Every generation seems to feel this same need to bring the Houdon bust down from its pedestal, to dust it off, and to interrogate again that quirky smile.

NOTES

1. V. Hugo, *Œuvres complètes, Politique*, ed. J.-C. Fizaine (Paris: Robert Laffont, 1985), p.989.
2. See H. H. Arnason, *The Sculptures of Houdon* (London: Phaidon, 1975), pp.49–53.
3. 'Do you sleep happy, Voltaire, and does your hideous smile still flutter above your fleshless bones?' ('Dors-tu content, Voltaire, et ton hideux sourire / Voltige-t-il encor[e] sur tes os décharnés?', Alfred de Musset, *Rolla*, 4th part). Compare the remark of the aphorist Joseph Joubert: 'Voltaire a, comme le singe, les mouvements charmants et les traits hideux. On voit toujours en lui, au bout d'une habile main, un laid visage' (*Textes choisis et commentés*, ed. V. Giraud, Paris: Plon, 1914, p.198).
4. G. Flaubert, *Le Dictionnaire des idées reçues*, ed. A. Herschberg Perrot (Paris: Livre de Poche, 1997), pp.126, 225.
5. V. Hugo, *Œuvres complètes, Politique*, p.987.
6. In Voltaire's lifetime, the label 'Romans, contes philosophiques' was used just once, in 1771, in the so-called quarto edition.
7. At the Théâtre Lucernaire, Paris, directed by Vincent Colin (February to April 2007).
8. R. Barthes, 'The Last Happy Writer', in *A Barthes Reader*, ed. S. Sontag (London: Vintage, 1993), pp.150–7 (p.157); the essay was first published ('Le dernier des écrivains heureux') in 1958.
9. I. Calvino, 'Candide: An Essay in Velocity', in *The Literature Machine*, trans. P. Creagh (London: Secker and Warburg, 1987), pp.175–81.
10. Voltaire, *Candide, illustré par Paul Klee* (Paris: Maisonneuve et Larose, 2001), p.10.
11. The film is directed by Norbert Carbonnaux; it is available on DVD (Éditions René Château, EDV 1102, 2004).
12. Recent productions include one directed by John Caird at the National Theatre in London (1999), in which Simon Russell Beale played the role of Voltaire.
13. E. Gibbon, *Memoirs of My Life and Writings*, ed. A. O. J. Cockshut and S. Constantine (Ryburn: Keele University Press, 1994), pp.112–13.

14. D. Diderot, *Rameau's Nephew and First Satire*, trans. M. Mauldon, Oxford World's Classics (Oxford: Oxford University Press, 2006), p.34.

15. N. Cronk, 'Une lettre de Voltaire à David Hume (D11499R)', *Revue Voltaire*, 8 (2008), 369–75 (p.369).

16. See N. Cronk, 'Voltaire autoplagiaire', in *Copier/coller: Écriture et ré-écriture chez Voltaire*, ed. O. Ferret, G. Goggi and C. Volpilhac-Auger (Pisa: Plus, 2007), pp.9–26.

17. See *OCV*, vol.82, pp.547, 647; D16136; and *The Oxford Dictionary of Quotations*, ed. E. Knowles, 6th edn (Oxford: Oxford University Press, 2004), p.816.

18. *OCV*, vol.81, p.351.

19. See M. Lilla, *The Stillborn God: Religion, Politics, and the Modern West* (New York: Knopf, 2007).

20. V. Hugo, *William Shakespeare*, in *Œuvres complètes, Critique*, ed. J.-P. Reynaud (Paris: Robert Laffont, 1985), p.418.

21. H. Feder, 'The Critical Relevance of the Critique of Rationalism: Postmodernism, Ecofeminism, and Voltaire's *Candide*', *Women's Studies*, 31 (2002), 199–219.

22. See H. Loichemol, *De l'horrible danger de la lecture [...], Morbleu! Une fatwa contre Voltaire?* (Montélimar: Voix d'encre, 2006).

23. H. Labroue, *Voltaire antijuif* (Paris, 1942).

24. For an overview of recent discussion of the 'problem' of Voltaire and the Jews, see A. Gurrado, 'Sei ebrei contro un cristiano: il problema Voltaire da Hertzberg a Schwarzbach', *Studi filosofici*, 28 (2005), 35–58.

25. The accusation was first made in a polemical pamphlet of 1877, *Voltaire, ses hontes, ses crimes, ses œuvres et leurs conséquences sociales*; it was signed with a pseudonym, Armel de Kervan.

26. See M. Duchet, 'L'anthropologie de Voltaire', *Anthropologie et histoire au siècle des Lumières* (Paris: François Maspero, 1971), pp.281–321; and J.-M. Moureaux, 'Race et altérité dans l'anthropologie voltairienne', in S. Moussa (ed.), *L'Idée de 'race' dans les sciences humaines et la littérature (XVIIIᵉ–XIXᵉ siècles)* (Paris: L'Harmattan, 2003), pp.41–53.

27. W. Blake, *The Complete Poems*, ed. W. H. Stevenson, 2nd edn (London: Longman, 1989), pp.483–4.

28. W. H. Auden, *The English Auden: Poems, Essays and Dramatic Writings: 1927–1939*, ed. E. Mendelson (London: Faber and Faber, 1977), p.240. Auden was prompted to write this poem after reviewing in *The Nation* two books about Voltaire by Norman Torrey and Alfred Noyes (see *The English Auden*, pp.386–9). The figure of Voltaire later reappears in Auden's 'New Year Letter'.

29. P. Porter, 'Voltaire's Allotment', *Times Literary Supplement*, 9 November 2007.

30. Salvador Dalí Museum, St Petersburg, Florida.

31. For example, Tom Stoppard writing in the March 2006 issue of *Index on Censorship*, and in *The Guardian*, 18 March 2006.

32. The phrase occurs in the context of a discussion of the Parlement's condemnation and the public burning of Claude-Adrien Helvétius's *De l'esprit*: 'The men who had hated it, and had not particularly loved Helvétius, flocked round him now. Voltaire forgave him all injuries, intentional or unintentional. "What a fuss about an omelette!" he had exclaimed when he heard of the burning. How abominably unjust to persecute a man for such an airy trifle as that! "I disapprove of what

you say, but I will defend to the death your right to say it," was his attitude now', S. G. Tallentyre (pseudonym of E. B. Hall), *The Friends of Voltaire* (London: Smith, Elder & Co., 1906), pp.198–9. See also E. Knowles (ed.), *What They Didn't Say: A Book of Misquotations* (Oxford University Press, 2006), p.55.

33. On Bernard Shaw and Voltaire, see M. W. Pharand, *Bernard Shaw and the French* (Gainesville, FL: University Press of Florida, 2000), pp.253–9.

34. Quoted by Pharand, *Bernard Shaw and the French*, p.259.

35. M. Holroyd, *Lytton Strachey* (London: Chatto & Windus, 1994), pp.533–4.

36. L. Sciascia, *Death of an Inquisitor and Other Stories*, trans. Ian Thomson (London: Harvill, 1994), p.23.

37. A. Rodin, *L'Art: Entretiens réunis par Paul Gsell* (Paris: Bernard Grasset, 1912), pp.159–60.

I

GEOFFREY TURNOVSKY

The making of a name: a life of Voltaire

Voltaire's eighteenth-century biographer Théophile Duvernet records an exchange from 1713 when the future *philosophe*, just 19 years old and completing his studies at the prestigious Jesuit Collège Louis-le-Grand in Paris, defies his father's insistence that he find a decent profession: 'I don't want any other than that of man of letters' ('je n'en veux pas d'autre que celui d'homme de lettres').[1] Two key points emerge from this remark.

Firstly, telling the story of the 'life of Voltaire' is, from the earliest years of that phenomenon, as much about describing the self-conscious construction and mythologisation of an intellectual identity as it is about enumerating the objective events that marked his career. One cannot offer so much as the date of his birth in 1694 without having to account for Voltaire's persistent manipulations of the fact in an effort to mould a particular image for himself. Baptismal records indicate 21 November; but the apparently concrete self-evidence of this detail is undercut by Voltaire's own assertions that he had actually been born nine months earlier on 20 February. Lest we let ourselves believe that a letter from later in his life suggesting that he always claimed the earlier date as a measure of self-protection – that is, by seeming older he was more likely to avoid persecution – offers solid insight into the 'true story' of the writer (D16346), it is worth recalling that Voltaire was, throughout his life, deeply invested in presenting himself as old, ailing and persecuted. His correspondence runs rife with references to his faltering health, imminent death and troubles at the hands of those hostile to his cause. In this respect, what had seemed to be a glimpse backstage into the real facts of the life of the *philosophe* turns out, typically, to be yet another scene in the staging of this life.[2]

Secondly, the exchange shows the extent to which Voltaire's entrance into 'literary life' rested on conforming to models of intellectual selfhood that he would have inherited from the seventeenth century. To declare in the early years of the eighteenth century an intention to become a 'man of letters' was in no way to foresee the kind of transcendent figure that Voltaire would later come to symbolise as a 'prototype of the modern intellectual' ('prototype de l'intellectuel moderne').[3] In the mouth of the young bourgeois still known by his given name of François-Marie Arouet, 'homme de lettres' designated a different kind of aspiration, namely that of elevating himself socially by his intellect. That is, Arouet was going to use his keen wit and poetic talent to integrate himself into the milieu of the high aristocracy, not as a professional serving their legal needs as his father wished, but as a bona fide member of their circles. In fact, his verse had already caught the eye of the cultural elites of Paris and Versailles. When he was still a student, a retired soldier came to the priests of Louis-le-Grand seeking help in petitioning the Dauphin for charity. Having won prizes at school for his poetry, Voltaire was entrusted with the task. He wrote a poem that touched the Dauphin, winning him, according to Duvernet, a 'grande célébrité'.[4] The famed writer and courtier Ninon de Lenclos, in her 80s, asked that he be presented to her; she would leave him 1,000 francs in her will, to be spent on books.

Thus, after initially submitting to his father's demands and beginning law school, Voltaire promptly abandoned these studies, and, as a wit and poet, insinuated himself into the leisured society of the aristocracy. He was pointedly self-inclusive when he remarked at a dinner hosted one day by the Prince de Conti, 'we are all of us here either princes or poets' ('nous sommes ici tous princes ou tous poètes').[5] But his wit proved to be a double-edged sword, for if it distinguished him in the relaxed climate of the early years of the Regency, it also all too often drove him across a fine line into impropriety. When he failed to win a contest sponsored by the Académie Française for the best poem celebrating a new choir at the Cathedral of Notre-Dame, he circulated verse ridiculing the winner. While the satire made clear Voltaire's superiority over the aged victor, the Abbé Du Jarry, it also appalled his father who sent his son away from Paris. Voltaire soon returned, but more satires followed. He was again exiled, this time on the orders of the Regent himself, who had become the target of some of this writing. The poet would be pardoned and allowed to return to Paris, but the cycle only continued; and ultimately, in the spring of 1717, Voltaire found himself arrested and locked up in the Bastille.

Voltaire's year-long stay in the state prison was, by all accounts, far from uncomfortable. The literary historian Gustave Lanson even went so far as to suggest that it might have been an honour for the striving man of letters to be treated with such seriousness by the authorities.[6] A police document from the time stating that Voltaire had 'no profession' might well signal his dissipation in these early years. But as recorded in the report of an interrogation, the statement can equally be imagined as the expression by Voltaire himself of a sense of self-made aristocratic pride. He had, after all, refused to adopt a profession. Certainly, he did not seem especially chastened on his release in April 1718, emerging more than ever determined to make a name for himself amongst the elites of the court. Literally indeed, for it was at this point that the writer reinvented himself with the ennobling moniker 'Arouet de Voltaire'. He went on to undertake projects that were astonishing for their audacity. He had been working on a new national epic for France since 1716, writing much of what would become *La Henriade* in prison. And he sought not just success as an author of tragedy, but to outshine both Corneille and Sophocles in choosing as the subject of his first play the classic story of Oedipus. The gamble paid off. First performed on 18 November 1718, *Œdipe* was a triumph, running for forty-five successive performances. The Regent rewarded him with a pension of 1200 livres.

With success, though, came further difficulties. A caustic remark made in the house of a minister earned him his first beating, on the Pont de Sèvres in 1722. And in February 1726 an infamous episode occurred that led not only to the second beating of his literary life, but to a dramatic reconfiguration of his intellectual trajectory. Accounts vary as to what exactly transpired when Voltaire encountered the Chevalier de Rohan-Chabot one evening in Paris, but the underlying conflict is unmistakable. Rohan, of ancient aristocratic stock, asked of the young poet whether his name was 'Arouet' or 'de Voltaire', evidently in an attempt to reveal the presumptuousness of the poet's claim to a place among nobles. Voltaire's actual response has been variously reported; however, in all the versions, it asserted the ascendancy of a new cultural and intellectual elite over a nobility of birth in marked decline.[7] A few days later, Rohan sent his lackeys to lure Voltaire out of the house of the Duc de Sully, where he was dining, and beat him with a cudgel in the street while Rohan watched from a carriage. Infuriated, Voltaire prepared to challenge Rohan to a duel, alarming members of the Chevalier's family who had Voltaire detained once again in the Bastille. He was released in May only when he made clear his intention to leave immediately for England, though he was keen to make known that he was never actually forced to leave the country (D291). This was not exile.

England

The Rohan episode is often seen as a turning point for Voltaire: his eyes were opened to the disdain that aristocrats really felt towards *gens de lettres*, and he could see the illusory nature of his early social ascendancy. He was stunned by the indifference of his elite friends to his humiliation; the Duc de Sully, for instance, politely refused to help Voltaire on the night of the beating, aligning himself with established hierarchy over the rising man of letters. It is, however, possible to discern not only disillusionment in Voltaire, but also a certain exasperation with the limitations of a model of intellectual activity that was so rooted in wit and in the writer's ability to please the privileged in their moments of free time. For if the opening-up of noble society to *belles-lettres* offered tremendous opportunities for educated bourgeois who desired to enhance their social stature, Voltaire discovered that there was, at the same time, nothing in the traditional ideal of the *bel esprit* to articulate the importance of the writer, who as a result remained, in the end, a dominated and expendable figure, even as he was valorised and celebrated in elite circles.

In England, Voltaire found an image of this importance, 'where all the arts are honoured and rewarded' ('où les arts sont tous honorez et récompensez', D299). He specifically esteemed the official positions that he saw conferred on writers. In the twenty-third of his *Letters Concerning the English Nation* (*Lettres philosophiques*), entitled 'On the Regard that ought to be shown to Men of Letters', he contrasts what he expects would have been the fate of Joseph Addison in France – he 'would have been elected a Member of one of the Academies, and, by the Credit of some Women, might have obtain'd a yearly Pension of twelve hundred Livres; or else might have been imprison'd in the Bastille' – with his life in England: 'Mr. Addison was rais'd to the Post of Secretary of State', going on to add that 'Sir Isaac Newton was made Warden of the Royal Mint. Mr. Congreve has a considerable Employment. Mr. Prior was Plenipotentiary.'[8] The obvious parallels between Addison's imagined French career and Voltaire's own trajectory are no doubt testimony to the depth of the latter's personal frustration at the time. They also begin to articulate a new kind of literary ambition, one that was expressed in political rather than social terms. The man of letters aspired, above all, to a role in government, as the advisor and mentor to rulers.[9]

Voltaire spent two and a half years in England, studying English philosophy and science, visiting English poets such as Alexander Pope, Jonathan Swift and Edward Young, and admiring the 'liberty' on which a religiously tolerant and commercial culture was built. To be sure, he had already observed much of what he would 'discover' in England, notably on earlier trips to Holland. In its celebration of industry and diversity, a letter written during a 1722 stay in The Hague anticipates more than a few pages of the *Lettres philosophiques*: 'Of the five hundred thousand men who live in Amsterdam, not one is idle . . . I see Calvinist ministers, Arminians, Socinians, Rabbis, Anabaptists, who all speak marvelously and, in reality, are right' ('De cinq cens mille hommes qui habitent Amsterdam, il n'y en a pas un d'oisif . . . Je voi des ministres calvinistes, des arminiens, de sociniens, des rabins, des anabaptistes qui parlent tous à merveille et qui en vérité ont tous raison', D128). Moreover, he had been introduced to the writings of John Locke and Isaac Newton in an epistolary exchange with Lord Bolingbroke in June 1724, fully two years before he set foot in London (D190).[10] Nonetheless, it is hard to escape the conclusion that when Voltaire returned to France in 1728, he was a changed man, who harboured different intellectual expectations from the one who had left two years earlier.

The nineteenth-century critic John Morley wrote: 'Voltaire left France a poet; he returned to it a sage.'[11] There are, of course, a variety of ways to understand this comment: as a reference to Voltaire's developing interest in scientific questions, to his shift from poetry to prose and the adoption of an ironic voice that he would have found in Swift, or to his mounting effort to command a more expansive, all-encompassing philosophical viewpoint. Certainly, it brings to light Voltaire's new sense of his mission as a writer and a thinker. It is at this point that he orients himself towards an ideal of literary selfhood that, in its claim to political influence and in its assertion of a critical perspective, is more clearly recognisable to us today as that of the *philosophe*. The articulations of this new identity were numerous, yet three key moves seem especially worthy of note: the forging of a new kind of relationship with monarchs and princes; the acquisition of wealth and property; and the cultivation of a public in whose eyes the legitimacy of the *philosophe*'s claims to authority, as a judge and a critic, would be reflected. Voltaire's 'life' from the moment of his return from England can be illuminated by tracing the development of these aspects of his literary endeavours.

Monarchs

Voltaire had never conceived of his literary life outside of his association with social and political elites. However, the exchanges had been dominated by the imperatives of aristocratic sociability and leisure. Voltaire now envisioned a different kind of relationship that was defined by an egalitarian collaboration in the responsibilities of governing. The *philosophe* was elevated as a trusted advisor with unique insights into wise administration; while the sovereign was transformed by the incorporation of this wisdom, ruling no longer as a tyrant but as a benevolent philosopher-king. The model had no doubt taken root in Voltaire's mind during his stay in England; in fact, he dedicated in English the 1728 London edition of *La Henriade* to the English Queen Caroline, wife of George II, invoking the example of Descartes who had offered his *Principia* to Elizabeth of Bohemia not because she was a princess but because she 'understood him the best, and loved Truth the most'.[12]

Voltaire's connection with Queen Caroline came to an end when he left England in 1728. But in August 1736 Voltaire received a letter from the crown prince of Prussia, Frederick, who had taken an interest in philosophy, and particularly in Voltaire's brand of anti-clerical irreverence. The two entered into an ingratiating correspondence in the course of the following years. Voltaire basked in the favour of the future king of Prussia, while Frederick laid claim through the relationship to the image of a new kind of prince. Voltaire was instrumental in this effort as he arranged for the publication of Frederick's enlightened treatise on the principles of governing, the *Anti-Machiavel*, publicising the appearance of the book in his letters to Paris just as Frederick acceded to the throne in 1740. Frederick meanwhile allowed Voltaire to see in himself the trusted friend of a monarch, an idea that quickly gained momentum as it circulated through his and others' correspondence, thereby entering into the public consciousness.

Of course, the relationship, along with the images that it reflected of its two protagonists, was idealised; and the ideal would collide with a reality to which it did not always conform. This was especially the case when Voltaire, following years of urging from Frederick, finally agreed, after the death of his long-time companion Émilie Du Châtelet, to settle at the Prussian court in Potsdam in 1750, where the king lavished him with distinctions and a pension of 20,000 livres. All started well, but Frederick soon grew impatient with Voltaire's impertinence, taking umbrage when the *philosophe* published a satire of the president of his newly formed Berlin Academy, Pierre-Louis Moreau de Maupertuis, with whom Voltaire had feuded. Voltaire in turn became disillusioned with the king's authoritarian tendencies. Frederick ordered a public burning of the satire, a gesture that did more than disgrace Voltaire because it struck at the very heart of his carefully moulded identity as a royal confidant. When Voltaire finally left Prussia in March 1753, having neglected to return his chamberlain's key along with a volume of Frederick's poetry, the king had him detained for five humiliating weeks in Frankfurt. Nonetheless, the ideal proved ultimately to be more powerful than this reality. Frederick and Voltaire were reconciled and resumed their correspondence, and a new reality took shape in which Voltaire triumphed in 'governing those who govern us', as the Abbé de Saint-Pierre advised him to do in 1740 when he began work on his history of the reign of Louis XIV.[13] Duvernet depicts the Voltaire of the 1770s receiving the tributes of a series of monarchs, and in particular those of the 'Sovereigns of the North' ('Souverains du Nord'): not only Frederick, but the kings of Sweden, Denmark and Poland, as well as the empress of Russia, Catherine the Great.[14]

The French king, however, is notably absent from the list. The publication in 1734 of a French-language edition of the *Lettres philosophiques* (first published in English a year earlier), and the circulation two years later of his epicurean poem *Le Mondain*, had forced Voltaire to keep his distance from Versailles in the years after his return from England. His status improved, though, as his friendship with the newly crowned Prussian king developed. French authorities saw potential benefits in the budding relationship; and, for his part, Voltaire seemed to jump at the chance to assume an official role as ambassador or spy. In his third-person 'autobiography', he plays up this service: 'the Secretary of State employed the man of letters in several important affairs during 1745, 1746 and 1747' ('le secrétaire d'État employa l'homme de lettres dans plusieurs affaires considérables, pendant les années 1745, 1746 et 1747').[15] In these same years, Voltaire was integrated into life at court, moving into an apartment at Versailles in April 1744. He was given the honorary post of Royal Historiographer – the same that Racine and Boileau had held – in 1745, and some months later was appointed as *gentilhomme ordinaire de la chambre du roi*, giving him greater access to the king. He had been entrusted with the charge of organising the festivities for the forthcoming marriage of the Dauphin with the Spanish Infanta, for which he wrote a short comedy that was well received. Finally, in 1746, on his second attempt, Voltaire was elected to the Académie Française.

Many commentators have seized on statements from his correspondence at this time about being 'the king's buffoon at fifty' ('boufon du Roy à cinquante ans') or dedicating himself 'so that the Dauphine nods at me as she passes' ('pour que la dauphine me fasse en passant un signe de tête'), as evidence of Voltaire's dissatisfaction with his life as courtier, in spite of his relative successes (D3073, D3015). The real picture seems a little more complicated. In fact, it is hard not to read underneath these coyly self-denigrating remarks a sense of the possibilities that were opening up with his long-desired rise in stature. And if in retrospect Voltaire gave voice to frustration with his life at Versailles, it is no doubt because ultimately those possibilities never did materialise. His first letters from Potsdam in 1750 express bitterness due not to the 'ridiculous life' that he claimed to have lived serving the king at the French court, but rather to the fact that, while he was honoured there with various kinds of distinctions, none of them reflected a sense of his importance to the king, nor his indispensability to the French state (D4206):

> The King never showed me the slightest kindness . . . The post of Historiographer was nothing but an empty title . . . In these circumstances, the King of Prussia, after a correspondence kept for sixteen years, has called me to his court, and is urging me to come to see him . . . Should I renounce the favour and the familiarity of one of the greatest kings of the earth, a man who will live on in posterity, in order to solicit at the royal toilet a word that I will not obtain?
>
> (Le roi ne me témoignait jamais la moindre bonté . . . La place d'historiographe n'était qu'un vain titre . . . Dans ces circonstances le roi de Prusse,

après une correspondance suivie de seize années, m'appelle à sa cour, me presse de le venir voir . . . Renoncerai-je à la faveur, à la familiarité d'un des plus grands rois de la terre, d'un homme qui ira à la postérité, pour aller briguer à une toilette un mot que je n'obtiendrai pas?

Thus, when Voltaire left Versailles and Paris in the spring of 1748, it was, for the second time, less under the specific threat of persecution than as rebuffed by indifference. As much as any ban on his presence, this official indifference to him would keep him away for almost thirty years.

Wealth and property

Voltaire praised the wealth of the English, returning to Paris determined to become rich; it was with remarkable efficiency that he undertook the project. In 1730, he came into possession of his share of the estate of his father, who had died seven years earlier. He then worked out with the mathematician, Charles-Marie de La Condamine, a scheme to win enormous pay-offs in the national lottery by studying the rules and exploiting loopholes that they discovered in the system: 'To make one's fortune in this country, one need only read the council's decrees' ('Pour faire sa fortune dans ce pays-ci, il n'y a qu'à lire les arrêts du conseil'), Voltaire boasts.[16] He and La Condamine were soon pulling in from 5 to 6 million livres a month, startling amounts that Voltaire was able to augment with investments in a variety of other opportunities.[17] By 1735, he was an immensely wealthy man.

Wealth was, of course, a mechanism of personal autonomy; it offered financial security and famously allowed Voltaire greater freedom in publishing since he was able to forego payment from publishers. But there was more to it than that. Jean Le Rond D'Alembert wrote that opulence was a 'guarantee of independence and credit' ('gage de l'indépendance et du crédit'), elevating not just one's material circumstances but also one's quality as an individual.[18] This in turn could multiply and deepen one's relationships with nobility. In other words, it was as much to proliferate his ties with the privileged and powerful as to feed himself without having to beg for pensions, that Voltaire became rich. 'One is less concerned about harassing an isolated being than a man who, by his renown and his great fortune, has an infinity of connections to society' ('on craint moins de molester un être isolé, qu'un homme qui, par sa renommée et ses grands biens, a une infinité de rapports avec la société'), remarks Duvernet, who points out that Voltaire lent significant sums to prominent noblemen such as the Ducs de Guise and Richelieu, as well as to foreign princes. He lost a fair amount to slow-paying and often bankrupt nobles, but this was trivial compared to the ascendancy that he gained over them as their creditors.[19]

Above all, his wealth allowed him to acquire estates. In his letters, he often referred to his properties as 'retreats' offering quiet workspaces far removed from the upheavals and persecutions of Paris, Versailles and Berlin. He had developed a taste for serene country living during the fifteen or so years, from 1734 when he left Paris after the publication of the *Lettres philosophiques*, and lived with Émilie Du Châtelet in the chateau of Cirey in Champagne, enjoying their shared intellectual pursuits. Françoise de Graffigny famously described the routine of work, science, sociability and theatre that made life at Cirey agreeable.[20] When his fraught departure from Prussia brought him to Geneva in 1755, Voltaire purchased a large house on the city outskirts overlooking the lake, explaining to the Marquis de Saint-Lambert: 'I hate cities; I can only live in the country' ('Je déteste les villes; je ne puis vivre qu' à la campagne', D7795). But there was more to it than rustic escape, for a distinct pleasure in property ownership began to play a defining role in his evolving sense of freedom and authority as an *homme de lettres*: 'Liberty! liberty! Your throne is in this place' ('Liberté! Liberté! ton trône est en ces lieux'), he exhorts in an epistle written in March 1755 as he moves into this lakeside house, which he named Les Délices.[21]

His correspondence repeatedly connects the themes of proprietorship and autonomy in two ways: property could free him from the obligations and dangers of subjecthood in a state; and it could transform him as a type of sovereign lord. The first idea followed from mounting hostility in certain factions of the Genevan political establishment to Voltaire's presence – spurred by the appearance in 1757 of D'Alembert's article 'Geneva' in the *Encyclopédie* – which convinced him to find residence outside the Republic. He had already bought a second home in Lausanne where, not wanting to install unsightly stoves at Les Délices, he spent winters.[22] In 1758, he purchased two more estates just over the border in France, at Ferney and at Tournay. He would write to the Chevalier de Brosses, from whom he bought Tournay:

> I persevere in my plans to own property in France, Switzerland, Geneva and even Savoy. It is said that one cannot serve two masters; I want to have four in order to serve none, and to enjoy fully the most beautiful prerogative of human nature, which we call liberty.
>
> (Je persiste toujours dans le dessein d'avoir des possessions en France, en Suisse, à Genève et même en Savoie. On dit, je ne sais où, qu'on ne peut servir deux maîtres; j'en veux avoir quatre pour n'en avoir point du tout et pour jouir pleinement du plus bel apanage de la nature humaine qu'on nomme liberté, D7913).

As he often did in this period, he signed the letter, 'the free Swiss V' ('le libre Suisse V', D7913).

The second figuration of liberty in and through property ownership is more surprising, for it articulates freedom not in the 'modern' language of natural rights but in the archaic vocabulary of noble privilege and entitlement, as these were conferred by the estate. When he purchased Tournay, Voltaire acquired, and indeed exercised, the right to call himself the 'Comte de Tournay', assuming ownership of the chateau on Christmas Eve 1758 in an elaborate feudal ritual.[23] He petitioned the administration to maintain Ferney's seigneurial exemptions, a wish that was granted in 1759 by decree (brevet) of Louis XV. Voltaire pointedly, and it might seem paradoxically, viewed this royal grace as an affirmation, not a denial, of his autonomy: 'you will see an entirely free man', he writes, urging his friend Nicolas-Claude Thiriot to visit, 'the king accorded me the confirmation of the privileges of my property which makes it entirely independent; I have reached what I have desired all my life, independence and rest' ('vous verrez un homme entièrement libre; le Roy m'a accordé la confirmation des priviléges de ma terre qui la rendent entièrement indépendante; je suis parvenu à ce que j'ai désiré toute ma vie, l'indépendance et le repos', D8348).

By 1756, he had adopted Ferney as his only residence, having divested himself of the other properties. He would hardly leave its confines until his return to Paris in the winter of 1778. Out of these years emerges an enduring picture of the self-styled 'seigneur de Ferney', reigning over his 'little kingdom' ('petit royaume'), surrounded by what he called his 'family' (his niece and lover Marie-Louise Denis), his friends, a constant stream of eminent visitors and acolytes who came from all over Europe to pay homage, as well as the peasants and villagers of his domain, in whose farming and artisanal activities he took a great interest. In the role of *philosophe-seigneur*, Voltaire again turned the tables: Duvernet notes how princes and aristocrats now paid court to him rather than the other way around, on terms that prioritised Voltaire's importance over their own: 'Foreign Princes rarely failed to visit him; most French nobles were pleased to go and see him . . . And as visitors knew that he was always busy, they were attentive not to inconvenience him' ('Les Princes étrangers manquaient rarement de le visiter; la plupart des Seigneurs Français se faisaient un plaisir de l'aller voir . . . Et comme on le savait toujours occupé, on était attentif à ne pas se rendre importun').[24]

The public and opinion

Voltaire's self-presentation as a *seigneur*, to the extent that it was not isolated from but integral to his evolution as an intellectual in the years after the Prussian debacle, is emblematic of his broader strategy as a writer, which was not so much to liberate himself from the framework of *ancien régime* possibilities, but rather, navigating within the traditional system, to claim that these possibilities meant something new. Thus, Frederick's patronage reflected not royal favour for an *homme de lettres* sharing in the monarch's glory, but a politicisation of the writer's role, and a transformation of the intellectual as an agent of reason who counsels and, if need be, limits the deployment of monarchical power. The success of the strategy rested on the credibility of the claim, and this in turn depended on the cultivation of a public willing to buy it. That contemporaries and subsequent biographers have to such a large extent been willing to repeat many of the things that Voltaire said about himself, often in the absence of any reason to believe these things other than that Voltaire said them, is evidence of how savvy the *philosophe* was in forming and mobilising such a public.

Who constituted Voltaire's public? It was, above all, a public formed by his writings, whether his letters, satires, poems, histories, stories or pamphlets. Thus it was a philosophical readership, not only sympathetic to the ideas that Voltaire propagated in his texts but receptive to the critical, authoritative voice that they projected. Given that his readers were largely drawn from the ranks of the social and political elite – Voltaire did not so much write for a 'mass' audience as for a more rarefied, educated network of princes, nobles, wealthy bourgeois and intellectuals – this public also comprised a self-consciously progressive and enlightened elite, one that was ready to downplay its own traditional prerogatives in order to uphold the 'modern' claims to authority and autonomy that were conveyed by Voltaire's texts. In this sense, the public became a crucial institution, for by reflecting and validating his largely self-proclaimed mandate to critique abuses of power and religious fanaticism, it rendered potent his denunciations.

One early indication of Voltaire's awareness of the power of a reading public to legitimise the Enlightenment project is found in a 1758 letter in which he reassures the Comte d'Argental, as the *Encyclopédie* was coming under attack from Church authorities and the Parlement, that its 3,000 subscribers would not stand for such a crackdown: 'the public outcry will make the persecutors execrable' ('le cri public rendra les persécuteurs exécrables', D7653). Two years later he again appealed to a community of subscribers in his efforts to help a distant relative of Pierre Corneille, who was living in poverty, with the publication of a luxurious edition of her ancestor's work. This undertaking anticipates a growing dedication in the 1760s to the task of deploying his influence with readers towards the righting of injustices, particularly those that were perpetrated by *ancien régime* courts beholden to religious prejudices. His intervention into the 1762 case of Jean Calas, a Protestant merchant wrongly executed by a judgement of the Parlement of Toulouse for murdering his son, allegedly in retaliation for the latter's conversion to Catholicism, furnishes what is undoubtedly the most outstanding image of the *philosophe* as a new type of intellectual, whose lack of any institutional basis for involvement in the case bolsters rather than undermines his moral authority to speak out by making this authority rest on his selfless and singular commitment to truth and justice. 'One man with no other support than the ascendancy of glory and talents resisted your persecutions for sixty years' ('Un seul homme, sans autre appui que l'ascendant de la gloire et des talents, a résisté soixante ans à vos persécutions'), the Baron von Grimm writes in his *Correspondance littéraire*, apostrophising Intolerance itself on the occasion of Voltaire's death in 1778.[25]

The key was to mobilise readers, which Voltaire did with an energetic campaign of letter-writing and by circulating documents: satires and self-justificatory pieces written in the name of Mme Calas and her two sons, as well as the records of the trial itself which Voltaire was able to have publicised over the objections of the Toulouse Parlement. In 1763 he published the *Traité sur la tolérance*, in which he integrates the Calas affair into the larger philosophical fight against religious and ethnic prejudice. Calas's cause, he would write, was not just that of his wife and sons but of the public and humanity (D10559). Subsuming the particularities of the affair in universal principles, and addressing the elite readers of his *Traité* as a lawyer would a jury, Voltaire offered himself as an advocate of humanity itself.[26] Calas was exonerated in March of 1765 by a decree of the royal council, and Voltaire turned to other instances of judicial travesty. In 1765 Pierre-Paul Sirven, another Protestant, was wrongly accused of murdering his daughter; a year later, the Chevalier de La Barre, a dissolute 20-year-old, was found guilty on highly questionable evidence of blasphemy, a crime for which he was tortured and executed. Tirelessly denouncing these and other injustices in the name of reason and human rights, Voltaire assumed what would certainly be his most important and influential role as the 'conscience of Europe', in Peter Gay's famous formulation.[27]

Conclusion

It is fitting that a man who had so triumphantly imposed his image and authority on the eighteenth-century public would put on a memorable last act. In February 1778, Voltaire left Ferney for Paris. His return, in the wake of the campaigns of the 1760s, is usually depicted as an apotheosis. According to Duvernet, the sensation of his arrival overshadowed the recent visits to the French capital of the kings of Sweden and Denmark.[28] On 30 March, after the performance at the Comédie-Française of his tragedy, *Irène*, he presided over a ritual coronation during which his bust was brought on stage and showered in garlands to the wild applause of the audience. Duvernet no doubt overstates the eminence of this audience, though, when he suggests that it was composed of the royal family, princes of the blood, ministers, ambassadors, dukes and peers, distinguished ladies, academicians and men of letters.[29] There is no shortage of mythologisation in the story of Voltaire's return. He himself was quick to publicise not just the events, but the events insofar as they marked a culmination of his philosophical trajectory. After his crowning at the Comédie-Française, Voltaire wrote exultantly to Frederick: 'It is thus true, sire, that at last men are becoming enlightened' ('Il est donc vrai, sire, qu'à la fin les hommes s'éclairent'). The letter also shows that even as he embraced his stature as a celebrity, Voltaire remained steadfastly committed to an image of his torments and of his persecution; indeed this was a key part of that celebrity: 'I have been busy avoiding two things plaguing me in Paris: whistles and death' ('J'ai été occupé à éviter deux choses qui me poursuivaient dans Paris, les sifflets et la mort', D21138). This characteristic ambivalence is illustrated by another illuminating gesture from his return to the capital. Arriving at the customs barrier to the city on 10 February, Voltaire was asked if he was smuggling anything in against the orders of the king. He replied that he had no contraband, 'except myself'.[30] If the Parisian adventure punctuated his dominance as an intellectual, it also most likely hastened his death. His health rapidly declined in the three and a half months that he spent in the city, and he died there on 30 May 1778.

NOTES

1. T.-I. Duvernet, *La Vie de Voltaire* (Geneva, 1786), p.24.
2. R. Pearson has recently suggested an alternative reading of the conflicting dates of Voltaire's birth, with the earlier one marking his illegitimate birth to his mother Marie-Marguerite and the Chevalier de Rochebrune (*Voltaire Almighty: A Life in the Pursuit of Freedom*, London: Bloomsbury, 2005, pp.9–18). The source for this obfuscation nonetheless remains Voltaire himself, who took great pleasure in emphasising the possibility of his illegitimacy.
3. N. Masson, 'La condition de l'auteur en France au XVIIIe siècle: le cas de Voltaire', in *Le Livre et l'historien: Études offertes en l'honneur du Professeur Henri-Jean Martin*, ed. F. Barbier *et al.* (Geneva: Droz, 1997), p.554.
4. Duvernet, *La Vie de Voltaire*, p.21.
5. Duvernet, *La Vie de Voltaire*, p.27.
6. G. Lanson, *Voltaire* [1906], ed. R. Pomeau (Paris: Hachette, 1960), p.23.

7. According to Duvernet, Voltaire retorted that 'he did not himself carry a great name but made the one that he had honourable' ('c'est un homme qui ne traîne pas un grand nom, mais qui fait honorer celui qu'il porte', pp.59–60). G. Desnoiresterres reports both this response and another, that Voltaire 'was just beginning to make his name while the Chevalier de Rohan-Chabot was ending his' ('qu'il commençait son nom et que le chevalier Chabot finissait le sien'), in *Voltaire et la société française au XVIIIe siècle*, 8 vols (Paris: Didier, 1867–76), vol.1, p.345.

8. Voltaire, *Letters*, pp.112–13.

9. Duvernet, *La Vie de Voltaire*, p.27.

10. The letter is cited in Lanson, *Voltaire*, pp.34–5.

11. Cited in A. O. Aldridge, *Voltaire and the Century of Light* (Princeton, NJ: Princeton University Press, 1975), p.79.

12. Dedication to *La Henriade* (London, 1728).

13. Cited in Aldridge, *Voltaire and the Century of Light*, p.130.

14. Duvernet, *La Vie de Voltaire*, p.261.

15. *Commentaire historique sur les oeuvres de l'auteur de 'La Henriade', avec les pièces originales et les preuves* [1776], Moland, vol.1, p.90.

16. Voltaire cites his own letter in the *Commentaire historique*, p.75.

17. See J. Douvez, *De quoi vivait Voltaire* (Paris: Éditions des Deux Rives, 1949), pp.52–9.

18. J. Le Rond D'Alembert, 'Essai sur la société des gens de lettres et des grands, sur la réputation, sur les mécènes, et sur les récompenses littéraires', in *Œuvres*, 5 vols (Paris: Belin, 1821–2), vol.4, p.342.

19. Duvernet, *La Vie de Voltaire*, p.77.

20. See *Voltaire et ses amis d'après la correspondance de Mme de Graffigny*, ed. E. Showalter in *SVEC*, 139 (1975).

21. 'L'auteur arrivant dans sa terre, près du lac de Genève', Moland, vol.10, p.365.

22. Aldridge, *Voltaire and the Century of Light*, p.236.

23. Aldridge, *Voltaire and the Century of Light*, p.247.

24. Duvernet, *La Vie de Voltaire*, p.203.

25. Grimm, *Correspondance littéraire, philosophique et critique par Grimm, Diderot, Raynal, Meister, etc.*, ed. M. Tourneux, 16 vols (Paris: Garnier, 1877–82), vol.12, p.110 (June 1778).

26. OCV, vol.56C, p.259.

27. P. Gay, *Voltaire's Politics: The Poet as Realist*, 2nd edn (New Haven, CT: Yale University Press, 1988), p.205.

28. Duvernet, *La Vie de Voltaire*, p.280.

29. Duvernet, *La Vie de Voltaire*, pp.290–1.

30. Cited in Aldridge, *Voltaire and the Century of Light*, p.399.

2

NICHOLAS CRONK

Voltaire and authorship

Voltaire was not simply the most celebrated European author of his day; his celebrity was of a wholly new type. It is impossible to understand the importance and influence of Voltaire's writing without also understanding the sort of writer that he was, or, to be more precise, the idea of the writer that he invented. All authors forge an identity and a sense of self within a literary field, that is to say within a network of institutions and social relationships, and it is through this field that they relate more widely to political authority and to the reading public.[1] This chapter will consider the entirely original manner in which Voltaire constructs his authorial self and strategically manages the creation of his authorial identity.

Voltaire and the status of the writer

In his article 'What is an Author?', Michel Foucault points to the eighteenth century as the decisive moment at which a writer's work became the 'property' of its creator.[2] Writers in the seventeenth century had typically enjoyed independent means or had depended on a pension paid by a person of position. Legislation to grant authors the legal copyright to their works was passed in France during the Revolution – much later than in England – and this meant that from the early nineteenth century writers typically lived off their earnings. The status of the man (and woman) of letters in the eighteenth century is a complex one.[3] On the one hand, a *philosophe* such as Diderot managed to make a living for himself from the *Encyclopédie*, though he never became rich; his collaborator, D'Alembert, on the other hand, complained often of poverty, and depended, for example, on a pension from Frederick II. The literary world of the eighteenth century was a highly complex one, in which each author had to negotiate his or her way between the often conflicting demands of patron, publisher and public, manoeuvring, as Roger Chartier puts it, 'between privilege and equality, protection and independence, isolation and sociability'.[4] Voltaire's position was an intriguing and paradoxical one, as he looked back nostalgically to the status of writers in the age of Louis XIV, even as he revelled in and reviled (in equal measure) the Grub Street culture of his own day.[5] From an early stage, Voltaire's strong instincts led him to act to protect his independence. The humiliating episode in 1726 involving the Chevalier de Rohan-Chabot was a cruel reminder of the poet's inferior social status, and even if Louis XV had liked him, which he did not, Voltaire was not suited to the life of a courtier. On just two occasions, he flirted with the idea of court life: in 1725 (when the king married) and in 1745 (when the king appointed him royal historiographer); both attempts ended quickly and predictably in failure.

Voltaire's solution to the problem of how to secure his independence was simple and radical: to become sufficiently wealthy not to need to be dependent on others. Born into a comfortable bourgeois family, he worked hard at becoming rich, mainly through shrewd investments and by making loans. To a close friend who was settling too easily into the life of the literary parasite, he wrote: 'Drink champagne . . . but do something that will enable you one day to drink wine of your own' ('Buvez du vin de Champagne . . . mais faites quelque chose qui vous mette en état de boire un jour du vin qui soit à vous', D875). From the mid-1750s, established first at Les Délices and then in his chateau at Ferney, Voltaire had become, literally, the king of his domain: 'I have made myself king at home' ('je me suis fait roi chez moi').[6] And in his *Mémoires*, which are for the most part quite unrevealing about himself, he makes a proud boast of his financial independence: 'I hear much talk of liberty, but I don't believe there has been in Europe an individual who has created for himself a liberty like mine. Let whosoever wants and whosoever can follow my example' ('J'entends parler beaucoup de liberté, mais je ne crois pas qu'il y ait eu en Europe un particulier qui s'en soit fait une comme la mienne. Suivra mon exemple qui voudra ou qui pourra').[7]

Voltaire and the book trade

Voltaire is acutely sensitive to the power of the book to influence readers' opinions, and explicit about how books in different formats will reach different readerships (D13235):

> I'd really like to know what harm a book costing a hundred écus can do. Twenty folio volumes will never cause a revolution; it's the small portable books that cost thirty sous that are to be feared. If the Gospels had cost 1,200 sesterces, the Christian religion would never have become established.
>
> (Je voudrais bien savoir quel mal peut faire un livre qui coûte cent écus. Jamais vingt volumes in-folio ne feront de révolution; ce sont les petits livres portatifs à trente sous qui sont à craindre. Si l'évangile avait coûté douze cents sesterces, jamais la religion chrétienne ne se serait établie.)

Voltaire possesses moreover a mastery of the practices of the book trade, and his understanding of how books are made comes through clearly in the detail of his letters to various printer-publishers, in particular to the Cramer brothers in Geneva, his favoured publishers in the last twenty years of his life, when he was living close by at Ferney.[8] The Cramer brothers wrote to Lambert, a prominent publisher in Paris: 'You know how carefully Voltaire always corrects his works. We're obliged to print them under his nose, and we can assure you that during printing, we have often had to revise the same sheet two or three times' ('Vous savez avec quel soin M. de Voltaire corrige toujours ses ouvrages. On est dans la nécessité de les imprimer sous ses yeux, et nous pouvons vous assurer que dans le cours de l'impression, nous avons été souvent obligés de refaire deux ou trois fois la même feuille', D7000). Voltaire was not always an easy author, and he expected Cramer to work as fast as he himself did: 'There is no scribbler more devoted to you than I. Print, print, print' ('Il n'y a point de griffonneur plus à votre service que moi. Imprimez, imprimez, imprimez', D9509). When he sends Cramer the manuscript of the *Traité sur la tolérance*, he gives precise instructions as to how the extensive notes are to be presented on the page (D10977); he often writes about the size of the margins, the typeface, the vignettes (D9541, D16388), always attentive to what will look best. Asked to comment on a friend's manuscript, he comments not just on the content, but also on the typographical presentation, urging him to turn the marginal notes into sub-titles: 'That relaxes the eye, and rests the mind' ('Cela délasse les yeux et repose l'esprit', D11051). For, as he remarks on another occasion, 'you don't print a book the way you sell cod in the market' ('on n'imprime point un livre comme on vend de la morue au marché', D14134). He made the same point, more elegantly, to Cramer, when he wrote to him in 1773: 'Believe me, the art of typography requires the whole man: you can't print works the way you invest in ships. A good printer is a man of letters' ('Croyez-moi, l'art de la typographie demandait un homme tout entier. On ne fait point imprimer des ouvrages comme on met de l'argent sur des vaisseaux. Un bon imprimeur est un homme de lettres', D18229). The Cramer brothers are, moreover, his brothers, Voltaire tells Damilaville, for – and this is the ultimate accolade – 'they are *philosophes*' (D11873).

Few other writers of the period took such pains with the physical appearance of their books, and perhaps no other writer manipulated and manoeuvred the printer-publishers with quite Voltaire's brio. He was, of course, much given to complaining about his treatment by unscrupulous publishers; Voltaire writes to the *pasteur* Élie Bertrand in 1756: 'Your publisher in Geneva seems an honest one. These gentlemen are for the most part the scourge of authors: everyone has his scourge in this world, every fly his spider, and this life is a struggle' ('Votre libraire de Geneve paraît un franc libraire. Ces messieurs là sont pour la plus part le fleau des autheurs: chacun a son fleau dans ce monde, chaque mouche a son araignée et cette vie est un combat').[9] In fact, Voltaire relished his struggles with his printers, and it was rare that they got the better of him.

Communication with printers abroad, for example in Holland, created a particular problem. In the second half of the 1730s, Voltaire was in frequent contact with Étienne Ledet in Amsterdam, in particular concerning a proposed collected edition of his works. After delays and suggestions that the printers would not accept Voltaire's corrections, Voltaire found himself obliged to travel from Brussels to Amsterdam, where he stayed with Ledet in 1736 in order to assert control over the situation (D1231). The four-volume collected edition, handsomely illustrated, was eventually published in Amsterdam in 1739, but it was marred by many blunders, leaving Voltaire bitterly disappointed. As part of his campaign to persuade Ledet to go to the expense of making the necessary corrections, Voltaire even published an article in an Amsterdam journal, the *Bibliothèque française*, publicly criticising his printer's careless errors, yet at the same time seeking to promote sales of the edition by drawing attention to what was new in the four volumes.[10] The journal was edited by Henri Du Sauzet, one of Ledet's principal rivals in Amsterdam. What Ledet could not have known is that Voltaire had also been in regular contact with Du Sauzet, having in December 1738 promised him a publishing scoop (D1692): 'You alone of all the Dutch publishers will have the exclusivity of the *Siècle de Louis XIV*, which I give you in advance, in the sure knowledge that a man of birth and feeling will not fail in the duties of friendship and gratitude' ('Vous seul des libraires de Hollande aurez le privilège d'imprimer mon histoire du *Siècle de Louis XIV*, dont je vous fais présent d'avance, bien sûr qu'un homme qui a de la naissance et des sentiments ne manquera jamais aux devoirs de l'amitié et de la reconnaissance', D1692). But a few years later, in 1740, when Du Sauzet passed off a minor play as the work of Voltaire, Voltaire would be less indulgent, referring to him in a letter to Cideville as 'Du Sauzet, the Dutch publisher, and so a double rascal' ('le Du Sauzet, libraire de Hollande, et par conséquent doublement fripon', D2201). In all these wrangles, it was usually Voltaire who won the day.

For the *philosophe* who did venture to have a book printed in eighteenth-century France, there were two evident perils: piracy and censorship. The problem with piracy was that, in a period when legal copyright did not exist, an author was only likely to earn income from the first edition of his or her book; pirate reprints of a best-seller were profitable for the printer who undertook them, but diminished the income of the rightful author. If Voltaire was really determined to prevent an early piracy of one of his works, he managed to do so. In publishing *Zadig*, for example, in order to avoid early piracies of his *conte* and so as to be able to distribute copies to his friends in advance of publication, Voltaire contrived to have one half of the sheets printed by Prault in Paris, and the other half by the Lefèvre press in Nancy, with each printer working in complete ignorance of the other.[11] Voltaire alone enjoyed the pleasure of putting the two halves together, and the pirated reprints appeared only when he was ready. For the most part, Voltaire turned the problem of piracy to his advantage. He was not in any case dependent on the editions for an income; his only concern was that his books, his message, should reach as wide a public as possible. To this end, the pirate publishers were a godsend, for in multiplying the number of editions in circulation, they helped Voltaire achieve his aim of maximising the number of his readers. One trick, for example, was to provide his printer with a succession of textual modifications as a pretext for multiple editions. In the case of the *Poème de Fontenoy*, which went through numerous editions, Voltaire over-played his hand and became a major target for satirists: one spoke ironically of a 'Final edition, with no corrections, no additions, and absolutely identical to the first' ('Dernière édition, sans correction, sans augmentation, et parfaitement semblable à la première'); another, more savagely, evoked a '77th edition, revised, corrected, and with two syllables and three notes taken under the tree of Cracow added' ('77me édition, revue, corrigée et augmentée de deux syllabes et de trois notes prises sous l'arbre de Cracovie').[12] In the case of the *Questions sur l'Encyclopédie*, Voltaire agreed with Cramer in Geneva to publish what was to be his last great multi-volume work, and then, as Robert Darnton has shown, came to an agreement with the director of the Société typographique de Neuchâtel, Ostervald, to supply him with a copy of Cramer's proofs, duly corrected and expanded, and all this, of course, behind Cramer's back.[13] These examples reveal his genius in handling his publishers – a skill which also served Voltaire well in his skirmishes with the censors.

Censorship in the *ancien régime* was unpredictably bureaucratic and came in various forms, from the Church, from the government and from the Parlement. A notorious example was the censorship by the Parlement de Paris of the *Lettres philosophiques*. The basic facts are well known. Voltaire entrusted the text to his close friend Thiriot, then in London, who oversaw the publication, first of the English translation in 1733, *Letters Concerning the English nation*, and then, early in 1734, of the French version, *Lettres écrites de Londres sur les Anglais*. Only after testing the market with these two London editions did Voltaire allow a French publisher, Jore in Rouen, to produce an edition on French soil; a second pirated edition soon appeared in Paris, and a scandal ensued. In June 1734, the Parlement de Paris, condemned the work to be burned, and for several months Voltaire lived in fear of arrest.[14]

Without question this was an uncomfortable time for Voltaire, and for a while he was almost certainly in some personal danger. Even so, his relentless campaign of letter-writing to influence those in authority did ultimately succeed, and the threat of arrest on account of the *Lettres philosophiques* was lifted. More importantly, the act of censorship was utterly ineffective in silencing Voltaire's voice. Too many copies of too many different editions were in circulation for the police to be able to act decisively; and the condemnation of the Parlement only served to give the *Lettres philosophiques* instant notoriety. Voltaire's correspondence of this period allows us to chart with some precision his strategy for publishing the *Lettres anglaises*. With the help of Thiriot he first ensured the safe publication in London of an English translation; its ambiguous preface, which Voltaire oversaw in proof, implies that the work is his own original English composition rather than a mere translation – a tactic to improve sales and ensure greater impact in the English capital.[15] The subsequent London edition in French made it possible for copies to begin to circulate outside England.[16] Meanwhile, another, slightly modified version of the French text was to be published clandestinely in France. Jore was a natural choice: Voltaire had worked with him already, and he was based in the relative security of provincial Rouen, where another close friend, Cideville, could act as Voltaire's representative. By May, the book was beginning to be produced in Rouen (D615), and in June Voltaire urged Cideville to give instructions to Jore that absolutely no trace of Voltaire's own writing must be kept (D620). Voltaire even invents an Englishman, Sanderson, who allegedly has supplied Jore with the text, and he asks the long-suffering Cideville to have Jore write two letters, one to Sanderson acknowledging receipt of the text, and another to Voltaire, replying to a (non-existent) letter which forbade him, Jore, from proceeding with the publication of any letters appearing in London under Voltaire's name (D620, D625). All this is worthy of an eighteenth-century epistolary novel, a genre which Voltaire professed to dislike. Meanwhile, it seems that Voltaire had published in the *Mercure de France* in June 1733 an article, 'Extrait d'une Lettre écrite de Londres, le premier Juin, concernant M. de Voltaire', which is in effect an extended advertisement for various Voltaire editions which were about to appear, most importantly the *Lettres*: this means that at the very moment when in his letters to Cideville Voltaire was urging the importance of confidentiality in order to protect Jore, he was also writing for the London editions a press announcement which could only bring publicity to the clandestine efforts of the Rouen printer. This is emphatically not the action of a man intimidated by the censors. And as the long *affaire* over the *Lettres philosophiques* dragged on, it was Jore who suffered, not Voltaire.

The circulation of the *Lettres philosophiques* was further boosted when later in 1734 a pirated copy of the Jore edition was produced in Paris by Josse. If we are to believe the conventional account, Voltaire made a foolish error. He entrusted one copy of Jore's clandestine edition to a Parisian bookseller, Jean François Josse, in order 'to have it bound'; the bookseller, predictably enough, made a copy of the work; and by April 1734, a pirated edition of the clandestine edition was on the market. In early June 1734, Voltaire writes to his close friend Formont: 'It seems highly likely that this François Josse, who ten weeks ago had one of my three copies in his hands for binding, abused the privilege, copied it and printed it with René' ('Il y a grande apparence que ce François Josse, qui a eu entre les mains un des trois exemplaires que j'avais, et qui me l'a fait relier, il y a deux mois et demi, en aura abusé, l'aura fait copier, et l'aura imprimé avec René', D752). Commentators have taken this testimony at face value and so completely missed Voltaire's *faux ingénu* voice. A close reading of the whole letter makes it abundantly clear that Voltaire has engineered a clandestine edition (another act of treachery with regard to Jore). No one would be so naïve as to entrust a clandestine book to a prominent Parisian printer simply 'to have it bound', as Formont knew perfectly well. Voltaire in this letter manages both to warn his friend about the clandestine edition, and also suggest a plausible alibi to be spread abroad when news of the Paris edition leaks out. Had the letter been intercepted, it is unlikely that a third party would have fully understood its cryptic irony; Formont, on the other hand, knew Voltaire well and so knew how to read between the lines. Voltaire's letters demand to be read as carefully as any of his (other) literary works.

Voltaire's control, through Thiriot, of the two London editions, his management, through Cideville, of the Rouen edition, and his engineering of the clandestine Paris edition, all combined to ensure that the number and spread of copies on the market would defeat any attempt by the police to limit the book's circulation; and Voltaire's planted announcement in the *Mercure de France*, followed by the unexpected bonus of condemnation by the Parlement de Paris, further ensured widespread demand for the book. In the face of this masterly manipulation of the various publishers, the *ancien régime* system of censorship was powerless: the more they tried, the more the censors gave Voltaire the publicity that he craved. Twenty years later, in 1756, Voltaire would comment laconically on the marketing benefits of censorship: 'Censorship by these gentlemen [the *parlementaires*] only helps sell a book. Publishers ought to pay them to burn everything they print'

('Une censure de ces messieurs fait seulement acheter un livre. Les libraires devraient les payer pour faire brûler tout ce qu'on imprime', D6946).[17] Voltaire's oriental tale *Zadig* is prefaced by a spoof oriental *approbation*, a parody of the official approvals granted to certain books by the government: the official censors could do nothing about it.

Voltaire turns manipulation of the book trade into an art form in its own right. Censorship, in all its vagaries, just occasionally seems to threaten his personal security, but it rarely prevents the books from circulating. On the contrary, Voltaire uses every means at his disposal, including correspondence and open letters to journals, as part of a publicity campaign in which rival publishers compete to multiply the editions of his works. This strategy of publication is neatly summed up in a dictum – conveniently cast in the form of a decasyllabic line – in a letter which Voltaire wrote near the end of his life, in 1772, to an 'authorised' biographer, Duvernet: 'Let whoever wants print me, and whoever can read me' ('M'imprime qui veut, et me lit qui peut', D17653).

Voltaire's authorial postures

When in 1768 Président Hénault found himself attacked by a fellow historian, he sought the support of his old friend Voltaire, who readily agreed to write a piece in his defence: 'Yes, I shall undoubtedly put my name to it, even though I have never put my name to any of my works. My pride is kept for special occasions, and I know of none more honourable than defending truth and your honour' ('Oui sans doute, j'y mettrai mon nom, quoi que je ne l'aie jamais mis à aucun de mes ouvrages. Mon amour propre se réserve pour les grandes occasions, et je n'en sais point de plus honorable que celle de défendre la vérité et votre gloire', D15278). It might seem surprising that Voltaire sets such store by the gesture of putting his name to a piece of writing. But we are accustomed to reading Voltaire in modern editions and translations, where his name appears as a matter of course on the cover of the book and on the title page. It was only at the end of the eighteenth century that it became standard practice for French books to name the author on the title page.[18] For that reason we need to go back and look at Voltaire's works as he published them to be reminded that he employed a whole range of strategies for (not) putting his name to a book.

We must not forget the continuing importance of manuscripts in this period in the circulation of clandestine thought. Manuscripts were generally anonymous, and they were not subject to censorship in the same way as books; indeed the existence of state censorship in France probably helped ensure the continuation of manuscript publication – in England, where there was no censorship of books, manuscript publication seems to have been notably less widespread. As a young writer, Arouet (before acquiring the identity of Voltaire) wrote a number of poems which circulated in manuscript and which were never intended to be printed; one of these, the *Epître à Uranie*, was printed with Voltaire's authorisation only in 1772, a full half-century after it had first circulated in manuscript.[19] The *Sermon des cinquante*, one of Voltaire's most outspoken attacks on Christianity, circulated for a long time in manuscript before appearing in print. This familiarity with manuscript publication persisted: as late as 1763 or 1764, Voltaire included a manuscript in a letter to the Marquis d'Argence, inviting him to circulate it as propaganda in the *philosophes*'s cause,[20] and he orchestrated from Ferney the diffusion of many manuscripts.[21]

Books too circulated anonymously, and works such as the *Éléments de la philosophie de Newton*, signed 'par M. de Voltaire' on the title page, or the *Histoire de Charles XII*, signed 'par M. de V***', are not entirely typical of his output as a whole. While Voltaire signs his works of science and history, he simply leaves unsigned his more controversial works such as the *Dictionnaire philosophique portatif*, the *Traité sur la tolérance* or *Le Philosophe ignorant*. In the case of works of fiction, fantasy is understandably to the fore: *Candide* is 'translated from the German of Dr Ralph' ('traduit de l'allemand de Mr. le docteur Ralph'), *L'Ingénu* is 'a true story, taken from the manuscripts of Father Quesnel' ('histoire véritable, tirée des manuscrits du Père Quesnel'), *Le Taureau blanc* is 'translated from the Syriac' ('traduit du syriaque').

The advantage of not signing a title page is very simple: it allowed Voltaire to deny authorship, and if the denial was not altogether convincing, so much the better – his style was, in any case, easily recognisable. An example of this game of cat-and-mouse is provided by the *Histoire du parlement de Paris*. This piece of contemporary history has some harsh words about Louis XV, and the first three editions are signed 'par Mr. l'abbé Big . . .'; the fourth edition 'par Mr. l'abbé Bigore'. To friend after friend, Voltaire wrote denying his authorship of the work, declaring himself the victim of a calumny, of an injustice.[22] 'I am used to taking the rap for others', he told Mme Du Deffand. 'I am rather like you ladies who are credited with twenty-odd lovers when you have only had one or two' ('je suis accoutumé à porter les iniquités d'autrui. Je ressemble assez à vous autres mesdames à qui on donne une vingtaine d'amants quand vous en avez eu un ou deux', D15758). In other letters he hints at the identity of the 'true' author, sometimes suggesting that the work was based on manuscripts which had been stolen from him. Then, as it becomes clear that it is the last two chapters which contain the principal causes of offence, he tries out a new line: that the book is clearly written by two different hands – in other words, he tacitly takes responsibility for chapters 1 to 65, but definitely not for the last two, which, he declares, are patently less well written (and therefore from a different pen). The comedy is played out in many dozens of letters over a number of months: clearly the letters were designed to influence opinion in Paris, and to the extent that no official moves were made against Voltaire, they may be said to have been successful. It sometimes suited Voltaire to play the role of the victim, and there was a strong element of play-acting in the whole charade, which Voltaire, and perhaps his correspondents, enjoyed. His playfulness, which begins by being strategic, ends up as an art form in its own right.

The same ambivalence affects his extravagant use of pseudonyms (the list of some 175 pseudonyms in the Bibliothèque nationale catalogue is far from complete). At the simplest level, a pseudonym can of course conceal the writer's true identity. Thus when, in 1736, Jean-Baptiste Rousseau published in the *Bibliothèque française* an article attacking Voltaire, a trenchant reply duly appeared in the same journal, signed by one 'de Molin' (D1134). We know nothing of this person, and can reasonably assume that it is a pseudonym designed to conceal Voltaire's own authorship. But when in 1767 *Les Questions de Zapata* first appeared, 'translated by sire Tamponet, a doctor of the Sorbonne' ('traduites par le sieur Tamponet, docteur de Sorbonne'), it seems unlikely that many readers would have been taken in; and even fewer two years later, when the same worthy cleric reappears as the translator of an epistolary fiction, *Les Lettres d'Amabed*, 'translated by the abbé Tamponet' ('traduites par l'abbé Tamponet'). In these last two cases, the invented name of the non-existent translator serves not to conceal Voltaire's authorship but rather to reveal and proclaim it. No writer of the century relished pseudonyms as much as Voltaire did, and altogether they number many hundreds. He had a predictable fondness for clerical garb, and signed various texts as a minister, a rabbi, a Quaker, even as the archbishop of Novgorod. In a collection such as the *Contes de Guillaume Vadé* (1764), a best-selling anthology of verse and prose tales and other short pieces, Voltaire puts on the title page a name which sounds half plausible, in that it alludes to Jean-Joseph Vadé (an author of light works composed in popular jargon) who had died in 1757. Voltaire then takes the game further within the same book and imagines the existence of relations of the fictitious Guillaume: a cousin Catherine Vadé signs the preface to the work, while a brother Antoine Vadé signs the *Discours aux Welches*. Voltaire's comedy *L'Écossaise* of 1760 is signed 'Hume', and a preface explains that the author is a priest and relative of David Hume; when David Hume arrived in Paris in 1763, Voltaire, unabashed, referred to the visiting Scottish philosopher as 'this Mr Hume, cousin of that other Hume, the charming author of *L'Écossaise*' ('ce Mr Hume, cousin de cet autre Hume, charmant auteur de L'Ecossaise', D11490).

Such proliferating pseudonyms are part of a game which Voltaire enjoys with his reader. More than that, they reflect a fragmentation of a single authorial and authoritative voice, an effect that leads us into the heart of the style and form of Voltaire's writing. In the polemical works in particular, Voltaire relishes all forms of literary device which multiply the voices within a single text. Thus the short chapters of the *Traité sur la tolérance*, composed in different and contrasting styles and even literary genres, create a dialogic effect which challenges the reader to pin down the author's 'real' voice. Another device, also found in this work, is that of the 'note', whereby Voltaire provides an often extensive commentary on his own work, forcing his reader to move between different registers of thinking and sometimes of language. He even invents a pseudonym, 'M. de Morza', specifically to sign the notes of certain works. Voltaire's use of self-quotation, especially in later works, is also a characteristic feature of his writing: as one Voltairean narrator quotes, and often re-writes, passages from another Voltairean work, the reader's sense of an authorial persona disappears behind the spectacle of a body of writing which is always in flux. At the level of form, this can lead to fragmented texts and miscellanies of self-reflecting patchworks of texts, far removed from the 'Classical' aesthetic that Voltaire notionally acknowledges.[23] No wonder that Voltaire was so often imitated and parodied, and that already in his lifetime there was a whole industry producing apocryphal works (such as the sequel, *Candide, seconde partie*). This was only to be expected, given that Voltaire seemed so often to be imitating and parodying himself.

After the *philosophe* Helvétius published *De l'esprit* to a storm of protest, Voltaire wrote to him, in 1760, with some fraternal advice (D9141):

> I can't get over the fact you published your book under your own name, but one has to deal with things as one finds them . . . Moreover one should never publish anything under one's own name; I didn't even write *La Pucelle*; Joly de Fleury [who denounced the *Encyclopédie* before the Parlement] can try to draw up an indictment, I shall tell him he's a slanderer, that he's the one responsible for *La Pucelle*, the work he is wickedly trying to pin on me.
>
> (Je ne me console point que vous ayez donné votre livre sous votre nom mais il faut partir d'où l'on est . . . Au reste il ne faut jamais rien donner sous son nom; je n'ai pas même fait *La Pucelle*; maître Joly de Fleury aura beau faire un réquisitoire je lui dirai qu'il est un calomniateur, que c'est lui qui a fait *La Pucelle*, qu'il veut méchamment mettre sur mon compte.)

Voltaire describes his strategy with untypical directness in the dedication to his comedy *L'Écossaise*:

> P.S. I am not putting my useless name at the end of this letter, because I have never attached it to any of my works; and when you see it at the start of a book

or on a poster, the responsibility lies entirely with the poster-writer or the printer

(*P.S.* Je ne mets point mon inutile nom au bas de cette épître, parce que je ne l'ai jamais mis à aucun de mes ouvrages; et quand on le voit à la tête d'un livre ou dans une affiche, qu'on s'en prenne uniquement à l'afficheur ou au libraire).[24]

As an author Voltaire makes his mark, literally and metaphorically, in a way that is altogether original. His contemporary Jean-Jacques Rousseau made it a point of honour always to sign his name to everything he wrote, insisting on an idea of authorship as a public activity.[25] Voltaire, by contrast, makes a literary virtue out of pretending to hide his name. 'Voltaire' – in itself, after all, an invented signature – becomes a brand name for a style of writing and a form of thinking. If it seems somehow to transcend and free itself from the person who originated it, that was surely François Arouet's intention. The much heralded 'death of the author', supposedly a hallmark of modernity, perhaps occurred earlier than we realised.[26]

'Voltaire': an invention of public opinion

The type of author that Voltaire became was only possible because of the expectations and ambitions of the reading public of his day. Since the mid-1980s, and influenced by the work of Jürgen Habermas,[27] Enlightenment scholars have been much preoccupied with the idea of an emerging 'public sphere' in which information could be exchanged between free rational individuals on a more or less egalitarian basis. The seventeenth-century republic of letters, essentially a network of scholars founded on personal relationships, came after 1750 to be replaced by a broader enlightened public sphere characterised by rational debate.[28] While the application of Habermas's ideas remains controversial, they have encouraged an increased awareness of the role of public opinion in the evaluation of what Voltaire wrote.[29] Already in the 1730s, Voltaire invokes the notion of 'opinion' by comparing Newton and Descartes: 'The Opinion that generally prevails in England with regard to these two Philosophers is, that the latter was a Dreamer, and the former a Sage'; and it is significant that in the French original of this passage, Voltaire uses the expression 'opinion publique'.[30] Later, in 1748, when he published the *Anecdotes sur Louis XIV* as a kind of trailer for his *Siècle de Louis XIV*, Voltaire explained to the Duc de Richelieu that this had been to test opinion: 'I flatter myself that this will not displease, especially after sounding out views and preparing public opinion' ('Je me flatte de ne point déplaire, surtout après avoir sondé les esprits et préparé l'opinion publique', D4561). With the Calas affair, Voltaire's engagement with public events acquired a higher profile than ever before, and he learned at first hand the importance of arousing and then guiding public opinion. When the Parlement of Toulouse refused to yield its papers to a Paris court, Voltaire wrote to an ally in Paris in July 1762 that it would be necessary to use royal powers to force the hand of the magistrates in Toulouse: 'We believe that a public outcry is the best means of achieving that' ('Nous croyons que le cri public est le meilleur moyen pour y parvenir', D10573). This expression 'le cri (du) public' occurs in Voltaire's correspondence for the first time only in 1758, then recurs on over fifteen occasions in the decade that follows:[31] testimony both of the extent to which Voltaire's activities in the 1760s depended on manipulating public opinion and of the central role of the correspondence in that campaign. In a work of 1764, *Conformez-vous aux temps*, Voltaire is adamant that it is the role of the *philosophes* to drive public opinion: 'Opinion rules the world; but it is the philosophers who in the long run steer this opinion' ('L'opinion gouverne le monde; mais ce sont les sages qui à la longue dirigent cette opinion') – Voltaire was clearly pleased with this formula, which he repeats twice in letters to d'Argental.[32]

One prime example of a book that took European public opinion by storm was Cesare Beccaria's *On Crimes and Punishments* (1764), a pioneering and influential work on penal reform: the French translation alone went through seven editions in the space of six months. An English translator, in his preface, comments on the reception of the work:

> It is not surprising then, that this little book hath engaged the attention of all ranks of people in every part of Europe. It is now about eighteen months since the first publication; in which time it hath passed no less than six editions in the original language . . . It hath been translated into French; that translation hath also been several times reprinted, and perhaps no book, on any subject, was ever received with more avidity, more generally read, or more universally applauded.[33]

Voltaire's decision to write a commentary on this work was motivated in part by his genuine engagement with the issues of political justice which it raised – and in part too by a desire to seize the moment and to exploit, and even share some part of, Beccaria's success. Voltaire did not like being in the shade. Very quickly, publishers with an eye on the market began producing combined editions, in which Voltaire's commentary follows Beccaria's text – no matter that Voltaire's 'commentary' is not really a commentary at all – and it was in this form that Voltaire's text became known to the English reading public. Following his by now usual practice, Voltaire had signed the *Commentaire* with a cryptic 'by a provincial lawyer' ('par un avocat de province') – a convoluted double-bluff, since in all probability part of the text really was written, or at least researched, by his young friend Christin, who genuinely was a provincial lawyer. Confusingly, Voltaire was for once (almost) telling the truth on the title page, and he could be confident that he would not be believed. The first English translation (1767) describes the *Commentaire* as 'attributed' to Voltaire, but from 1778 the translations simply say 'by' Voltaire. Here is how one English translator deals with this problem:

> With regard to the Commentary, attributed to Monsieur de Voltaire, my only authority for supposing it to be his, is the voice of the public, which indeed is the only authority we have for most of his works. Let those who are acquainted with the peculiarity of his manner judge for themselves.[34]

It is, claims the translator, the 'voice of the public' that allows us to attribute this work to Voltaire. This is, of course, the ultimate achievement of Voltaire's notion of authorship. He does not need to sign his works: his voice, 'the peculiarity of his manner', is immediately recognised by readers across Europe. The pseudonym 'Voltaire' designates not a person, not even a precise body of writing: it comes to stand for a way of writing and a way of looking at the world.

NOTES

1. See A. Viala, *Naissance de l'écrivain: Sociologie de la littérature à l'âge classique* (Paris: Minuit, 1985); and É. Walter, 'Les auteurs et le champ littéraire', in *Histoire de l'édition française*, 4 vols, ed. R. Chartier and H.-J. Martin (Paris: Promodis, 1984), vol.2, pp.382–400.
2. M. Foucault, 'What is an Author?', in *The Foucault Reader*, ed. P. Rabinow (New York: Pantheon, 1984), pp.101–20 (p.108); the essay was first published ('Qu'est-ce qu'un auteur?') in 1969.
3. An excellent overview of recent debates in this area is found in G. S. Brown, *A Field of Honor: Writers, Court Culture, and Public Theater in French Literary Life from Racine to the Revolution* (New York: Columbia University Press, 2002). Available online: www.gutenberg-e.org.
4. R. Chartier, in S. Ginet (ed.), *Le Statut de l'homme de lettres au XVIIIe siècle* (videocassette, Paris: Arts et éducation, 1994).
5. See N. Cronk, 'Voltaire au pays des folliculaires: une carrière littéraire entre deux siècles', in H. Duranton (ed.), *Le Pauvre Diable: Destins de l'homme de lettres au XVIIIe siècle* (Saint-Étienne: Publications de l'Université de Saint-Étienne, 2006), pp.25–38.
6. Moland, vol.1, p.45.
7. Moland, vol.1, p.55.
8. See the Introduction to *Lettres inédites de Voltaire à Gabriel Cramer*, ed. B. Gagnebin (Geneva: Droz, 1952); B. Gagnebin, 'La diffusion clandestine des œuvres de Voltaire par les soins des frères Cramer', *Annales de l'Université de Lyon, Lettres* 39 (Paris: Les Belles Lettres, 1965), pp.119–32; and G. Barber, 'Voltaire et la présentation typographique de *Candide*', in his *Studies in the Booktrade of the European Enlightenment* (London: Pindar Press, 1994), pp.37–55.

9. G. Banderier, 'Une lettre inédite de Voltaire au pasteur Élie Bertrand (Besterman, D6793b)', *French Studies Bulletin*, 83 (Summer 2002), 10–12.

10. *OCV*, vol.18B, pp.411–29.

11. See *Zadig, ou la destinée*, ed. H. T. Mason, *OCV*, vol.30B, p.71.

12. Quoted by J. R. Iverson, 'Voltaire, Fontenoy, and the Crisis of Celebratory Verse', *Studies in Eighteenth-Century Culture*, 28 (1999), 207–28 (p.217). Voltaire had long been sensitive to criticism on this matter: when he asked Thiriot to delay the publication of the *Lettres anglaises* in order to add the twenty-fifth letter on Pascal, he explained that it would be no good adding this to a second edition: 'Those who will have acquired the first edition at a fairly high price will be most displeased to have to buy it a second time for the sake of a small addition, and . . . the literary hacks will be sure to say it's a trick to make people buy the same book twice at an inflated price' ('Ceux qui auraient acheté la première édition qui se vendra assez cher, seront très fâchés d'être obligés de l'acheter une seconde fois pour une petite augmentation, et . . . les misérables insectes du parnasse, ne manqueront pas de dire que c'est un artifice pour faire acheter deux fois le même livre bien cher' (D631)).

13. See R. Darnton, 'The Science of Piracy: A Crucial Ingredient in Eighteenth-Century Publishing', *SVEC* 2003:12, 3–29.

14. See *Histoire de l'édition française*, ed. R. Chartier and H.-J. Martin, vol.2 (Paris: Fayard, 1990), pp.94–6. For a full list of condemnations of the *Lettres philosophiques*, see F. Weil, *Livres interdits, livres persécutés 1720–1770* (Oxford: Voltaire Foundation, 1999), pp.126–7.

15. The *Letters* would have seemed all the more plausibly 'English' given that their form was strongly reminiscent of the English periodical, in particular Addison's *Spectator*; see N. Cronk, 'Voltaire rencontre Monsieur le Spectateur: Addison et la genèse des *Lettres anglaises*', in *Voltaire en Europe: Hommage à Christiane Mervaud*, ed. M. Delon and C. Seth (Oxford: Voltaire Foundation, 2000), pp.13–21.

16. This publishing strategy is discussed further in N. Cronk, 'The *Letters Concerning the English Nation* as an English Work: Reconsidering the Harcourt Brown Thesis', *SVEC* 2001:10, 226–39.

17. This idea recurs twice in the *Notebooks*: see *OCV*, vol.81, pp.134 and 351.

18. See F. Moureau, 'L'auteur n'est pas celui que l'on croit', in *La Plume et le plomb: Espaces de l'imprimé et du manuscrit au siècle des Lumières* (Paris: Presses universitaires Paris-Sorbonne, 2006), pp.87–101.

19. See N. Cronk, 'Arouet, poète épicurien: les voix de l'épicurisme de la poésie de jeunesse de Voltaire', *Dix-Huitième Siècle*, 35 (2003), 153–66; and 'L'*Épître à Uranie* de Voltaire: stratégies de publication d'une œuvre clandestine', in *Poétique de la pensée: En hommage à Jean Dagen* (Paris: Champion, 2006), pp.275–84.

20. See M.-H. Cotoni, 'Sur les juifs: hypothèses sur un manuscrit de Voltaire', *La Lettre clandestine*, 11 (2003), 77–90.

21. See Moureau, *La Plume et le plomb*, 'L'Agence Voltaire de Ferney et d'ailleurs', pp.445–58.

22. See the comments of J. Renwick, in his edition of this work, *OCV*, vol.68, pp.99–113.

23. See N. Cronk, 'Les dialogues de Voltaire: vers une poétique du fragmentaire', *Revue Voltaire*, 5 (2005), 71–82; and 'Auteur et autorité dans les mélanges:

l'exemple des *Lois de Minos, tragédie avec les notes de M. de Morza et plusieurs pièces détachées* (1774)', *Revue Voltaire*, 6 (2006), 53–70.

24. OCV, vol.50, p.346.

25. See C. Kelly, *Rousseau as Author: Consecrating One's Life to the Truth* (Chicago, IL: University of Chicago Press, 2003).

26. R. Barthes, 'The Death of the Author', in *Image, Music, Text*, selected and trans. S. Heath (London: Fontana, 1977), 142–8; the essay was first published ('La mort de l'auteur') in 1968.

27. J. Habermas's *Strukturwandel der Öffentlichkeit* first appeared in German in 1962; the work began to influence Enlightenment scholars after the publication of translations into French (*L'Espace public*, 1978) and English (*The Structural Transformation of the Public Sphere*, 1989).

28. See A. Goldgar, *Impolite Learning: Conduct and Community in the Republic of Letters, 1680–1750* (New Haven, CT: Yale University Press, 1995).

29. On public opinion generally, see J. A. W. Gunn, *Queen of the World: Opinion in the Public Life of France from the Renaissance to the Revolution* (Oxford: Voltaire Foundation, 1995), SVEC 328; and P.-E. Knabe (ed.), *Opinion* (Berlin: Berlin Verlag Arno Spitz, 2000). For an example of how public opinion can influence Voltaire's writing, see O. Ferret, *La Fureur de nuire: Échanges pamphlétaires entre philosophes et antiphilosophes (1750–1770)*, SVEC 2007:03, pp.395–411.

30. *Letters*, p.64; *LP*, vol.2, p.5 (letter 14).

31. See D7653, D7661, D7708, D9534, D10554, D10556, D10567, D10573, D10588, D10636, D10679, D10849, D10925, D11040, D12559, D13308 and D14606.

32. Moland, vol.25, p.318; D13082 and D13139.

33. *An Essay on Crimes and Punishments by the Marquis Beccaria ... with a Commentary by M. de Voltaire* (Edinburgh: James Donaldson, 1788), 'Preface of the translator', pp.iii–iv.

34. *An Essay on Crimes and Punishments*, 'Preface of the translator', p.v.

3

DAVID BEESON AND NICHOLAS CRONK

Voltaire: philosopher or *philosophe*?

For one historian of ideas, Isaiah Berlin, Voltaire is 'the central figure of the Enlightenment'; while for another, John Gray, 'Voltaire's writings on philosophical questions are unoriginal to the last degree ... Few of the entries in his *Philosophical Dictionary* are concerned with philosophical questions.'[1] The problem lies in part with the word *philosophique*, which Gray here (perhaps mischievously) misunderstands. The French word *philosophe* is not easily translated into English: in the specific context of the eighteenth century, it refers to those authors – Montesquieu, Voltaire, Jean-Jacques Rousseau, Diderot – who through their writings helped popularise the Enlightenment values of reason, empiricism, toleration and humanity. More broadly, the French word can also refer to any philosopher, such as Descartes or Kant. The ambivalence of the term reflects an ambivalence in our image of Voltaire. Is he an original philosophical thinker? Or is he simply a vulgariser and publicist for the thought of others?

On the one hand, Voltaire was the first to admit that he was no analytical philosopher: to his friend Thiriot, he wrote in 1760 that 'I have never pretended to have an orderly mind like a Newton or a Rameau. I would never have discovered the root of the chord or integral calculus' ('Je n'ai jamais prétendu avoir une tête organisée comme un Newton, un Rameau. Je n'aurais jamais trouvé la basse fondamentale ni le calcul intégral', D9489). Voltaire is no Locke, no Newton: but in the *Lettres philosophiques* he did play a decisive role in introducing both those thinkers to a wide European audience. His skills as a writer and as a publicist of ideas mean that he did perhaps more than any other single author to shape the course of Enlightenment thought.

On the other hand, we should not underestimate the extent to which Voltaire was steeped in the philosophical tradition of his time. One recent study which does treat Voltaire seriously as a thinker takes as its starting point his relationship to Cartesianism; other recent research has revealed, for example, the extent of Voltaire's knowledge of George Berkeley.[2] A further consideration is that there is a tipping point in works popularising the thought of others at which they cease to be 'mere' vulgarisation and become genuinely original. What can be said of Voltaire is that he gave expression, forcefully and militantly, to a set of values. We find in his writings a series of recurring themes and a picture of the world which, disconcertingly, leaves much unexplained. That incompleteness is a consequence of his very approach. One of the constants of Voltaire's outlook is empiricism: his epistemology is based on the principle that nothing can reach the intellect other than through the senses and anything unobserved is necessarily unknown (and possibly unknowable).[3] Doubt is an essential element of Voltaire's philosophy – a lesson that he learned from Pierre Bayle[4] – and there are areas of ignorance that we simply have to accept. If doubt is inevitable, then dogmatism is impossible and so is intolerance. How can we oppress others for their views if we cannot be certain of our own? That same empiricism underlies what we now regard as the essential methodology of science. Voltaire witnessed the beginnings of the scientific revolution brought about by the impact of Newton's work. Himself an enthusiast for Newton, Voltaire became an active participant in the scientific revolution around him; he played a key role in spreading knowledge of Newton in continental Europe, and even attempted to become a practising scientist himself. Though that attempt failed, his scientific work marked his thinking and moulded the philosophical legacy he has left us, a legacy more complex than appears at first sight.

The problem of Voltaire's deism

Any discussion of Voltaire as a thinker begins with consideration of his ideas on religion. When René Pomeau, one of the leading specialists on Voltaire in the second half of the twentieth century, published his thesis *La Religion de Voltaire* in 1956, the title was intended to surprise, even shock. The nineteenth-century view of Voltaire as an opponent of Catholicism, an atheist, the Antichrist even, was then still prevalent, so to speak of 'Voltaire's religion' must have seemed like a provocation. Through a detailed chronological overview of a wide range of texts, Pomeau distilled the references to religion and was able to demonstrate Voltaire's abiding – one might say, obsessive – adherence to the notion of a 'supreme being' who had created the universe, and who punished evil and rewarded good. The evidence for the existence of this god – we are no longer really speaking of the Christian God – is found in the argument from design (sometimes also called the argument from final causes): the 'architecture' of the universe implies the existence of an architect. In 1745, Voltaire first used the formulation of the idea with which his name has ever since been linked, that of God as watchmaker (he may have found the metaphor in a clandestine manuscript

by Robert Challe, best known under its later title of *Le Militaire philosophe*).
We examine a watch and understand that the cogs and springs did not come
together by chance: 'I shall always be convinced that a watch proves the
existence of a watchmaker and that the universe proves the existence of a
God' ('Je serai toujours persuadé, qu'une horloge prouve un horloger et que
l'univers prouve un Dieu').[5]

Pomeau's thesis that Voltaire was a sincere deist has found broad acceptance. One rare critic was Theodore Besterman, who in the 1960s argued
against Pomeau that it would be more accurate to describe Voltaire as an
agnostic, if not quite an outright atheist.[6] There are clear hints, for example
in Letter 13 on Locke in the *Lettres philosophiques*, that Voltaire was
tempted by the atheist hypothesis;[7] but the intellectual temptation was
tempered always by social pragmatism: 'If you've got a town to govern, it
must have a religion' ('Si vous avez une bourgade à gouverner, il faut qu'elle
ait une religion').[8] Simply applying a label to Voltaire's religious beliefs
does not in any case help advance the debate: what is important is not so
much what Voltaire thinks as how he writes and argues. In other words, the
interpretation of Voltaire's religious thinking is as much a matter for the
literary critic as for the historian of ideas. Pomeau's thesis, enormously
important as it remains, is now half a century old, and its methodology has
evident limitations. In particular, it tends to treat literary texts as historical
documents; and it sometimes describes Voltaire's ideas without adequate
contextualisation. We will examine these points in turn.

Firstly, there is the question of the proper use and interpretation of literary
texts. The complexity of Voltaire as a writer lies in the fact that he speaks
through many voices and masks. While this feature makes Voltaire such a
fascinating author to read, we have to beware of quoting out of context any
single passage as though it represented the author's considered and unme-
diated view. Voltaire's *Traité sur la tolérance* concludes with a celebrated
'Prayer to God' ('Prière à Dieu', chap.23): 'It is no longer men that I am
addressing, it is you, God of all beings, of all worlds and of all times'
('Ce n'est donc plus aux hommes que je m'adresse, c'est à toi, Dieu de tous
les êtres, de tous les mondes et de tous les temps').[9] This certainly seems like
an uncomplicated expression of belief in a deist god, and Pomeau quotes the
'Prière' as 'the great lesson of the Calas affair'.[10] But when we examine this
chapter more closely, we discover that it is entirely unlike the others in the
same work. All the other chapters – we might call them short essays – are
dialogic, containing interposed voices, often in quotation marks or italics;
the final chapter of this highly fragmented work is oddly monologic and so
stands quite apart from the others. As José-Michel Moureaux has shown,
this 'Prière à Dieu', when read in the context of the work as a whole, is not at

all the conclusion that it pretends to be.[11] Certainly, the narrator of the 'Prière' assumes a deist voice; but whether this voice is also Voltaire's is another matter.

Secondly, the question of contextualisation: Pomeau describes at length Voltaire's commitment to deism, yet does not situate this belief in the debates of the period. Deism, influenced by thinkers in England and Holland, was important in France broadly in the first half of the eighteenth century (we shall return to this below); thereafter, radical thinkers were less inhibited in expressing materialist or atheist views. Here is Voltaire putting forward a familiar deist argument: 'You can be a very good philosopher and believe in God. The atheists have never answered the argument that a clock proves the existence of a clockmaker' ('On peut être très bon philosophe et croire en Dieu. Les athées n'ont jamais répondu à cette difficulté, qu'un horloge prouve un horloger', D15189). The difficulty with this statement lies simply in its date. It occurs in a letter which Voltaire wrote in 1768, at a time when deism and the argument from design had long since ceased to be a focus of debate.[12] Voltaire's deism was a personal and idiosyncratic creed which, as the years passed, seemed increasingly out of step with the times. In 1770, the Baron d'Holbach published anonymously his *Système de la nature*, a comprehensive (if shallow) exposition of atheist materialism. Voltaire was incensed, and in his late 70s responded with a series of works re-asserting the case for deism in the face of the growing tide of atheism. His strident rejection of atheism is emotional as much as intellectual. Voltaire's passionate attachment to deism does not, and cannot, evolve.

English thought in the *Lettres philosophiques*

The first prose work in which Voltaire openly presented himself as a *philosophe* was his *Lettres philosophiques*. The letters were begun while Voltaire was in England in the 1720s, and the title of the first English edition, *Letters Concerning the English Nation*, might give the impression that they are a traveller's view of England; in reality, Voltaire offers often idealised vignettes of English life designed to make philosophical points and implicitly suggest ways in which France needed to change.

If doubt breeds tolerance, then certainty breeds bigotry, and nowhere is that clearer than in established religions. The first seven *Letters* deal with religion, and their key sentiment is freedom: 'An *Englishman*, as one to whom liberty is natural, may go to heaven his own way' ('Un Anglais comme homme libre, va au Ciel par le chemin qui lui plaît').[13] England practises freedom of belief, creating a society based on religious tolerance. (Of course, this is an idealised picture, and Voltaire realised that reality fell short of the ideal, admitting in Letter 5 that it is only within the Church of England that a career in public service could be made.) To Voltaire, tolerance and prosperity are linked, a point demonstrated by the description in Letter 6 of men of many faiths conducting their business together in the Royal Exchange: commerce unites where religion divides.[14]

This plea for toleration is grounded in a philosophical approach. When he turns to philosophy proper, the contrast between England and France provides another orthodoxy to attack, that of the all-embracing system. Generous in his tribute to Descartes's achievements, he is uncompromising in denouncing his faults: Descartes's preference for 'hypotheses' over 'geometry' meant that his 'Philosophy was no more than an ingenious Romance' ('sa Philosophie ne fut plus qu'un roman ingénieux').[15]

England, in contrast, has produced Locke:

> Such a Multitude of Reasoners having written the Romance of the Soul, a Sage at last arose, who gave, with an Air of the greatest Modesty, the History of it . . . He every where takes the Light of Physicks for his Guide. He sometimes presumes to speak affirmatively, but then he presumes also to doubt.
>
> (Tant de raisonneurs aïant fait le roman de l'âme, un sage est venu, qui en a fait modestement l'histoire . . . Il s'aide partout du flambeau de la Phisique; il ose quelquefois parler affirmativement, mais il ose aussi douter.)[16]

The courage to doubt and the notion of the 'light' or torch of physics are recurring ideas in Voltaire's thought. He applauds Locke's rejection of Descartes's innate ideas, and endorses the Lockean view that ideas can only be derived from sense impressions, the fundamental assumption of empirical science, in which observation is central.[17] This discussion therefore leads naturally into the scientific material of the *Lettres*.

Descartes's followers accorded only a limited role to experiment. Newtonians, on the other hand, felt that scientific propositions had to be based entirely on experiment. Newton explicitly rejects Cartesian belief in the legitimacy of abstract thought in the words of his *Scholion Generale* to the *Principia Mathematica*, 'hypotheses non fingo' ('I feign no hypotheses'). What he could not advance by induction from observation, he would not attempt to explain by speculation. Voltaire had fully adopted this distinction by the time he wrote the *Lettres*. He points out that Cartesian gravitational theory, based on the idea that bodies are driven downwards by vortices of ethereal matter, has the merit of simplicity. He warns however that facile explanations can be treacherous: 'In Philosophy, a Student ought to doubt of the Things he fancies he understands too easily, as much as of those he does not understand' ('En philosophie il faut se défier de ce qu'on croit entendre trop aisément, aussi bien que des choses qu'on n'entend pas').[18] For example, no Cartesian had been able to propose a structure in which the rotating matter would cause objects to fall rather than push them sideways. The simplicity of the assumption is belied by the difficulty of the detail. Newton, by contrast, came up with a more complex model of nature, whereby all bodies seem to gravitate towards each other and do so even though there is no mechanical contact between them. This principle of gravitational attraction leads to startling simplicity when we observe what happens in nature. The way bodies fall on the surface of the Earth follows this law, but so do the planets in their orbits around the Sun or the Moon in its orbit around the Earth, and so does the ebb and flow of the tides. A difficult assumption generated a unifying and simplifying view of several phenomena that had previously seemed disparate. The *Lettres philosophiques* thus represent the first attempt in France to argue the superiority of Newtonian over Cartesian physics, a gesture which was widely seen as unpatriotic – and which only added to the storm which greeted the publication of the work.

Cirey and science

Following the appearance of the *Lettres philosophiques*, it was dangerous for Voltaire to remain in the capital. Mme Du Châtelet, who was to remain his companion until her death fifteen years later, provided Voltaire with a refuge in her husband's chateau at Cirey. It was there that they would pursue their studies together, both in philosophy and in science, for the next few years.[19] Voltaire followed up the *Lettres philosophiques* with a work intended only for Mme Du Châtelet and not published until after his death, the *Traité de métaphysique*. Because it remained unpublished, he could safely go further in developing many of the unorthodox ideas that he had announced in the *Lettres*.

The principal concern of the *Traité* is man as a social being, the theme to which the whole work builds in its concluding chapter. Yet this material is not a deduction by speculative reason from stated premises. On the contrary, Voltaire remains assertively empirical:[20]

> It is clear that we should never advance a hypothesis; we should not say: Let us start by inventing some principles with which we shall try to explain everything. Instead we should say: Let us analyse things exactly and then attempt to see with great trepidation if they obey certain principles.
>
> (Il est clair qu'il ne faut jamais faire d'hypothèse; il ne faut point dire: Commençons par inventer des principes avec lesquels nous tâcherons de tout expliquer. Mais il faut dire: Faisons exactement l'analyse des choses, et ensuite nous tâcherons de voir avec beaucoup de défiance si elles se rapportent avec quelques principes.)

Beyond what we can learn from observation we must accept that there is only ignorance: 'If we can make use neither of the compass of mathematics, nor of the torch of experiment and of physics, then we can certainly not take a single step forwards' ('Quand nous ne pouvons nous aider du compas des mathématiques, ni du flambeau de l'expérience et de la physique, il est certain que nous ne pouvons faire un seul pas').[21] Once more we meet the torch of physics. As for 'expérience', two pages later he will refer to 'experience founded on reason, the only source of our knowledge' ('l'expérience appuyée de raisonnement, seule source de nos connaissances'),[22] surely as neat a definition as any of what in English we call 'experiment'.

Mme Du Châtelet pursued her scientific studies at Cirey, but with a tutor, Samuel König, who also communicated to her his enthusiasm for the philosophy of Gottfried Wilhelm Leibniz. Voltaire, too, continued his scientific work in collaboration but also in rivalry with her, since each submitted a paper to the 1738 prize competition of the Paris Academy of Sciences, on the nature of fire, without the other knowing.[23] Neither won but the Academy published their submissions alongside that of the winner.

This was Voltaire's only venture into experimental science. During this Cirey period, he did however pursue other, more theoretical scientific study. In particular, he produced a comprehensive overview of Newton's science and philosophy, the *Éléments de la philosophie de Newton* (1738). Between 1738 and 1785 it went through no fewer than twenty-six editions. In its purely scientific chapters, the *Éléments* were a popularisation of Newton's work in optics and on gravitational theory. They reveal a remarkable understanding by Voltaire of complex scientific issues. Particularly interesting, however, is his discussion of the metaphysical implications of Newtonian science. Left out of the original edition of 1738, in a vain attempt to get it past the censor, it was published separately as the *Métaphysique de Newton* in 1740 and then as the prologue of the 1741 edition of the *Éléments* (it is this third version that we quote here). Newton's subordination of the universe to a single set of laws subject to rigorous mathematical analysis is for Voltaire nothing less than the most striking proof of the directing mind of God: 'The movement of the heavens . . . offered [Voltaire] some hopes that his own activities in the cause of rational enlightenment, toleration and humanity were not out of keeping with the essential nature of the cosmos.'[24]

Voltaire also returns repeatedly to the need to accept ignorance and refuse speculative explanation. For example, on the effect of the soul on the body, he writes that 'this action is to be numbered among those things whose mechanism will always remain unknown' ('cette action est du nombre des choses dont le mécanisme sera toujours ignoré');[25] on how elementary particles join to form bodies: 'this is perhaps one of the secrets of the creator, which will be forever unknown to men' ('peut-être est-ce un des secrets du créateur, lequel sera inconnu à jamais aux hommes').[26] Most striking of all are his words on Newton's lack of a position on the relationship between matter and soul: 'What was known in this field to the man who subjected the infinite to calculation, and who discovered the laws of weight? He knew how to doubt' ('Que savait donc sur cette matière celui qui avait soumis l'infini au calcul, et qui avait découvert les lois de la pesanteur? Il savait douter').[27] Where previously Voltaire had talked of daring to doubt, we are now in the realm of learning to doubt. Overall, the *Métaphysique de Newton* drew extensively on the *Traité de métaphysique*. It must have irked him not to have been able to publish the *Traité*, and the later work gave him an outlet for many of its ideas. So it deals with the problem of both human and divine liberty, the nature of man as a social being, and the nature of good and evil derived from that social existence.[28]

Much of this discussion is contained in new arguments against Leibniz, no doubt inspired by Voltaire's working in such close proximity to the newly converted Leibnizian, Mme Du Châtelet. He decisively rejects monads, the pre-established harmony, live force and other central tenets of Leibniz's thinking. When he deals with the problem of liberty he argues against Leibniz for a freedom of indifference. God exercises his freedom to create as he chooses, subject to no constraint; thus such decisions as the direction in which the planets rotate are arbitrary. Similarly, Voltaire himself reserves the right 'that the Creator has given me to want, and to act with no other reason than my will itself' ('que m'a donné le créateur de vouloir, et d'agir en certains cas sans autre raison que ma volonté même').[29] This may seem another simple proclamation of liberty, but it specifically targets Leibniz's belief that there is no action, including divine action, without sufficient reason, which excludes purely arbitrary choice. Voltaire saw this as an unacceptable restraint on God's and even man's freedom. The *Métaphysique* in 1741 is a bold and relatively optimistic statement of a Newtonian outlook on the world. An empirical methodology that accepts doubt allows us to develop a picture of the universe based on order. We have the capacity to understand God's wisdom and this gives us a means to control our physical world through scientific advance, and to govern ourselves better by promoting the application of good laws.

The *Éléments* was Voltaire's last scientific work, but he continued to revise it for later editions. The final version, which appeared in the Cramer collected edition of 1756, was prepared after the Lisbon earthquake of 1755. This event had shaken Voltaire's optimism and his confidence in the ability of scientific knowledge to help man control his surroundings, which is one reason why he began to lose interest in the physical sciences.[30] We are left with a disordered text in which some of the scientific insights, on the movement of the moon and the planets for instance, are simply missing. The result is a picture of a disordered world in which mankind no longer has any real control. In turn, this means that Voltaire's scientific thinking has become less relevant to his thinking about humanity.[31]

The *Éléments* represent a major scientific achievement: more than mere vulgarisation, this is a work of synthesis requiring real depth of knowledge.[32] The early version of this work marks the summit of Voltaire's achievement as a philosopher (rather than as a *philosophe*), an achievement which Jonathan Israel sums up in this way:

> The decisive period of Voltaire's formation as a philosopher was the years 1732–38 when he worked painstakingly to fashion a coherent system for himself and succeeded in reconfiguring, and briefly dominating, the French intellectual stage as a whole. By the mid 1730s, he could look forward to presiding over a wide-ranging programme of reform and renewal in French philosophy, science and scholarship as well as the world of literature, based on Lockean-Newtonian principles.[33]

In the *Éléments* Voltaire certainly establishes empirical principles deriving from Locke and Newton as the basis for future enquiry, whether in physical or moral sciences. It is significant, however, that by the final version, after the Lisbon earthquake, there is no longer the same firmness of principle nor the same faith in scientific method as a means of discovering truth with certainty. If initially Voltaire's sense of the importance of observation and the philosophical value of doubt had gone hand in hand with his adoption of a scientific method based on empiricism, in his later years the scientific method is lost, leaving only the reliance on observation and, above all, doubt.

Berlin: The dispute with Maupertuis

During his stay in Berlin as guest of the 'philosopher king', Frederick II, Voltaire crossed swords with Pierre-Louis Moreau de Maupertuis, his erstwhile ally and mentor in Newtonian science, and now president of the Prussian Academy of Sciences.[34] The spark that caused the latent hostility between them to explode was provided by the same Samuel König who had won over Mme Du Châtelet to Leibnizianism. In 1751, König published a paper which attacked the scientific principle that Maupertuis claimed as his own most important discovery, that of 'least action'. Paradoxically, given that he was questioning it, König also supported the rival attribution of the principle to Leibniz.

It seems a relatively minor dispute, but Maupertuis's reaction caused it to escalate. Instead of replying to König's arguments, he concentrated on the claim of Leibnizian precedent and demanded that König produce the original of the letter which supposedly proved his argument. When neither König nor anyone else succeeded in turning up any trace of it, Maupertuis called the Academy into plenary session on 13 April 1752 to hear a charge of forgery against König. The Academy complied and provided Maupertuis with the condemnation of König that he sought. Yet the Academy was not a court of law and had no authority to sit in judgement on König. Maupertuis's behaviour represented precisely the kind of abuse of power that Voltaire regularly denounced.

Voltaire took up the cause with energy and brilliance. His most effective work was the series of short satirical pieces that together form the *Histoire du Docteur Akakia et du natif de St-Malo*. Instead of reasoned argument, we have finely crafted invective, as in the *Diatribe du Docteur Akakia, médecin du Pape* in which the fictional doctor is ostensibly warning the president (Maupertuis) that a young man is trying to pass off his own, inferior works as the president's. Akakia quotes outlandish statements made by the young man, all of which are in fact drawn from Maupertuis's works. So he tells us the young man had 'claimed that children are formed in the mother's womb by attraction, that the left eye attracts the right leg, etc.' ('affirmé que les enfans se forment par attraction dans le ventre de la mère, que l'oeil gauche attire la jambe droite, etc.').[35] Maupertuis had argued that a foetus is formed from mixing 'parts' from the two parents, where each part is attracted towards parts corresponding to those that had been close to it before. This is speculation based on thin evidence but it was hardly as naïve as Akakia suggests.

Frederick II could not stand idly by as the president of his own Academy came under attack. Voltaire was to discover that a king could wield real oppressive power, far beyond any Maupertuis could exercise. The *Akakia* was officially condemned in Prussia and burned by the public executioner on Christmas Eve of 1752, in the same way as the *Lettres philosophiques* had been burned in Paris. The 'philosopher king' had behaved like the French authorities. Voltaire's stay in Germany ended in bitterness.

From our point of view, what is most significant about the *Akakia* is that it shows Voltaire moving beyond a theoretical exposition of the principles of his social philosophy to practical action to support it; for Voltaire, 'thought and writing were above all forms of action'.[36] The powerful use of a fictional framework and caricature to make philosophical points also marked a new development. These were to become his weapons of choice in the *contes* that he wrote alongside his campaigning pamphlets: the two genres are in fact convergent.[37] The most successful pamphlets mixed reality and fiction, just as in the *contes* reality appeared through the veil of fiction. In both, the narrative is not to be taken seriously but serves to make a particular human idea or attitude more concrete, the better to reveal its absurdity.

Écrasez l'Infâme: Campaigning for justice and tolerance

All the elements were now in place for Voltaire to compose the works that would mould the image we now have of him, the image which emerged from his campaign against social abuse under the slogan *Écrasez l'Infâme*. One of the major weapons of that campaign will be the *contes*, another the campaigning pamphlets such as those he wrote for the Calas case. In 1762 Jean Calas, a Protestant citizen of Toulouse, was tortured and executed for allegedly murdering his son who was said to be considering conversion to Catholicism. The trial that condemned him was deeply flawed and it is highly unlikely that Calas committed the offence. Voltaire, though suspicious of the Calvinists whom he regarded as intolerant sectarians, saw the case as bringing together many of the greatest evils of social life: religious intolerance, injustice and the abuse of power. He launched a campaign not just to rehabilitate Calas himself but to ensure that the surviving members of the family could reunite and enjoy a reasonable life.

A major work in Voltaire's campaign was his *Traité sur la tolérance* of 1763. He declares that tolerance is at the root of the natural order of relations between people, ultimately based on the precept that we should not do to others what we would not have them do to us. He supports this with examples of tolerance down the ages: the Romans tolerated heterodox thought, as did the Jews and the early Christians. It is even among the principles proclaimed by the modern Catholic Church. Voltaire is once more acting inductively, deriving his principles from observation, not deducing them from pre-ordained principle. The conclusion is that the intolerance shown to unorthodox thought in France, in particular in the Calas case, is an aberration that needs to be resisted.

The central point in Voltaire's thinking is this desire for an ordered society, in which well-meaning non-conformity is tolerated. In words reminiscent of the *Lettres philosophiques* he proclaims that 'the more sects there are, the less dangerous each is' ('plus il y a des sectes, moins chacune est dangereuse').[38] Persecution is the root cause of the very disorders it sets out to prevent:

> The university of Alsace is in the hands of the Lutherans; they hold a number of municipal offices; there has never been the slightest religious quarrel to disturb the peace of the province since it has belonged to our kings. Why? Because no one is persecuted. Don't set out to hurt hearts, and all hearts will be yours.

(L'université d'Alsace est entre les mains des luthériens; ils occupent une partie des charges municipales: jamais la moindre querelle religieuse n'a dérangé le repos de cette province depuis qu'elle appartient à nos rois. Pourquoi? C'est qu'on n'y a persécuté personne. Ne cherchez point à gêner les cœurs, et tous les cœurs seront à vous.)[39]

A Lockean empirical outlook had led Voltaire both into an early interest in science and also into a lifelong understanding of the need to accept doubt and ignorance. Doubt and ignorance undermine dogmatism and favour tolerance. These themes come together once more in *Le Philosophe ignorant* of 1766. The book's title couples philosophy and ignorance, and its first edition was structured as a series of 'Doubts'. Voltaire again underlines his Lockean view that much of the traditional subject matter of philosophy is unknowable. The book begins with a brief statement of the fundamental questions of metaphysics: who are we, where do we come from, what are we doing, what will we become? This leads to an extensive review of attempts to answer these questions. What emerges is that there are few things of which we can be sure. One is the existence of God, creator and legislator of the universe, because we know that the universe is subject to laws, and such law requires intelligence to apply it. Otherwise, philosophical speculation leads to little other than obscurities which bring no practical benefit for mankind.

This argument builds up to a eulogy of Locke, the master thinker, who is modest enough to appreciate that there are some things we do not know and others that we cannot know. In an appealing image, Voltaire talks of returning to Locke after his visits to other thinkers, like a prodigal son returning to his father.[40] As well as revisiting some truths that we have already seen him draw from Locke, such as the impossibility of knowledge drawn from anywhere but the senses or the impossibility of knowing the substance of things, Voltaire also draws on Locke for a view of freedom that has changed since the *Traité de métaphysique*. He no longer argues for freedom of indifference – the freedom to choose between indistinguishable alternatives. He now accepts that there will always be a reason to choose one alternative over the other; thus our will is determined by factors outside it. This leads him to conclude that 'free' is simply not a qualifier that one can apply to 'will': I am not free to will what I will. Freedom instead is the ability to do what one wills, with no external constraint.

The impossibility of answering more than a small number of questions of speculative philosophy leads to a scepticism that relativises all philosophy. That obliges him to assert the absolute independence of morality from philosophy. For, as John Gray argues, Voltaire embodied a belief common to the Enlightenment that ultimately man was progressing, whatever the setbacks, towards a model of civilisation which embodied aspirations common to all of humanity. This requires him to demonstrate the universality of those values, a position in stark contrast to the relativisation of morality that Locke had proclaimed.

It is the objective of the next argument of *Le Philosophe ignorant* to make this point. Voltaire starts by turning his guns against Locke's argument that the adoption of different standards in different societies demonstrates the relativism of moral values. To Voltaire, there are certain principles that are common to all cultures, principally the concept of justice. Those who point to the apparently unjust, cruel or barbarous behaviour of men in different circumstances fail to take into account that the perpetrators themselves feel justified in what they are doing: for instance, soldiers massacre people they see as enemies. A further review of many authorities, this time covering a wide range of cultures, shows that they all espouse essentially the same set of values.

Since ideas are not innate, Voltaire explains this universality as deriving from the order with which God has imbued the universe. He quotes Newton's principle 'natura est semper sibi consona' ('nature is always consistent with itself'),[41] as an argument for constancy in human nature against Locke's claim that nature varies, revealing that Voltaire's admiration for Newtonian science still had influence on his thinking generally. Since men have received reason from God, they are able to appreciate the underlying order of the world and deduce the same moral values from it, and it is true that Voltaire is a great deal closer in this work than in earlier ones to seeing in God not simply a Creator but also a legislator for human affairs. In one of the longest of the 'Doubts', dealing with Spinoza, Voltaire is particularly outspoken in his criticism of the new, and to him unwelcome, trend towards atheism among Enlightenment thinkers.[42]

Thus Voltaire has asserted the existence of God and of a universal moral code derived from him. We end up with a single commandment: 'Worship heaven and be just' ('Adorez le ciel et soyez justes').[43] This is not a speculative statement but a practical guide to life on Earth. So it is appropriate that *Le Philosophe ignorant* concludes with a call to action:

> Should we remain idle? Or should we light a flame at which envy and calumny will once more set alight their torches? For my part, I believe that truth should no longer hide from these monsters, that one should not stop feeding oneself for fear of being poisoned.
>
> (Faut-il rester oisifs? Ou faut-il allumer un flambeau auquel l'envie et la calomnie rallumeront leurs torches? Pour moi, je crois que la vérité ne doit plus se cacher devant ces monstres, que l'on ne doit s'abstenir de prendre de la nourriture dans la crainte d'être empoisonné.)[44]

'Dare to think for yourself'

Jonathan Israel's recent work on the Enlightenment distinguishes two parallel currents in the eighteenth century: on the one hand the atheistic 'Radical Enlightenment', derived from Spinoza; and on the other, the deistic 'Moderate Enlightenment', deriving from Locke and Newton, which grew up in the late seventeenth and early eighteenth centuries to counter the latent atheism of the radicals.[45] This interpretation, which goes against the more traditional view that argued for the emergence in the eighteenth century of a single radical, 'philosophical', current of thought, encourages us to reassess Voltaire's standing as an Enlightenment thinker.

Voltaire played a key role in explaining and establishing the importance of Locke and Newton in continental Europe. He was not their first spokesman, but he was the most influential, and his work in explaining Newton in the *Éléments* went well beyond mere vulgarisation. Thus Voltaire's role in spreading 'moderate Enlightenment' from England and Holland to France was a crucial one. His enduring influence can be seen, for example, in the 'Discours préliminaire' (1751) of the *Encyclopédie*, written by his friend (and later protégé) D'Alembert. The *Éléments* bear witness to his considerable knowledge of the scientific debates of the time.[46] In the 1730s and 1740s, he can reasonably be said to have been a leading progressive thinker, who even aspired – admittedly with only moderate success – to be an experimental scientist.

For a number of reasons the situation changed after the 1740s. For one thing, experimental science quickly grew more sophisticated, and became the privileged domain of specialists.[47] In an article 'Gens de lettres' published in the *Encyclopédie* in 1757, Voltaire described the ideal modern intellectual, equally at home in grammar, geometry, philosophy, history, poetry and eloquence. No true man of letters could specialise in just one area, yet Voltaire recognised that it was no longer possible to be a polymath: 'Universal science is no longer within the reach of man: but true men of letters make incursions into these different terrains, even if they cannot cultivate them all' ('La science universelle n'est plus à la portée de l'homme: mais les véritables *gens de lettres* se mettent en état de porter leurs pas dans ces différents terrains, s'ils ne peuvent les cultiver tous').[48] This had undoubtedly been his own ideal during the Cirey years, but by the time Voltaire's article was published in the late 1750s, this portrait of the man of letters as a quasi-Renaissance man was already beginning to look dated. Another significant change after the 1740s was the growing confidence and assertiveness of the exponents of atheistic materialism, which made it increasingly difficult to hold on to the compromise position of physico-theology derived from Locke and Newton. And finally there were undoubtedly personal factors at work too. The unexpected death in 1749 of Mme Du Châtelet brought to an abrupt end the time of their collaboration at Cirey, the place where Voltaire had had his scientific laboratory and where he had discussed Newton (and the Bible) with a privileged companion. He would now move to a different country and a new phase in his life would begin.

Voltaire's life took a different turn in Berlin, and even the unfortunate quarrel with Maupertuis – in a sense marking the end of Voltaire's career as a serious scientific thinker, whatever the rights and wrongs of the case – led to the satire *Akakia* and the new literary possibilities of short satirical fictions. Increasingly Voltaire was attracted to practical action. The Lisbon earthquake of 1755 marked what was possibly a turning point in the way he responded to the question of evil, and we should never underestimate the emotionalism that lies just below the surface of Voltairean reason: where *Zadig* (1747) deals with evil as a somewhat dry theoretical question, *Candide* (1759) treats evil as part of some absurdist nightmare. Throughout, Voltaire clung to the deist beliefs of his youth, and of course he has been criticised for this. But in a sense he had no choice: his deism was intricately bound up with the philosophical stances of Locke and Newton; the alliance of natural philosophy and natural theology did not really outlive the *Éléments*;[49] but having been a pioneer advocate of their cause in continental Europe, Voltaire was not inclined to renege on his former positions.

Instead, his thinking takes a more practical turn, and through the 1760s his involvement with a series of judicial causes célèbres encourages him to become more closely interested in questions of legal and judicial reform, as he emerges as a robust champion of free speech and tolerance. A cynic might say that Voltaire had been overtaken as a radical thinker and that his interest in practical, common-sense causes was an expedient designed to keep him at the centre of the action. But this would not be quite fair. It is true that the deist Voltaire cuts an old-fashioned figure by the 1760s; but his grasp of the evolving book trade and of the possibilities of using articles and pamphlets to influence public opinion – we would now call it being 'media savvy' – was unequalled. He emerges in this period as a journalist of genius, using not just the verbal and rhetorical skills of the writer but also his grasp of the publishing medium as a means to carry his message to the widest public, in France and beyond.[50] Bertrand Russell freely admitted the influence Voltaire had had, 'not so much on my opinions themselves as on the manner of conceiving them and the tone of professing them'.[51]

As the 'patriarch of Ferney' in his later years, he took a paternalistic interest in the local peasants, and expended vast energy in setting up a local watch-making industry to help the local economy: having spent all his life defending the notion of a God-watchmaker, he ends up himself as a seigneur-watchmaker. So a part of Voltaire's legacy is a practical one: this is after all one sense of the conclusion to *Candide*, with its injunction to 'cultivate the garden'. In his late poem addressed to Horace, the *Épître à Horace* (1772), Voltaire declares, with an understatement that has little to do with modesty, 'I've done a little good; it's my best work' ('J'ai fait un peu de bien; c'est mon meilleur ouvrage').[52]

It is true that Voltaire hardly qualifies as a philosopher in our modern sense of the term. But that is in part because much of what we would now regard as the baggage of a philosopher he would dismiss as idle and useless speculation. He limited his philosophy to a small number of principles that guided action. He derived from them a programme to build on the Enlightenment values of humanity, tolerance, justice, freedom of thought, that he supposed were universal. That Enlightenment programme has continued to inform us down to the present day: when we set out to extend 'Western values' to other societies we are wittingly or unwittingly acting on the programme that Voltaire favoured. However effectively we achieve that goal, however desirable or undesirable it may be, we are guided by habits of thought that originate with Voltaire.

In his article 'Liberté de penser' ('Freedom of Thought', 1765) in the *Dictionnaire philosophique*, Voltaire stages a dialogue between two aristocrats, the English 'milord' Boldmind and the Portuguese count Médroso (his name means 'Fearful'), an officer of the Inquisition. It is, of course, an unequal match, and Boldmind is uncomprehending of a man who does not strive to assert independence of thought:

> It's simply up to you to learn to think; you were born with intelligence; you are a bird in the Inquisition's cage, the Holy Office has clipped your wings, but they can grow back. If you know no geometry, you can learn it; any man can teach himself; it is shameful to place your soul in the hands of those you wouldn't trust with your money: *dare to think for yourself.* [my emphasis]
>
> (Il ne tient qu'à vous d'apprendre à penser; vous êtes né avec de l'esprit; vous êtes un oiseau dans la cage de l'Inquisition, le Saint-Office vous a rogné les ailes, mais elles peuvent revenir. Celui qui ne sait pas la géométrie peut l'apprendre; tout homme peut s'instruire; il est honteux de mettre son âme entre les mains de ceux à qui vous ne confierez pas votre argent: osez penser par vous-même.)[53]

This last dictum is borrowed from Horace (*sapere aude*, 'dare to know').[54] It is a good motto: Kant famously made it the starting point of his essay 'What is Enlightenment?' (1784), but Voltaire got there first, in this 1765 addition to the *Dictionnaire philosophique*. It is his unfailing sense of the telling expression that helps make Voltaire the consummate *philosophe.*

NOTES

1. I. Berlin, *Against the Current: Essays in the History of Ideas* (Oxford: Clarendon Press, 1991), p.88; J. Gray, *Voltaire* (London: Phoenix, 1998), p.3.

2. É. Martin-Haag, *Voltaire: Du cartésianisme aux Lumières* (Paris: Vrin, 2002); S. Charles, 'La figure de Berkeley dans la pensée voltairienne', *Dix-Huitième Siècle*, 33 (2001), 367–84.

3. See R. Niklaus, 'Voltaire et l'empirisme anglais', *Revue internationale de philosophie*, 48 (1994), 9–24.

4. See, for example, Moland, vol.9, p.476.

5. *Éléments de la philosophie de Newton*, OCV, vol.15, p.755.

6. T. Besterman, 'Voltaire's God', *SVEC*, 55 (1967), 23–41. R. Pomeau replied to this article in the 'Postface' to the revised edition of *La Religion de Voltaire* (Paris: Nizet, 1969).

7. See *Letters*, p.57, p.184–5; and C. Porset, 'La "philosophie" de Voltaire', *Europe*, 781 (May 1994), 53–62.

8. Article 'Religion' in the *Questions sur l'Encyclopédie* (1771), Moland, vol.20, p.341.

9. OCV, vol.56C, p.251.

10. R. Pomeau, *La Religion de Voltaire*, new edn (Paris: Nizet, 1969), p.333.

11. J.-M. Moureaux, 'Place et présence de Dieu dans le *Traité sur la tolérance*', in F. Bessire and S. Menant (eds), *Lectures d'une œuvre: 'Traité sur la tolérance' de Voltaire* (Paris: Éditions du temps, 1999), pp.82–99.

12. See N. Cronk, 'Voltaire (non) lecteur de Nieuwentijt: le problème des causes finales dans la pensée voltairienne', *Revue Voltaire*, 7 (2007), 169–81.

13. Letter 5; *Letters*, p.26; *LP*, vol.1, p.61.

14. Letter 6; *Letters*, p.30; *LP*, vol.1, p.74.

15. Letter 14; *Letters*, p.65; *LP*, vol.2, p.6.

16. Letter 13; *Letters*, p.56; *LP*, vol.1, pp.168–9.

17. Letter 13; *Letters*, p.56; *LP*, vol.1, p.169.

18. Letter 15; *Letters*, p.67; *LP*, vol.2, p.17.

19. On this period generally, see W. H. Barber, 'Voltaire at Cirey: Art and Thought', in *Studies in Eighteenth-Century French Literature Presented to Robert Niklaus*, ed. J. H. Fox, M. H. Waddicor and D. A. Watts (Exeter, University of Exeter Press, 1975), pp.1–13.

20. OCV, vol.14, p.440.

21. OCV, vol.14, p.442.

22. OCV, vol.14, p.444. The French word 'expérience' translates both 'experience' and 'experiment' in English.

23. See the Introduction by W. Smeaton and R. Walters to *Essai sur la nature du feu, et de sa propagation*, OCV, vol.17, pp.3–22.

24. W. Barber and R. Walters, OCV, vol.15, p.58.

25. OCV, vol.15, p.227.

26. OCV, vol.15, p.240.

27. OCV, vol.15, p.232.

28. Barber and Walters argue that a difference between the *Traité de métaphysique* and the *Métaphysique de Newton* is that in the latter 'Voltaire claims to accept Newton's vision of God both as the creator of the cosmic order and the

benevolent if stern father of mankind, who expects obedience to divinely prescribed moral law' (*OCV*, vol.15, p.112). But Voltaire seems to make the same point in the *Traité* when he writes that 'It is evident, since all men live in society, that there is in their very being a secret link by which God intended them to be connected one to another. Now if at a certain age, ideas acquired through the senses by men all organised in the same way, did not give them all more or less the same principles necessary to any society, it is then absolutely evident that those societies would not survive' ('il est certain, puisque tous les hommes vivent en société, qu'il y a dans leur être un lien secret, par lequel Dieu a voulu les attacher les uns aux autres. Or si à un certain âge les idées venues par les mêmes sens à des hommes tous organisés de la même manière, ne leur donnaient pas peu à peu les mêmes principes nécessaires à toute société, il est encore très sûr que ces sociétés ne subsisteraient pas' (*OCV*, vol.15, p.219)).

29. *OCV*, vol.15, p.215.
30. *OCV*, vol.15, p.136.
31. *OCV*, vol.15, p.140.
32. See V. Le Ru, *Voltaire newtonien: Le combat d'un philosophe pour la science* (Paris: Vuibert – ADAPT, 2005), chap.4.
33. See J. I. Israel, *Enlightenment Contested: Philosophy, Modernity, and the Emancipation of Man, 1670-1752* (Oxford: Oxford University Press, 2006), p.751.
34. See D. Beeson, *Maupertuis: An Intellectual Biography*, SVEC 299 (1992).
35. Voltaire, *Histoire du Docteur Akakia* , ed. J. Tuffet (Paris: Nizet, 1967), p.5.
36. Barber and Walters, *OCV*, vol.15, p.58.
37. Voltaire, *Histoire du Docteur Akakia*, p.cix.
38. *OCV*, vol.56C, p.154.
39. *OCV*, vol.56C, p.149.
40. *OCV*, vol.62, p.70.
41. *OCV*, vol.62, p.86.
42. *OCV*, vol.62, pp.57–64 (Doute xxiv).
43. *OCV*, vol.62, p.91.
44. *OCV*, vol.62, pp.104–5.
45. See J. I. Israel, *Radical Enlightenment: Philosophy and the Making of Modernity, 1650-1750* (Oxford: Oxford University Press, 2001); and *Enlightenment Contested*.
46. See Le Ru, *Voltaire newtonien*, p.54, note 92.
47. See F. de Gandt (ed.), *Cirey dans la vie intellectuelle: La réception de Newton en France*, SVEC 2001:11, 'Préambule', p.4.
48. *OCV*, vol.33, pp.121–2.
49. See Le Ru, *Voltaire newtonien*, p.97.
50. See J. Vercruysse's article on Voltaire in J. Sgard (ed.), *Dictionnaire des journalistes: 1600-1789*, 2 vols (Oxford: Voltaire Foundation, 1999), vol.2, pp.995–7.
51. B. Russell, 'Sous l'influence de Voltaire', *La Table ronde*, 122 (1958), 159–63 (p.159).
52. *OCV*, vol.74B, p.282.
53. *OCV*, vol.36, p.300.
54. Horace, *Epistles*, 1.2.40. See R. Goulbourne, 'Horace au siècle des Lumières: *Sapere aude* et la pré-histoire de la devise kantienne', SVEC 2006:12, 167–83.

4

MIGUEL BENÍTEZ

Voltaire and clandestine manuscripts

The importance of clandestine manuscripts in the diffusion of early Enlightenment thought was first suggested by Gustave Lanson at the beginning of the twentieth century. Ira Wade's classic study *The Clandestine Organization and Diffusion of Philosophical Ideas in France from 1700 to 1750* (1938) marked a decisive advance in our understanding of this phenomenon, and since then this area has become a major focus of Enlightenment research. Radical ideas about religious belief circulated from the second half of the seventeenth century, very often in manuscript form, and after 1700 these works either found their way into print or influenced other printed works.[1] We think of Voltaire primarily as an actor in the world of the printed book; but to fully understand the nature and sources of his polemical thought, we need also to study his familiarity with the culture of clandestine manuscripts and their influence on the production of his own books and pamphlets.

Voltaire believed, unlike Fontenelle, that it was the duty of the *philosophes* to teach the truth. From early on, he taught by example. In April 1726, a certain Abbé accused Voltaire of having preached for a good ten years or more 'naked deism in the boudoirs of our young gentlemen' ('le déisme tout à découvert, aux toilettes de nos jeunes seigneurs'), and of declaring himself an 'enemy of J. C.' ('ennemi de J.-C.').[2] Voltaire had already begun at this date to compose works in verse and prose destined for private reading and for circulation in manuscript. Later, his library as well as his own writings reflect his familiarity with the manuscript works which circulated clandestinely. The years of his struggle against *l'Infâme*, between 1762 and 1777, mark a decisive evolution in Voltaire's relationship to this clandestine culture: even if he remains careful to maintain the cloak of anonymity, he senses that the moment has come to move beyond the limited group of the *philosophes* and to reach out, if not to the people, then at least to a broader public. In the tradition of the clandestine *côteries*, Voltaire steadily built up a philosophical network which he employed to produce simple texts, accessible to a wide audience. Although remaining just within the clandestine world, this strategy marked a decisive step away from the manuscript and the printed work of limited print-run – collectors' items for bibliophiles – and towards the small book, cheap or even free of charge, diffused in hundreds of copies. In the second half of the eighteenth century, the manuscript copy became increasingly rare, until eventually it existed only to copy printed books.

The young Voltaire as freethinker

During his visits to Brussels and The Hague in 1722, Voltaire reportedly gave readings of his *Épître à Julie*, a poem probably written for Mme de Rupelmonde. If we are to believe the poet Jean-Baptiste Rousseau, in a letter published in the *Bibliothèque françoise* in 1736 (D1078), this poem was 'tinged with the blackest impiety' ('marquée au coin de l'impiété la plus noire'), so much so that Voltaire was alleged subsequently to have 'toned down the phrasing of this infamous poem' ('mitigé les expressions de cette infâme poésie'). The new version was given the title by which the poem remains best known, the *Épître à Uranie*. The text was soon circulating in manuscript, there was a first clandestine printing in 1738, and copies multiplied.[3] In this deist poem preaching natural religion, his first major statement of religious belief, Voltaire opposes the 'for' and 'against' of Christianity: on the one hand, it is presented, as some length, as a barbaric religion deeply rooted in Jewish superstition; on the other, a few verses present the clichéd defence of Christian apologetics. The structure seems artificial, and we may suspect that the handful of lines in favour of Christianity were added as an afterthought, a hypothesis strengthened by the existence of one manuscript in which precisely these verses are missing.[4]

In his letter 'Sur M. Locke' a few years later, a work dealing with the controversial subject of the immateriality of the soul, Voltaire experiments with alternative versions in manuscript and print. An early version, whose composition probably dates back to his time in England, circulated in manuscript, before being printed in 1736.[5] Meanwhile, a more 'moderate' version appeared in print, as the thirteenth letter in the *Letters Concerning the English nation* (1733) and the *Lettres philosophiques* (1734). In the manuscript, the idea that the soul might be material is made to depend on the parallel natures of men and animals: animals are endowed with life and feeling, like men, and they are composed purely of matter. But since God is all-powerful, he could have endowed organised matter with the faculties of feeling and thinking. Such a solution undermines the idea of the immortality of the soul, and Voltaire proposes that God could have preserved the faculty of thought in the matter which gives life to the body. It remains to be explained how this immortal 'thinking matter' can be the object of rewards and punishments . . . Hinting at explanations which did away with the immortal soul was a delicate business, and one can readily understand why Voltaire, in the printed version, sought, as he put it, 'to obscure' Locke (D542). A close reading of this version shows that it adopts in fact a more radical position. To begin with, it ignores completely the issue of the immortality of the soul, as being nothing more than a matter of faith. Furthermore, if Voltaire can say categorically that God endowed matter with the capacity of feeling and thinking, it is because animals can feel, but also and more importantly, because he has implicitly reduced man to his body.

It is not surprising therefore that the freethinking Voltaire, in contact with the clandestine networks, asked his friend Thiriot in 1735 for the manuscript of that Curé 'as philosophical as Locke' (D951), that is, the *Mémoire des pensées et sentimens de Jean Meslier*, which circulated widely, both in its original form and in various extracted versions. In all probability Thiriot never sent the manuscript,[6] for there is no mention of it subsequently in the correspondence. Nor does Voltaire seem to have acquired the work by other means, for we find no trace in his writings of a reading of the complete *Mémoire*. When, much later in 1763, he wrote to Jean-François Marmontel saying that 'this work had always struck him' (D11271), he is probably speaking not of its contents but rather of the example of a priest who wrote against religion and on his deathbed repented for having misled mankind.

A manuscript work often attributed to Voltaire is a *Commentaire sur la Bible*,[7] a systematic critical reading of the forty-two books which following the Council of Trent made up the Catholic Bible. Probably composed around 1740, a note added to one copy attributes the work to Voltaire, while another manuscript has a note claiming it to be the autograph of Mme Du Châtelet. In 1759, Voltaire spoke of 'a work of Mme Du Châtelet' which 'has not been printed', containing a critique of religion, 'the best thing that's been written on these subjects' (D8037). A few months later, he wrote to Mme Du Deffand that Du Châtelet 'had commented' on the Bible 'from one end to the other' (D8484). Later Grimm reports rather doubtfully how during the Cirey period Voltaire and Mme Du Châtelet 'used to read a chapter of the holy scriptures every morning at breakfast, and each would comment on it in his or her own way, then the bard of *La Pucelle* [Voltaire] gave himself the job of writing up the discussion' ('on lisait tous les matins, pendant le déjeuner, un chapitre de l'Histoire Sainte, sur lequel chacun faisait ses réflexions à sa manière; et le chantre de *la Pucelle* s'était chargé d'en être le rédacteur').[8] Grimm sees in these discussions the remote origins of *La Bible enfin expliquée* (1777), but his description of the Cirey discussions seems better to fit the long manuscript biblical commentary. It may be that the work was indeed the result of a collaboration between Voltaire and Émilie Du Châtelet, but there are reasons for doubting this.[9] It could be argued moreover that Voltaire would have published the text if it had been in his possession, especially during the years of his fight against *l'Infâme*, when he made use of every weapon which came to hand. Finally, when in 1763 he invited Helvétius to write a book exposing the flagrant contradictions in the Bible, 'this scandal of the human mind' ('ce scandale de l'esprit humain', D11444), he made no mention of the *Commentaire sur la Bible* – a surprising lapse if he was indeed familiar with the work, since it corresponds precisely to the project he was submitting to his friend.

Clandestine manuscripts in Voltaire's library

Voltaire's personal library contains considerable evidence of his interest in clandestine manuscripts. He owned a copy of a work by the priest Pierre Cuppé, *Le Ciel ouvert à tous les hommes*,[10] but he does not seem to have been much interested in this system of Christian rationalism which preaches the salvation of all men; perhaps he acquired it as being, as the title page announces, 'a very rare and curious manuscript' ('manuscrit très rare et très curieux'). He also possessed an *Extrait d'un livre intitulé Discours sur les miracles de Jésus Christ traduit de l'anglais*,[11] a work including commentaries, often integrated into the main body of the text, translated directly from Thomas Woolston's *Discourses on the Miracles of Our Saviour* (1727–9).

Voltaire was familiar with the writings of Benoît de Maillet, and he owned a copy of his *Telliamed*, which teaches that all living beings emerged from the ocean.[12] This must have been copied before the work's (posthumous) publication in 1748, since in his *Dissertation sur les changements arrivés dans notre globe* of 1746, Voltaire speaks of 'the opinion of the Indians' ('l'opinion des Indiens') that 'all the habitable earth had previously been sea, and that the sea had for a long time been earth' ('toute la terre habitable avait été mer autrefois, et que la mer avait longtemps été terre').[13] In *Le Siècle de Louis XIV*, Voltaire remarks that Maillet had written 'manuscript works of daring freethinking' ('des ouvrages manuscrits d'une philosophie hardie').[14] He is doubtless referring here to, among other texts, the *Extrait de Maillet*, which also figures among the manuscripts in his library.[15] This work of biblical criticism is no more than a literal translation of sections of Spinoza's *Tractatus theologico-politicus* concerning the attribution of the historical books of the Old Testament.

Another manuscript, entitled *Religion. Par Du Marsai*,[16] is an incomplete copy of *La Religion chrétienne analysée*, containing only the last part of the text, with a few of the proofs added at a later stage. Some remarks made to Damilaville in 1765 would seem to prove that Voltaire had read this work (D13026):

> I don't know who wrote this manuscript which is circulating and which is very well done. The gross errors of an interesting chronology are developed in column after column. One can deduce that if God is the creator of Hebrew ethics, as we believe unquestionably, he certainly isn't the creator of their chronology.
>
> (Je ne sçais de qui est une analise qui court en manuscrit et qui est très bien faite. Les erreurs grossières d'une chronologie assez intéressante, y sont développées par colonnes. On y voit évidemment que si Dieu est l'auteur de la morale des Hébreux, comme nous n'en pouvons douter, il ne l'est pas de leur chronologie.)

Voltaire's library also contains an *Examen de la religion chrétienne, par du Marsais*, in fifteen chapters,[17] and it is his knowledge of this manuscript which explains his reaction to the printed edition of 1763 which reproduces the version in eleven chapters first published in 1745: 'I had known for a long time the book attributed to Saint-Évremond', he wrote to Damilaville in 1763. 'It is by Dumarsais, but heavily abridged, and horribly printed' ('Je connaissais, depuis longtemps, le livre attribué à Saint-Évremond . . . Il est de Dumarsais, mais il est fort tronqué, et détestablement imprimé', D11535). He repeats his view in a note which he writes on the title page of the printed book: 'There are many things left out in this printed version. The manuscript is much fuller' ('Il y a bien de choses oubliées dans cet imprimé. Le manuscrit est bien plus ample'). On the title page of his own copy of the manuscript, Voltaire wrote: 'This work is written in a cold, languid and diffuse style, and is perhaps not sufficiently thorough; it is not worth printing' ('Cet ouvrage est d'un stile froid languissant et diffus. et n'est peutetre pas assez aprofondi il ne merite pas l'impression').

Voltaire also owned two manuscripts of works by Nicolas-Antoine Boulanger, one called *Gouvernement historique, politique, religieux, ancien, et moderne* (a résumé of *Recherches sur l'origine du despotisme oriental*), and the other *Dissertation sur Élie et sur Enoch*,[18] and so he knew these works prior to their appearance in print. In 1762, he wrote to Damilaville that he had confused *Recherches sur l'origine du despotisme oriental*, published by d'Holbach in 1761, with a text which he had 'read in manuscript' (D10295): the manuscript in question must surely be his own copy, on which he had written 'obscure hotchpotch, foolish, riddled with errors and solecisms' ('fatras obscur, insensé, plein d'erreurs et de solécismes'). He is similarly critical of the Boulanger's *Dissertation*, writing to Damilaville in 1764 to acknowledge receipt of several examples of the work: 'I've received the Enochs, that's not to the public's taste' ('J'ai reçu des Enocs, cela n'est pas publici saporis', D12208).

Finally, Voltaire had in his library at Ferney a work entitled *Traité sur l'Apocalypse*. Ms, clearly a copy of Firmin Abauzit's *Discours historique sur l'Apocalypse*. We know that Jacob Vernes had loaned him a manuscript of this work, and in late 1757 Voltaire asked to borrow it again (D7545): it was doubtless at this moment that he had the work recopied.

Reading and editing clandestine manuscripts

Voltaire's familiarity with clandestine manuscripts extends beyond those we know to have been in his library. During his stay at Les Délices in 1765, Damilaville promised to send the manuscripts circulating under the name of Fréret; Voltaire had not received them two months later (D12938, D12984), and they seem never to have arrived. Meanwhile, Voltaire appears to have heard that the *Lettre de Thrasybule à Leucippe* had been printed, and he asked both the printer Cramer and Damilaville to acquire it for him (D12959, D12989). He finally received the book and wrote to Damilaville on 30 November (D13014):

> I've read *Thrasibule*, dear friend; there are some very good things in it, and some very sound arguments. It's not at all in the style of Fréret, but no matter where the light comes from, so long as it illuminates. It would have been easier for the reader if the work had been split up into several letters.
>
> (J'ai lu Thrasibule, mon cher ami; il y a de très bonnes choses et des raisonnements très forts. Ce n'est pas là le stile de Fréret, mais n'importe d'où vienne la lumière pourvu qu'elle éclaire. Il eût été plus commode pour le lecteur que cet ouvrage eût été partagé en plusieurs Lettres.)

From late December he continued to ask Damilaville for Fréret (D13066), suggesting that he had heard of the printing of another work, the *Examen critique des apologistes de la religion chrétienne*. Voltaire again questioned whether this book was the work of Fréret, but he considered it 'the best book yet written on these questions' ('le meilleur livre qu'on ait encore écrit sur ces matières', D13369). He sent it to his friends, and immediately proposed to Cramer another edition, on the pretext that the first was faulty (D13342).

When *Le Militaire philosophe* appeared anonymously in 1767, Voltaire informed the Marquis d'Argence that it had long been known in manuscript, information probably gleaned from the preface, adding: 'It's a work in the style of the Curé Meslier' ('C'est un ouvrage dans le goût du curé Mêlier', D14639). The comment is not surprising, since the deism which emerges from the problems which the 'soldier philosopher' puts to Père Nicolas Malebranche recalls the ideas expressed in Meslier's extracted *Mémoire*. From the moment of its publication, Voltaire informed a number of his correspondents about the qualities of the work, 'perhaps the most effective writing yet against fanaticism' ('ce qu'on a fait peut être de plus fort contre le fanatisme', D14730); he praised its eloquence and insisted on the rigour of its reasoning, which leaves Malebranche with no room to reply – perhaps for the very good reason, Voltaire suspected, that the latter shared the views of the 'militaire philosophe' concerning the nature of divinity.

Voltaire seems not to have known any of the various manuscript versions of the *Traité des trois imposteurs* which had been in circulation since the beginning of the eighteenth century. He speaks of this work for the first time in April 1768, when it is published by Marc-Michel Rey. It does not appeal to him, and a year later he writes a verse epistle *A l'auteur du livre des Trois imposteurs* in which he lambastes atheism. He describes his poem in a letter to Mme Du Deffand as 'a little work against atheism' ('un petit ouvrage contre l'athéisme', D15517), while to another correspondent he speaks of his 'Epistle against the Atheists' ('Épitre contre les athées', D15540). Given that the work he was refuting promoted not atheism but pantheism, and since he was more than capable of distinguishing between the two, we may wonder whether Voltaire ever read the work at all.

Voltaire read the clandestine manuscripts which he managed to obtain and then circulated them among his friends; more than that, he edited and reworked certain texts. The case of the *Sermon des cinquante*, a violent attack on the Scriptures, remains controversial. It seems likely that the first edition, antedated to 1749, was published by Cramer only in 1762, even though versions of the text had then been in circulation for a decade. In May 1752, Voltaire heard that 'a sort of philosophical sermon' ('une espèce de sermon philosophique'), circulating both in print and in manuscript ('imprimé et manuscrit'), was being attributed to him, and he in turn immediately attributed it to Julien Offroy de La Mettrie (D4900). Laurent-Angliviel de La Beaumelle, informed by Maupertuis, openly accused Voltaire in 1753 of being the author, and Jean-Jacques Rousseau repeated the accusation the following year in his *Lettres de la montagne*. At least one of the manuscript copies of the work reflects this rumour in its title.[19] Voltaire denied his own paternity of the work, which he claimed to find written 'in a crude style' ('d'un style grossier') and lacking 'any trace of intelligence' ('nul trait d'esprit', D12300). He even attributed the work to Frederick II in his correspondence and in certain of his works dating from 1768, such as the *Examen important de Milord Bolingbroke* and the *Instructions à Antoine Jacques Roustan*. The Prussian king never reproached him in the least for this attribution, possibly because Voltaire had rewritten the *Sermon des cinquante* at his suggestion.[20] The work itself gives us few clues, but it is clear at the very least that Voltaire took an active part in its diffusion.

Also attributed to Voltaire is an *Extrait des sentiments de Jean Meslier*, published in 1762, and derived from the *Mémoire des pensées et sentimens de Jean Meslier* which had been in circulation since the 1740s. The 'Extract' in question turns the atheist Meslier into a deist devoted to natural religion, and it is now argued that Voltaire pieced together the printed text from two different extracts from the *Mémoire*, adding a few passages of his own for good measure.[21] None of these added passages is clearly 'Voltairean', however, and the text contains many errors, so it is possible that Voltaire simply published a copy which had come into his possession.

Voltaire was involved not only in the editing of individual texts but in the publication of collections of clandestine texts. He seems to have collaborated – though this has been disputed – with Marc-Michel Rey in the publication of the *Évangile de la raison* (1764), made up of five works, of which four are by or attributed to Voltaire (*Saül et David*, *Testament de Jean Meslier*, *Catéchisme de l'honnête homme* and the *Sermon des cinquante*). The fifth text, the *Examen de la religion*, may have been reworked by Voltaire (though there is cause for doubt since in comparison with the manuscript version in his library, this printed version is abridged and lacks the final two chapters). The following year, 1765, appeared the *Recueil nécessaire*, published by Cramer in Geneva (with 'Leipsik' on the title page). This included six 'Voltairean' texts (including, again, the *Catéchisme de l'honnête homme*, and the *Sermon des cinquante*), the *Vicaire savoyard* extracted from Jean-Jacques Rousseau's *Émile*, and the *Analyse de la religion chrétienne*, here attributed to Dumarsais. Again, Voltaire is suspected of having 'rearranged' the *Analyse*, but this version lacks its preface and is divided into chapters, a practice followed by several copyists, but which seems to go against Voltaire's judgement that the work was well constructed, so he may not have been closely involved in its preparation. These matters are impossible to determine with certainty, especially since Voltaire is always careful to cover his traces with attributions which are deliberately misleading, if not entirely fanciful. Finally, in his collection *Les Lois de Minos* (1773), Voltaire edited *Le Philosophe*, which he attributes to Dumarsais. The original version had had a distinctly materialist tinge, but in Voltaire's bowdlerised abridgement, the essay emerged as a deist work, conveniently so at a time when Voltaire was preoccupied with combating atheism.

The fight against *l'Infâme*: Voltaire's use of clandestine manuscripts

Between 1762 and 1777, Voltaire wrote prolifically. He himself produced some of the pamphlets or 'scraps' ('rogatons') which he also encouraged his friends to write, always with the aim of *écraser l'Infâme*. In writing these 'philosophical' works, he took material wherever he found it, without worrying too much about its originality: as he wrote to Damilaville in 1764, 'I harvest my fields and a few scattered truths in some bad books' ('Je moissonne mes champs, et quelques vérités éparses dans de mauvais livres', D11985). Clandestine manuscripts were among the sources that he harvested, and there are debts in his writing, some more important than others, to such texts as the *Examen de la religion*, the *Mémoire de Jean Meslier* or *La Religion chrétienne analysée*.

The *Dictionnaire philosophique*, published in 1764, illustrates perfectly Voltaire's strategy in this respect. To anyone who would listen, he would explain poker-faced that the author of this work attributed to him had simply assembled texts from different places. Far from being the author of the work, he was one victim among others of this calamity, since, as he explained to Damilaville in 1765, the work contained entire sentences lifted word for word from his own works (D12618). He informed several correspondents that the article 'Apocalypse' was by Firmin Abauzit, and later explained that it was extracted from Abauzit's *Discours historique sur l'Apocalypse*. In fact it seems likely that Voltaire himself is the author of the article, a patchwork of extracts from the original work.

Voltaire had no liking for the ideas of Benoît de Maillet, too metaphysical for his taste, and too prone to theories which could be used to defend the Flood. But though he did not agree with its arguments, he made use of *Telliamed* in *La Philosophie de l'histoire* (1765). On no occasion does Voltaire cite passages literally from Maillet, so it is hard to assess the precise use which he made of his manuscript. He borrows several examples of the sea having covered areas which are now dry land, but believes that the retreat of the ocean in these cases is compensated by the flooding of other areas; and if he speaks of the disappearance of a few stars in the immensity of space, it is simply to demonstrate the great changes which have taken place in the solar system, and not because he subscribes to the cosmology of the Indian Telliamed.

In the article 'Miracles' in the *Questions sur l'Encyclopédie*, Voltaire summarised the ideas of Woolston on miracles. He believed him to be a sincere Christian who rejected out of hand the theology of priests and their literal interpretations of the Scriptures. Voltaire saw in Woolston another Meslier, and reproduced literally Woolston's disparaging remarks. There is however no trace in this summary of the commentaries in the manuscript extract of Woolston's work to be found in Voltaire's library. Finally, even if Voltaire found the style of Boulanger's works not accessible to everyone, he nonetheless made use of his dissertation in the article 'Élie et Énoch' in the *Questions*, in which he alluded to the author (without naming him) as 'a very learned man' ('un très-savant homme') and an 'inventive and profound writer' ('l'écrivain ingénieux et profond').[22]

The fight against *l'Infâme*: The manuscript circulation of pamphlets

Some of the texts published by Voltaire in this period also circulated in manuscript. Such copies were understandably not numerous, since the large number of printed editions of Voltaire's works made this other form of diffusion less necessary. These works were intended for clandestine printing from the beginning, and it would seem that the manuscript copies which have been discovered were generally made from the scarce printed editions. The *Sermon du rabbin Akib* was apparently published, as stated on the title page, in late 1761.[23] It is certain however that the copy belonging to the Portuguese doctor Ribeiro Sanches, full of errors and with certain passages summarised, was not made from a printed book: the owner described the work as a manuscript and attributed it to Voltaire: 'They say that Voltaire is the author, and that he sent it to Helvétius, author of the condemned work *De l'esprit*' ('On dit que M˙ de Voltaire est l'auteur, et qu'il l'a communique à M. Helvétius, auteur de *l'Esprit* livre condamné').[24] Another copy, appearing in Grimm's *Correspondance littéraire* in 1762, introduces the work by pointing out that the text is from Les Délices, Voltaire's home.[25] A third manuscript, based on a printed source, places the text immediately after the 'Essai sur les facultés de l'âme', and so makes it share that title.[26]

Voltaire attributed the *Catéchisme de l'honnête homme, ou dialogue entre un caloyer et un homme de bien*, published in 1763,[27] to 'a certain Abbé Durand' ('un certain abbé Durand', D11383), and, more fancifully, to Jean-Jacques Rousseau (D11433). There was widespread rumour that Voltaire had written the work himself, and one copyist of a manuscript wrote in a note that 'we believe Voltaire to be the author of this work' ('On croit M. de Voltaire auteur de cet ouvrage').[28] The doctor Ribeiro Sanches confined himself to copying brief extracts from the printed work;[29] while another copyist provided fragments from the edition allegedly published in 1758, remarking that 'this book appeared here in 1764, and was confiscated' ('Ce livre a paru ici en 1764, et a été confisqué').[30]

The *Dialogue du douteur et de l'adorateur* also dates from this period. Voltaire included this brief work, of which there is no mention in the correspondence, in the *Recueil nécessaire*, and we know also of one manuscript.[31] Voltaire was writing the *Questions de Zapata* in February 1767 (D13922), and printed copies were in circulation by April (D14123). All the known manuscript copies derive from the printed work;[32] the one exception is a fragmentary text which stops at the thirty-eighth question, and which claims simply that these 'questions' are 'traduites par le Sieur Tamponet, Docteur de Sorbonne'.[33] Finally, the *Dîner du comte de Boulainvilliers* appeared in December 1767.[34] Suspected of having written this work, Voltaire started the rumour that it was by Thémiseul de Saint-Hyacinthe, who, as he explained to Marmontel in 1768, 'had had it printed in Holland in 1728' ('le fit imprimer en Hollande en 1728', D14694); and to confound his accusers further still, he arranged with Cramer to have printed an edition antedated to that year. Among the participants in this dialogue, Voltaire introduces the historian and Spinozist Henri de Boulainvilliers and the academician Nicolas Fréret; even the grammarian Dumarsais has a walk-on role at the end. This is a fitting and witty homage to the authors who had lent their name to influential clandestine manuscript works which had all, in differing ways, nourished Voltaire's own writing.

translated by Nicholas Cronk

NOTES

1. For a survey of recent studies of clandestine literature, see M. Benítez, *La Face cachée des Lumières* (Oxford: Voltaire Foundation, 1996); the Spanish translation of this work includes an updated inventory of clandestine philosophical manuscripts: *La cara oculta de las Luces* (Valencia: Biblioteca Valenciana, 2003), pp.13–172. See also J. S. Spink, *French Free-Thought from Gassendi to Voltaire* (London: Athlone Press, 1960), chaps.14–15; R. Niklaus, 'Clandestine Philosophical Literature in France', in *The Encyclopedia of Philosophy*, ed. P. Edwards (New York: Macmillan, 1967), vol.2, pp.114–18; M.-H. Cotoni, 'Aperçus sur la littérature clandestine dans la correspondance de Voltaire', in *Materia actuosa: mélanges en l'honneur d'O. Bloch*, ed. M. Benítez, A. McKenna, G. Paganini and J. Salem (Paris: Champion, 2000), pp.635–55; G. Artigas-Menant, 'De l'austérité au sourire: Voltaire et les manuscrits philosophiques clandestins', in *Du secret des clandestins à la propagande voltairienne* (Paris: Champion, 2001), pp.305–19; B. E. Schwarzbach, 'Manuscrits philosophiques', in *Dictionnaire général de Voltaire*, ed. R. Trousson and J. Vercruysse (Paris: Champion, 2003), pp.783–6; and J. I. Israel, *Radical Enlightenment: Philosophy and the Making of Modernity, 1650–1750* (Oxford: Oxford University Press, 2001), chap.36, 'The Clandestine Philosophical Manuscripts'.
2. *Archives de la Bastille: Documents inédits recueillis et publiés par François Ravaisson: Règnes de Louis XIV et Louis XV (1709 à 1772)* (Paris: Durand, 1881), vol.12, pp.132–3.
3. To the copies noted by I. O. Wade (1932) and H. T. Mason (*OCV*, vol.1B, 2002) should be added those described by M. Benítez in 'Voltaire libertin: l'*Épître à Uranie*', *Revue Voltaire*, 8 (2008), 99–135. We now know forty-seven copies in all, of which three are fragmentary, in addition to the manuscript translations of the poem into English, German, Russian, Italian and Latin. On the successive editions of the poem, see N. Cronk, 'L'*Épître à Uranie* de Voltaire: stratégies de

publication d'une œuvre clandestine', in *Poétique de la pensée: Études sur l'âge classique et le siècle philosophique: En hommage à Jean Dagen*, ed. B. Guion *et al.* (Paris: Champion, 2006), pp.275–84.

4. Rouen-BM Montbret 553[2] (all manuscript references will be given in this form).

5. Paris-Arsenal 2557 (edited by G. Lanson in *Lettres philosophiques*, vol.1, pp.190–205); Paris-BnF fr 12634; Paris-BnF Rés. PZ 1196; Roma-BAV Patetta 827.

6. See C. Porset, 'Voltaire et Meslier: état de la question', in *Le Matérialisme du XVIII*[e] *siècle et la littérature clandestine*, ed. O. Bloch (Paris: Vrin, 1982), pp.193–201.

7. Three manuscripts have been identified (Brussels-BR 15188–15189, Troyes-BM 2376–2377, private collection); none of these bears an original title.

8. Grimm, *Correspondance littéraire, philosophique et critique*, 16 vols. ed. M. Tourneux (Paris: Garnier, 1877–82), vol.11, p.348 (September 1776).

9. See B. E. Schwarzbach, 'Les études bibliques à Cirey', in F. de Gandt (ed.), *Cirey dans la vie intellectuelle: La réception de Newton en France*, SVEC 2001:11, 26–54.

10. The full title is *Le Livre d'or ou Le ciel ouvert à tous les hommes dans lequel sans rien déranger des Pratiques de la Religion on prouve solidement par l'Ecriture Sainte et la Raison que tous les hommes seront sauvés*; St Petersburg-RNB Voltaire 205 (XI).

11. St Petersburg-RNB Voltaire Oct. 221. See the critical edition, Thomas Woolston, *Six Discours sur les miracles de Notre Sauveur: Deux traductions manuscrites du XVIII*[e] *siècle dont une de Mme Du Châtelet*, ed. W. Trapnell (Paris: Champion, 2001), pp.333–79.

12. St Petersburg-RNB Voltaire Oct. 239. The manuscript is entitled *Nouveau Systeme du Monde, ou Entretiens de Teliamed Philosophe Indien, avec un Missionaire françois au passage que fit au Caire ce Philosophe aux années 1715 et 1716 écrits par le Missionaire en 1724 a un de ses amis.*

13. OCV, vol.30C, p.29.

14. *OH*, p.1183.

15. St Petersburg-RNB Voltaire 240 (P 5), f.97r–102r (OCV, vol.81, pp.420–6).

16. St Petersburg-RNB Voltaire 240 (IX), f.449–464; the title is probably that of Voltaire's secretary, Wagnière.

17. St Petersburg-RNB Voltaire Oct. 821.

18. St Petersburg-RNB Voltaire 240 (IX), f.304–334; St Petersburg-RNB Voltaire 240 (IX), f.335–364.

19. *Sermon des Cinquante, Prononcé dans la Ville de *** Par Mr de Voltaire. En 1760. Lausanne 1763* (Moscow-Historic Museum 342, op.1, no 135). On the manuscript diffusion of the work, see J. P. Lee, 'Le *Sermon des cinquante* de Voltaire: manuscrit clandestin', in *La Philosophie clandestine à l'âge classique*, ed. A. McKenna and A. Mothu (Oxford: Voltaire Foundation, 1997), pp.143–51.

20. See J. Lavicka, 'La genèse du *Sermon des cinquante*', SVEC, 256 (1988), 49–82.

21. See the critical edition by R. Desné, *Testament de Jean Meslier*, OCV, vol.56A.

22. Moland, vol.18, pp.511, 513.

23. Barnard Castle-Bowes Museum FO/91 Re; Gotha-FuLB Cart B 1138[d]; Grenoble-BM 4051; Paris-BHVP Rés 54 (Rés 2026); Paris-EM 2017; Paris-Mazarine 1192; Paris-private collection F. Moureau; Stockholm-K.B. Holm Vu 29:3. See J. P. Lee, 'The Genesis and Publication of Voltaire's *Sermon du rabbin Akib*', SVEC, 347 (1997), 627–31.

24. Paris-Faculté de Médecine 2017.
25. Stockholm-KB Holm. Vu 29:3.
26. Paris-Mazarine 1192.
27. Barnard Castle-Bowes Museum FO/91 Re; Cambridge-Harvard University, Houghton Lib. FR 79; Gotha-FuLB Cart B 1138e; Moscow-Historic Museum Fond 342, op. 1, no 135; Paris-EM 2017; Reims-BM 2472; Rouen-BM M 74; Wittenberg-Evang. Predigerseminar Man. 58.
28. Rouen-BM M 74.
29. Paris-Faculté de Médecine 2017.
30. Wittenberg-Evang. Predigerseminar Man. 58, f.31–34.
31. Montpellier-BM 338.
32. Budapest-OSK Duod. Gall. 2; Darmstadt-Hessische Staatsarchiv Abt. D 4 Nr. 558/4; Halle-UuLB Misc. Quart. 12; Halle-UuLB Stolberg-Wernigerode Zl 44; Cracow-PAN 720; Montpellier-BM 338; Wittenberg-Evang. Predigerseminar A III 20. See critical edition by J. Marchand, *OCV*, vol.62.
33. Cracow-PAN 720.
34. Bordeaux-BM 828 (XXXVI); Paris-private collection F. Moureau. See critical edition by U. Kölving and J.-M. Moureaux, *OCV*, vol.63A.

5

JOHN LEIGH

Voltaire and the myth of England

'It's a sad state of affairs . . . that while the University of Cambridge produces admirable books every day, astute foreigners regard France as nothing more than the whipped cream of Europe' ('C'est une chose déplorable . . . tandis que l'université de Cambridge produit tous les jours des livres admirables, les étrangers habiles ne regardent la France que comme la crème fouettée de l'Europe', D901). Voltaire's appreciation of English intellectual achievements, recorded here in a letter of 1735, serves a typical purpose. English habits and practices are validated chiefly insofar as they offer a contrast with, and reproach to, the French modus vivendi. Voltaire's enthusiasm for England recurrently nourishes and justifies his satirical disaffection with France, a nation, the analogy seems to suggest, given to frivolity ('cream') yet subject also to persecution ('whipped'). But if England provides Voltaire with a useful foil to France, it disconcerts, challenges and illuminates him in more profound and lasting ways. England's own contradictions and idiosyncrasies reveal, or perhaps elicit, different facets of Voltaire's thought.

England had already been deemed an acceptable destination for French thinkers by the time Voltaire disembarked in 1726. He was following in the footsteps of writers such as the Seigneur de Saint-Évremond. A journey across the English Channel was to become practically de rigueur for a self-respecting French thinker in the eighteenth century. Even Jean-Jacques Rousseau, Voltaire's faithful adversary, who professed to dislike travel in general and England in particular, would make the journey. But Voltaire's sojourn produced a *frisson* without precedent: he was, for one thing, one of the first foreigners in history to write and bring to publication a work in the English language.

Voltaire's seemingly effortless acquisition of the English language has been the subject of some myth. The *Lettres philosophiques*, first published in English as the *Letters Concerning the English Nation* (1733), and apparently announced as a work of Voltaire's in their own right, were once considered testimony to Voltaire's precocious gift for the language. Now they are considered rather to offer evidence of the usual liberties taken by translators from French into English.[1] Nevertheless, Voltaire's *Essay on Epic Poetry*, which enjoyed a similar dual life in English and French, was first written by Voltaire in English. He would spend as long in Germany (principally of course at the French-speaking court of Frederick the Great) as he did in England, but knew barely enough German to get by in conversation with postillions (D3248). Voltaire also learned Italian, a language with which he was, he sighed, 'unhappily in love' ('infelicemente innamorato', D3351), and the ideal vehicle for otherwise potentially embarrassing love letters to his niece. But it is clear that Voltaire learned English with particular enthusiasm. Whether cause or effect, he perceived the English language to fit the English people. Voltaire valued especially the simplicity and forcefulness that he saw as characterising the language. These properties seemed for Voltaire to inhere, irrespective of the contingencies of context or speaker. The English tongue seemed to permit freedoms not countenanced by the French language. No doubt the acquisition of another language does in any case afford some sort of alter ego, permitting those who learn it to feel less than entirely responsible for what they are saying. But Voltaire found in the English language the opportunity to speak all the more boldly and plainly.

Nevertheless, not long after his return to France, Voltaire taught English to his mistress, Mme Du Châtelet. Although this was ostensibly so that she might read Locke and Pope, it also afforded them new conversational possibilities in front of the servants. Just as, later, the Italian tongue spiced furtive messages to his niece, so Voltaire found that, in English, there was no such thing as indiscretion. Voltaire, on this evidence, deployed the language acquired as much to confound the French as to comprehend the English.

Voltaire wished to speak English not only to ask directions, but to become a writer, an English writer. The *Notebooks* testify to his early efforts in learning the language. The writing he copied was chiefly poetry, the most illustrious and assimilable of forms, where the rhymes assist and direct the memory. These fragments are not the banalities of conversational English, but the cadences of an aspiring writer. Voltaire's 'first masters', he explained subsequently, were 'Shakespeare, Addison, Dryden, Pope' (D2890).

Alexander Pope in particular exerted an especial influence on Voltaire, who, by the time he came to England, had achieved a reputation as a poet and dramatist. Pope had not only heard of Voltaire but had commended him to Lord Bolingbroke in 1724 as 'no less a Poet for being a Man of Sense' (D197). Armed at first with his unsteady, phonetic English, Voltaire made his way to 'Tuitnam' (Twickenham), near 'Chizeek' (Chiswick), to see the bard. The nineteenth-century historian John Morley suggested, more memorably than accurately, that Voltaire arrived in England as a poet and departed as a philosopher. Indeed, Voltaire's ambitions and achievements as a poet might seem to preclude the endeavours of the philosopher, and he periodically announces to friends that he is hanging up his lyre to concentrate on philosophy. But Pope's blessing and the example of his *Essay on Man*, which in its turn radiated such good sense to Voltaire, may have given him ideas. Perhaps they reassured him that there need be no necessary tension between poetry and philosophy. The poetry Voltaire learns is indeed enlisted in the service of all kinds of writing. He weaves poetic allusions into the fabric of his own prose, including his correspondence. When Voltaire comments in a letter to a friend that 'life is but a dream full of starts of folly and of fancied and true miseries' (D303), the sentiments and syntax clearly owe something to Shakespeare. Bored in Brussels, Voltaire writes to his friend Sir Everard Fawkener in the summer of 1740 that he 'wants two provisions . . . necessary to make that nauseous draught of life go down' (D2175), namely books and friends. Yet even as he laments the absence of books, Voltaire quotes from one in his head, refashioning some lines of Rochester:

> Love . . .
> That cordial drop, heav'n in our cup has thrown,
> To make the nauseous draught of life go down.[2]

Voltaire's writing in English is often a mosaic of pre-fabricated poetic insights. But he is, as this borrowed line goes to show, adventurous in adapting to his own ends. Voltaire, having been brought up to believe in and adhere to rigorous partitions between forms and genres, savoured a new licence. He was at liberty to transfer words and phrases from one context to another, made possible by a less regulated trade across the genres. It was in England that Voltaire realised that poets did not, in a strictly French sense, have to be poetic, remarking that 'only in London are poets allowed to be philosophers' ('il n'est permis aux poètes d'être philosophes qu'à Londres', D2648). London has also been called the capital of prose, and it was here that Voltaire first seems to have conceived of new horizons for himself as a writer.[3] While in England, Voltaire published *An Essay upon the Civil Wars of France and also upon the Epick Poetry of the European Nations* (1727), and he worked, at least in a preparatory way, on his *Histoire de Charles XII* (1731) and, of course, on the 'English letters' or *Lettres philosophiques*.

This latitude was not easily understood by Voltaire's compatriots. Voltaire, already in October 1726, and in his best new English, tries to attract his old friend Thiriot to 'this unaccountable nation' with the following promise:

> You will see a nation fond of their liberty, learned, witty, despising life and death, a nation of philosophers, not but that there are some fools in England, every country has its madmen. It may be French folly is pleasanter than English madness, but by God English wisdom and honesty is above yours. (D303)

The perceived English attitude to death was familiar enough, but Voltaire took an unusual interest in the extent of folly that reigned in the respective nations and in its differing manifestations. 'You know England', remarks Candide to Martin, 'are they as mad there as in France?' ('Vous connaissez l'Angleterre; y-est-on aussi fou qu'en France?'). England is characterised by 'another form of madness' ('une autre espèce de folie'), replies Martin, before outlining the enormous expenses that a colonial war waged over 'a few acres of snow somewhere near Canada' ('quelques arpents de neige vers le Canada') is incurring for both France and England. Candide is told bluntly, as the ship nears the shores of England: 'I only know that in general the people whom we are going to see are very bilious' ('Je sais seulement qu'en général les gens que nous allons voir sont fort atrabilaires').⁴ This naked cliché dangles rather forlornly. However, it is duly substantiated by the sight that follows. Admiral Byng is being shot on deck 'to encourage the rest' ('pour encourager les autres'). Candide's party sails on, having seen enough of England. Not only is this nation characterised by a certain belligerence but the dry nonchalance of the 'explanation' is also characteristically English. This insouciance surfaces as a cliché which Voltaire is content to inherit and pass on. Amazan, in Voltaire's story *La Princesse de Babylone*, visits England and makes for 'the capital of Albion', where he is invited to dinner by 'Milord What-then' ('Milord Qu'importe'). We are told, almost as bluntly as he himself might tell us, that the Milord 'drank a lot and did not utter a word' ('but beaucoup et ne dit mot').⁵

Voltaire does not challenge many of the clichés about the distinctive English national character in the eighteenth century, nor the notion that there might be such a thing as national character at all. Indeed, the anachronistic allusion to Albion reinforces the suggestion that national character is in essence immutable. But, although an archetypally taciturn Englishman may preside over the dinner, we learn that 'there were people of all types' present at it. Voltaire, typically, offers a brief conjectural socio-political explanation for this diversity. Since England had only ever been governed by foreigners, 'the families that had come with these monarchs had all brought customs of their own' ('les familles venues avec ces princes avaient toutes apporté des moeurs différentes'). Furthermore, the hostess has 'nothing of that affected and clumsy air, that stiffness, that false modesty that was held against young women from Albion' ('rien de cet air emprunté et gauche, de cette roideur, de cette mauvaise honte qu'on reprochait alors aux jeunes femmes d'Albion').⁶ Characteristically, Voltaire, without discrediting the cliché, is pleased to look beyond it.

Voltaire harboured some nostalgia for a time when those foreigners governing England were French. Although, ever strategic with the dedications that headed his works, Voltaire humbly offered the London edition of *La Henriade* to Queen Caroline, George II's consort, and did his best to ingratiate himself with the Hanoverian royal family, he longed, at least once he had left England, for a state more sympathetic to the French. In the first canto of *La Henriade*, he goes to the trouble of organising a fictional visit for his hero Henri IV (the father of Henrietta Maria) to Elizabeth I in England. It would not take much for such Anglo-French longings to look suspiciously like Jacobite sympathies. In 1745, Voltaire reportedly wept as he read out news of the ordeal of Bonnie Prince Charlie, though he recovered sufficiently to compose a manifesto for the Young Pretender (*Manifeste au roi de France en faveur du prince Charles Édouard*).

In the time it took to travel out to Pope's villa at Twickenham, Voltaire will have had the leisure to think about the constraints under which Roman Catholics had to live in England. Voltaire could not fail to realise that religious freedom in Britain was in fact heavily circumscribed, yet, in the interests of exposing French intolerance, he mythologised the situation in England. Voltaire was prepared to exaggerate English religious freedoms in order to make the French feel all the more keenly their own shackles.

Such is his desire to put the French in their place, Voltaire's praise of the English can seem inordinate. He claimed that the English clergy, educated in Oxford and Cambridge 'far from the corruption of the capital', were more virtuous than their French counterparts, yet when he came to describing the capital, Voltaire did not mention, let alone discuss, corruption. On the contrary, he then praised the capital's institutions, such as the Royal Exchange, for their indifference to the corrupting influence of clerical controversies. Voltaire is surely the only French author to have written a work about Joan of Arc, his mock-epic *La Pucelle d'Orléans*, which is barely critical of the English.[7]

In his first, faltering words of English, penned in the *Notebooks*, Voltaire wrote: 'England is meeting of all religions'.[8] Where accounts of English life might typically open with a description of the monarchy or Parliament, Voltaire, in what must have seemed a perverse opening gambit, began the *Lettres philosophiques* with a description of his encounter with a Quaker. When they first meet, the narrator Voltaire bows obsequiously to this curious fellow, only to find that his courtesy is met with curtness. The Quaker is beholden to no one. And he can defend his views vigorously. Voltaire thus opens his account of the English nation (and he sustains this over the next few letters) by exchanging views with the exponent of a minority religion. This move, made with an eye to the suffocating orthodoxies of French religion, itself constitutes a refusal to generalise about the English and England. Quakers are a 'people' unto themselves, characterised by their own principles, their own history. There seems, on this evidence, to be no such thing as a typical Englishman. The Quaker may oblige some French preconception of the gruff awkwardness of the English but also forces us to revise notions of Englishness. By subscribing to or indeed promoting a cliché that the English are free to be themselves, you necessarily banish other clichés about England, a nation of individuals.

Voltaire cherishes these freedoms sanctioned by an incipient form of constitutional monarchy. In a memorably neat formulation in the eighth of the *Lettres philosophiques*, Voltaire writes approvingly of the constitutional arrangements that result in the king's hands being constrained from doing evil but remaining free to do good. Voltaire echoes Montesquieu's praise of the division and balance of power in England between the legislative, the executive and the judiciary, and this three-part structure is neatly folded into a laudatory couplet or two in *La Henriade*.[9] These new checks and balances had at long last guaranteed stability, after a turbulent history best left to the executioner to write up: 'this slippery throne from which a hundred kings have fallen' ('ce trône glissant dont cent rois descendirent') had finally become more adhesive.[10]

In another axiom that invites us to remember it and turn it into a cliché, Voltaire pointedly remarks in the fifth of the *Lettres philosophiques* that 'an *Englishman*, as one to whom liberty is natural, may go to heaven his own way' ('Un Anglais comme homme libre, va au Ciel par le chemin qui lui plaît'). But it is helpful to read on. In the next line Voltaire adds:

> Nevertheless, tho' every one is permitted to serve God in whatever mode or fashion he thinks proper, yet their true religion, that in which a man makes his fortune, is the sect of Episcopalians or Churchmen, called the Church of England, or simply the Church, by way of eminence. No person can possess an employment either in England or Ireland, unless he be rank'd among the faithful, that is, profess himself a member of the Church of England. This reason (which carries mathematical evidence with it) has converted such numbers of dissenters of all persuasions, that not a twentieth part of the nation is out of the pale of the establish'd church.
>
> (Cependant quoi-que chacun puisse ici servir Dieu à sa mode, leur véritable Religion, celle où l'on fait fortune, est la Secte des Episcopaux, apellée l'Eglise Anglicane, ou l'Eglise par excellence. On ne peut avoir d'emploi ni en Angleterre, ni en Irlande, sans être du nombre des fidéles Anglicans; cette raison qui est une excellente preuve, a converti tant de Non-conformistes, qu'aujourd'hui il n'y a pas la vingtiéme partie de la Nation qui soit hors du giron de l'Eglise dominante.)[11]

In this way Voltaire's agreeable aphorism is duly qualified by the delicious ironies that follow, and the particular order of these words, in which the axiom is not really borne out, is designed to wrong-foot the unsuspecting reader.

Voltaire is adept at twisting and turning when comparing England to France. He is quite happy to draw on the sort of comparative schema by which eighteenth-century travel writers regularly help out their readers. Thus Swift is the 'English Rabelais', Pope praised as 'the English Boileau', and William Congreve 'their Molière'.[12] These approximations always implicitly pay tribute to the French component in the comparison, a stable referent against which the novelty may be measured. Voltaire appreciates these writers as interchangeable exponents of an essentially Classical aesthetic. As he says: 'I know nothing more useful, for the purposes of improving taste, than the comparison of those great geniuses who have worked in the same areas' ('Je ne sçai rien de plus utile pour se perfectionner le goût, que la comparaison des grands génies qui se sont exercés sur les mêmes matières').[13]

The French geniuses who had dominated the seventeenth century, 'the century of Louis XIV' as Voltaire named it, constitute for him an imperishable touchstone. However, the comparative approach falters when Voltaire tries to describe to his French readers the experience of seeing and reading Shakespeare. Not only has Shakespeare no French counterpart, but he enforces a revision of the very criteria by which other writers and indeed writing itself may be judged. Voltaire recognises genius without being able to apprehend it. When he speaks of Shakespeare, Voltaire's language crashes into oxymorons, the refuge of a writer unable to gainsay the contradictions before him. So Shakespeare is, intractably, 'a lovable barbarian, a seductive madman' ('un barbare aimable, un fou séduisant', D6562).

In a similar vein, the science of Newton would at first seem to be a symmetrical equivalent to the system devised by France's Descartes, 'our René', as Voltaire facetiously puts it. The fourteenth of the *Lettres philosophiques*, 'Sur Descartes et Newton', seems superficially to do justice to the two competing cosmologies. Gradually it emerges that Newton has displaced and supplanted Descartes. Voltaire seems to shelter behind the somewhat anodyne form of the travel account to propound insights that are damaging to French intellectual self-esteem. England, Voltaire suggests, is a nation that recognises and protects talent.

The *Lettres philosophiques* celebrate the mysterious collusion between national character, political freedom and philosophical insights. Did Locke and Newton just happen to be English? It seems that Voltaire is drawn to the English on account of Newton and Locke, but he is equally drawn to Newton and Locke because they are English. It is Voltaire's conviction that intellectual development and liberty form an interdependent and mutually encouraging pair of qualities.

Disposed as he is to enthuse about English intellectual life, probably from the day he disembarked, a sunny day as it happens, there is a countervailing thrust which is silently, but no less influentially, present. It is noticeable, when looking at his choices of textual illustration, that Voltaire alights on extracts which are overwhelmingly the accents of a first-person voice, perhaps implicit testimony to Voltaire's view of a boldly individualistic culture. But there is also in the *Lettres philosophiques* an unremitting, if tacit, emphasis on the joylessness of the English. Voltaire's quotations gravitate universally to the same bleak and melancholic truths. In Letter 18, Voltaire selects as his chief example from Shakespeare, Hamlet's 'To be or not to be' soliloquy; then, as an example from John Dryden, he cites this passage:

> When I consider life, 'tis all a cheat
> Yet fool'd by hope, men favour the deceit.

In Letter 19, he cites William Wycherley's *Plain Dealer*, which imitates Molière's *Misanthrope*, then in Letter 21 quotes Edmund Waller's poem on Oliver Cromwell. Finally, in Letter 22, Voltaire comes to his friend Pope and selects a passage from his comic poem, *The Rape of the Lock* – and even here he alights on a moment of introspection. By discussing only the formal properties of these majestically gloomy passages, leaving the content to speak for itself, Voltaire conveys a message about the English in which the incidental or even subliminal quality of these observations helps to guarantee their force. Voltaire is seemingly trying to impart an unpalatable truth about the English which is not only concomitant with their freedoms but shapes their art. Perhaps this is the reason why Voltaire would never return to England. Or why, indeed, he subsequently professes a wish to die in England more often than he expresses a desire to live there (D5160).

Voltaire instead moved to Geneva and Lausanne and became a 'Suitzerman', before settling in Ferney. He contentedly signed himself 'V the Swiss' ('le Suisse V') in correspondence from his residences there. In these places, Voltaire found a climate that was kinder to his constitution than was the English air. But, more importantly, he also found, at least for a while, an ideal synthesis of English and French attributes: 'They speak in French but they think as in English' ('On y parle français, on y pense à l'anglaise', D5780). English thought is not then confined to England. The freedoms prevailing in England, sometimes insufficiently regulated, are tempered here by French grace. Switzerland provides the ideal marriage of French and English attributes.

Voltaire's love for England is never more nor less than an affection for English individuals. As long as English people visited and entertained him, his Anglophilia could withstand extended absence from the nation, war between England and France, and even the loss of his teeth – a problem which meant that Voltaire whistled when he tried to pronounce English words. If Voltaire could not travel to England, a nation, so he claimed, he loved but could not live in (D5244), England would come to him. Even if he was 'damnably sick', as he explained to his English visitors (D7069), he was no less hospitable, his visitors no less curious. Voltaire was vividly, sometimes painfully, aware of the extent to which the characteristics of a nation could be exaggerated beyond its boundaries. But if Englishness could be exported from England and embodied beyond its shores, Voltaire was increasingly hostile to the England which wielded colonial power detrimental to French interests. Already in *La Henriade*, the threat of British hegemony overseas had been hinted at; English activities abroad became more controversial and unpalatable in Voltaire's eyes as the struggles of which they were a part became more pervasive, more devastating, more pointless.

Voltaire's appointment as *historiographe du roi* in 1745 committed him to celebrate such French victories as might come to pass. Voltaire yearned for a success with which he could ingratiate himself with Louis XV and justify his appointment. And when the French delivered, winning the Battle of Fontenoy in 1745, Voltaire in a triumphant frenzy composed his *Poème de Fontenoy*. But in this poem the French seem to have won over an enemy that is barely mentioned. The English do not seem to have lost this battle. Voltaire initially designates the English with a generous periphrasis:

> Above all this proud people who across so many seas
> See their commerce and glory embrace the universe.
>
> (Surtout ce peuple altier qui voit sur tant de mers
> Son commerce et sa gloire embrasser l'univers.)[14]

Voltaire, in a footnote to the poem, is furthermore careful to specify that the English officers are every bit as generous as their French counterparts.[15] Often rather sceptical of anecdotes, he is content to recycle the story that the French offer, at the onset of battle, the first volley to the English with the gallant invitation: 'Messieurs les Anglais, tirez les premiers.'

Voltaire at this point is endeavouring to ensure that praise of the French does not necessitate scorn for the English. But this even-handedness slowly, inexorably, declines. A turning point in this regard occurred early on in the Seven Years War, when, much to the delight of Voltaire, the French regained from the British the island of Minorca. Admiral Byng was held responsible for this disaster. He was consequently court-martialled and, under the noses of Candide and company, executed. As Candide observes, it seems a little unfair to execute the admiral for keeping his distance from the French enemy when, necessarily, they were at the same distance from the English foe.[16] This fictional gag barely does justice to a very real and urgent anxiety on Voltaire's part to exonerate Byng. Voltaire, wishing to believe that both sides could fight an honourable and courageous battle irrespective of the result, mobilised his military acquaintances and had letters sent to England, pleading for the life of Byng, on the basis that there was no dereliction of duty. French valour did not mean English deficiency. But these letters from France, orchestrated by Voltaire, had no effect and may indeed have helped cost Byng his life, such were the fears of treason. Voltaire seems to have learned from this strategic error that there was no point, no possibility even, in trying to have it both ways. With the stakes raised higher than previously, a French success could only mean an English failure, and vice versa. The nations were henceforward starkly polarised.

Moreover, these struggles, waged with commercial rather than ideological interests uppermost, had consequences for all citizens. English victories sent up the price of Voltaire's sugar, as he informed his correspondents with undisguised consternation at this relatively trivial by-product of a savage war. Some of Voltaire's shares and investments were also hurt by British military interventions (D7131). In 1748, Voltaire was already upset with the English, but no more than with the French: 'The French are persecuting me on land, the English are pillaging me at sea' ('les Français me persécutent sur terre, les Anglais me pillent sur mer', D3665). In 1757, he commented more ruefully that 'I was an Englishman . . . I am one no longer since they have been assassinating our officers in America and are pirates on the seas and I wish a fitting punishment to those who trouble the peace of the world' ('J'étais anglais . . . je ne le suis plus depuis qu'ils assassinent nos officiers en Amérique, et qu'ils sont pirates sur mer, et je souhaite un juste châtiment à ceux qui troublent le repos du monde', D7310).

These colonial struggles, at once baffling and distressing, form a new backdrop to Voltaire's later tales in which the tighter interdependence of particular destinies and international battles is dizzying. *L'Ingénu*, written in 1767, concerns a clear-thinking, straight-talking, heroic Huron who becomes a French citizen. Although set in the seventeenth century, the story also allows Voltaire to give some expression to the contemporary vogue for *sensibilité*. Following the success of Rousseau's *La Nouvelle Héloïse* (1761) and Richardson's *Clarissa* before it, the emotions of innocent people, explored in novelistic form, became favoured subjects. Voltaire remarked that Pope, 'the sad Englishman' ('le triste Anglais'), omitted all consideration of love from his admirable *Essay on Man*. The bilious English offered a foil to the delicacies of these emotions. Mme de Kerkabon, a character in *L'Ingénu*, is assigned a cliché that, in its exasperation with the uncouth godlessness of the English, is familiarly French: 'They will always set more store by a play of Shakespeare, a plum pudding and a bottle of rum than the Pentateuch' ('Ils feront plus de cas d'une pièce de Shakespeare, d'un plumbpouding et d'une bouteille de rhum que du Pentateuque').[17] Mme de Kerkabon, as her name implies, is obsessed with the proprieties of the Church, but where, previously, the comparative indifference to religious orthodoxy in England had been found entirely laudable, here it seems to be a symptom of a nation whose freedoms veer towards licence. The English, a paradigm for modernity, have now become an anonymous, belligerent force. Mirroring Voltaire's own changing allegiances, the Ingénu announces that, despite having lived with them and learned their language, he will fight his 'former friends' the English. In the title of chapter 7, we are told that 'the Ingénu repels the English' ('l'Ingénu repousse les Anglais'). The enemy now is no longer, as in the poem about Fontenoy, merely incidental. The Ingénu, who is after all named Hercule, kills precisely three Englishmen and injures an admiral to boot. There is no better proof of his valour and maturity than fighting for the French against the English, a faceless, motiveless force who deserve to be on the receiving end of his guile and courage. Voltaire just about allows a lingering sense that, even if he ends up their sworn enemy, the Ingénu might not have become quite such a rounded paragon without the assistance of the English. He is by no means the last man to become a greater hero of the French for having first been a prisoner of the English.

A few years later, the *Histoire de Jenni ou l'athée et le sage* (1775), probably Voltaire's last tale, yields a more positive view of the English, still within a similar military and transatlantic context. This time, Voltaire places at the centre of the story an Englishman who goes by the auspicious name of Dr Freind. As his name suggests or rather shouts out, Freind is a model of good sense (the name Goudman, which belongs to another nice Englishman in a Voltaire story, is equally unsubtle). His sang-froid is repeatedly tested by the misadventures of various people, not least of his son. Freind is certainly not virtuous because he is English, but he is virtuous in a distinctively English way. When people are free to think of atheism, Voltaire becomes rather worried by freethinking, and, on behalf of Voltaire, Freind seeks to expose the fallacies and dangers of this way of thinking. It is not by chance that the philosophical conversations which ensue should be entertained by Englishmen. It is perhaps above all in England that the fine line Voltaire sees between freedom and permissiveness can be traced. Freind turns out, in Voltaire's story, to be the grandson of William Penn, recalling the Quakers or Society of Friends, one of whom Voltaire had first encountered at the start of the *Lettres philosophiques*. The world had since become more complex and dangerous, making new demands on man. But those steadfast virtues, celebrated by Voltaire many years earlier, remained inviolable.

Montesquieu suggested that the English did not like foreigners for the simple reason that they did not like anyone, not even one another.[18] But

Voltaire found lasting admirers and friends in England. And England warmed quickly to Voltaire: he was elected to the Royal Society in 1743, three years before he made it to the Académie Française. If Voltaire mythologised England, England was pleased to return the favour. Voltaire continues to be cherished by the English as their version of the archetypal French writer, both satisfyingly *engagé* and a debonair fount of *bons mots* which confirm suppositions about France and her writers. Yet Voltaire, characterised by an outlook that can be both empirical and cynical, has as often been welcomed as an honorary Englishman. Tobias Smollett, writing in the preface to his edition of Voltaire's works in 1772, recognised a 'congenial affinity' between Voltaire and the English nation, a truly exclusive bond: 'But how much so ever [Voltaire] may be admired in other countries, he seems to be peculiarly adapted by nature, for the entertainment of the English people.'[19] Voltaire cannot be made to serve as the counterpart to any English author. Instead, he himself becomes a surrogate Englishman.

Aware of the ambivalence of this form of dual citizenship, Voltaire in the *Histoire de Jenni* alludes to himself at one point by mentioning 'un philosophe *frenchman*'.[20] On these terms, Voltaire contrives to remain a Frenchman even while he looks to England for his self-definition. Voltaire once assured his old friend and 'worthy Englishman' Everard Fawkener, in a statement that is both emphatic and vague: 'I retain for my life something of the English in me' (D3418). Unusually, Voltaire was not talking about his indigestion nor was he alluding to English puddings. That mysterious 'something', an extraordinarily rich and complex import, continues to tease and intrigue readers on both sides of the Channel.

NOTES

1. See N. Cronk, 'The *Letters Concerning the English Nation* as an English Work: Reconsidering the Harcourt Brown Thesis', *SVEC*, 2001:10, 226–39; and J. P. Lee, 'The Unexamined Premise: Voltaire, John Lockman and the Myth of the *English Letters*', *SVEC*, 2001:10, 240–70.
2. See 'A Letter from Artemiza in the Towne to Chloe in the Country', *The Works of John Wilmot, Earl of Rochester*, ed. Harold Love (Oxford University Press, 1999), p.64. Curiously, Dr Johnson later uses these very words from Rochester in the same way as Voltaire in likewise emphasising the primacy of friendship rather than love (Boswell, *Life of Johnson*, Oxford: Oxford University Press, 1969, p.1020; 24 April 1779).
3. C. Connolly, 'One of My Londons', *Previous Convictions* (London: Hamish Hamilton, 1963), p.393.
4. *RC*, p.209 (*Candide*, chap.23).
5. *RC*, p.390.
6. *RC*, pp.389–90.

7. Joan of Arc is designated 'the shame of the English' ('la honte des Anglais') in *La Henriade* (*OCV*, vol.2, p.525); but *La Pucelle* is not consistently or overtly anti-English.

8. *Notebooks*, *OCV*, vol.81, p.51.

9. *OCV*, vol.2, p.382.

10. *La Princesse de Babylone*, *RC*, pp.390–1, and *La Pucelle*, *OCV*, vol.7, p.381.

11. Letter 5; *Letters*, p.26; *LP*, vol.1, p.61.

12. Letter 22; *Letters*, p.108; *LP*, vol.2, p.135; and Letter 24; *Letters*, p.117; *LP*, vol.2, p.172.

13. Letter 21; *Letters*, p.101; *LP*, vol.2, p.124.

14. Moland, vol.8, p.385.

15. Moland, vol.8, p.391.

16. *RC*, p.210.

17. *RC*, p.294.

18. 'Comment les Anglois aimeroient-ils les étrangers? Ils ne s'aiment pas eux-mêmes' (Montesquieu, *Notes sur l'Angleterre*, *Œuvres complètes*, ed. R. Caillois: Paris, Gallimard, 1949, 2 vols, vol.1, p.876).

19. T. Smollett, *The Works of M. de Voltaire* (Dublin: Moncrieffe, 1772), vol.1, p.iv.

20. *RC*, p.631.

6

RUSSELL GOULBOURNE

Voltaire's masks: theatre
and theatricality

In 1944, on the 250th anniversary of Voltaire's birth, the poet Paul Valéry praised him as 'a man who tried his hand at every literary genre, who had a go at everything, tragedy, epigrams, history, epic, short fiction, essays, and that vast correspondence' ('un homme qui s'est essayé dans tous les genres, qui a touché à tout, tragédie, épigramme, histoire, épopée, contes, essais, et cette correspondance innombrable').[1] Valéry's account recalls that of the eighteenth-century actor-cum-historian Claude Villaret, who as early as 1759 sought to explain the success of 'this ingenious and sublime author' ('cet auteur ingénieux et sublime'): 'Superior in almost every literary genre, it is above all through the beauty in the detail that he is able to captivate his readers and enchant his audiences' ('Supérieur presqu'en tout genre de littérature, c'est surtout par les beautés de détail qu'il sait trouver l'art d'attacher ses lecteurs et de charmer les spectateurs').[2]

Perhaps the most surprising, and certainly the most telling, feature of both of these appreciations of Voltaire the polymath is the specific mention of his work as a dramatist. Surprising, because today perhaps the most common image of Voltaire is that of the satirical story-teller. We have forgotten that his fame in his lifetime, both in France and abroad, was largely based on his reputation as a dramatist, and that the theatre occupies a substantial place in his vast output. Whereas in the story *Le Taureau blanc* (1772) the character Mambrès, usually seen as an image of Voltaire, claims that 'telling stories is the only way to get on in the world' ('ce n'est que par des contes qu'on réussit dans le monde'),[3] Voltaire himself, if the word of one of his secretaries is to be believed, thought that science, history, theology and the writing of fiction were whimsical pastimes compared with the serious work of writing plays.[4]

This change in popular perception of Voltaire notwithstanding, it is worthwhile revisiting Voltaire's theatre, and in particular his innovations in the writing and staging of both tragic and comic drama, in the context of his writing as a whole. For what emerges from a consideration of a wide range of Voltaire's writing is an underlying preoccupation with theatricality.

Voltaire's theatre and his broader concern with theatricality need to be studied together, because role-playing and the ludic wearing of masks are generally pervasive devices in the Voltairean corpus.

Theatre

Voltaire was France's, even Europe's, greatest dramatist in a stage-struck age. The theatre was the royal route to fame and consecration as a writer in the eighteenth century, through both performance and printed editions. As Voltaire observes in the 1765 preface to his tragedy *Adélaïde du Guesclin*: 'The book-buying public numbers forty or fifty people for serious books, four or five hundred for entertaining books, and about eleven or twelve hundred for plays' ('Le public, en fait de livres, est composé de quarante ou cinquante personnes, si le livre est sérieux, de quatre ou cinq cents lorsqu'il est plaisant, et d'environ onze ou douze cents s'il s'agit d'une pièce de théâtre').[5] Voltaire wrote fifty plays: twenty-six tragedies; eighteen comedies; four opera libretti; and two small-scale *divertissements* for private royal entertainment. For him, and for his contemporaries, his theatre was his most significant literary monument. His public and literary persona is effectively framed by his successes in the tragic theatre: from *Œdipe* in 1718, when Voltaire was only 24, to *Irène*, for the fourth performance of which he returned to Paris in triumph in March 1778, just two months before his death, his apotheosis signalled symbolically by the crowning of the dramatist's bust on the stage of the Comédie-Française at the end of the performance.

The success of *Irène* at the end of Voltaire's career suitably echoed that of *Œdipe* near the beginning. Whereas the average number of total performances for a tragedy in the first half of the eighteenth century was just over nine, *Œdipe* had thirty performances in its first run alone (between 18 November 1718 and 21 January 1719), and it was performed more in its first two years than any other eighteenth-century tragedy; it earned greater profits for its author than any previous play had done; and it remained in the repertory of the Comédie-Française until 1852.[6]

Despite the undeniable success of many of Voltaire's tragedies in the eighteenth century, modern critics tend to dismiss them as pale imitations of the works of his more famous seventeenth-century forebears Corneille and Racine. *Œdipe* is a case in point, so the complaint runs. It is a play that shows Voltaire trying to write a tragedy precisely in the so-called 'Classical', seventeenth-century mould, choosing not just any subject from the ancient world, but the archetypal subject of tragedy and one which Corneille himself had already treated in 1659, derived, of course, from Sophocles and Seneca.

However, while it is true that Voltaire was greatly influenced by the theory and practice of seventeenth-century tragedy – like Racine, for example, he followed Aristotle in arguing that the primary aim of tragedy was to move the audience to tears by stirring the emotions of pity and fear[7] – he was also an innovator in a number of important respects.

One of Voltaire's major innovations in tragedy was in the domain of subject matter. Whereas earlier French tragic dramatists had always exploited subjects from the history and mythology of ancient Greece and Rome, Voltaire more innovatively exploited some subjects linked to French national history. He first did this in *Zaïre* (1732), a tragedy set in the Crusades and about the struggle to free Jerusalem from the Muslim infidel in the thirteenth century. With *Zaïre* Voltaire managed to beat his existing record of success: between 1732 and 1936 it was performed at the Comédie-Française no fewer than 488 times, and within a few years of its publication the play had been translated into Spanish, Italian, German and English (the second of the known English translations, by Aaron Hill, was very successful when it was first produced at Drury Lane in January 1736, running for fourteen performances and thereafter establishing itself as the most frequently acted adaptation of all Voltaire's plays on the English stage).[8] In the light of this success, Voltaire experimented further with medieval settings for his tragedies *Adélaïde du Guesclin* (1734), set during the Hundred Years War; *Tancrède* (1759), set in eleventh-century Syracuse; and *Don Pèdre* (1761), set in fourteenth-century Toledo.[9]

In comedy, too, Voltaire was an innovator. His eighteen comedies are more varied than is usually conceded: no two are alike.[10] In particular, he sought to extend the possibilities of the comic genre and to write comedies which were not like those of his predecessors and contemporaries. He experimented with the forms, settings, characters and themes of comedy. Beginning with *L'Indiscret* (1725), a comedy about a pompous *petit-maître* set in eighteenth-century Paris, he went on to write comedies about, *inter alia*, a lascivious sea captain (*Les Originaux*, 1738), a hack journalist (*L'Envieux*, 1739) and religious hypocrites (*La Prude*, 1739; *Le Dépositaire*, 1769), and with settings as diverse as ancient Athens (*Socrate*, 1759), eighteenth-century London (*L'Écossaise*, 1760) and the French provinces in the sixteenth century (*Charlot*, 1767). He also wrote comedies involving music and dance, most notably *La Princesse de Navarre*, a *comédie-ballet* written in collaboration with the composer Jean-Philippe Rameau for a royal command performance at Versailles in 1745.

La Princesse de Navarre also highlights another of Voltaire's innovations in comedy, and arguably the most important: his experimentation with tone. He certainly wrote comedy with the example of the seventeenth-century

French comic tradition in his mind, particularly the laughter-provoking comedies of Molière: *La Princesse de Navarre*, for instance, is a self-conscious attempt to recreate the sub-genre of the *comédie-ballet* pioneered by Molière and Jean-Baptiste Lully. But he also sought to innovate by experimenting with tone, amalgamating the comic and the sentimental, and thereby distinguishing his plays from the contemporary vogue for sentimentality, a vogue illustrated by the plays of Philippe Néricault Destouches, Pierre-Claude Nivelle de La Chaussée and Diderot. Voltaire's comedies are, in different ways, tools of critical response to contemporary drama: he sought not to follow trends, but to set new ones.

And in doing so he enjoyed some major successes. His fourth comedy, *L'Enfant prodigue*, for instance, was first performed in October 1736 at the Comédie-Française, where it had a first run of 22 performances, compared to the average number of total performances for a comedy in the first half of the eighteenth century of just over 10; and in the second half of the century it was second only to *Tancrède* as Voltaire's most popular play, performed 157 times, compared to only 52 performances of La Chaussée's *Le Préjugé à la mode* (1735).[11]

Voltaire's contemporary success as a dramatist might be attributed not just to his ability to shape and satisfy public taste, but also to his keen theatrical sense and his practical understanding of the theatre as a performance art.[12] He was first and foremost a man of the theatre, writing to his niece Mme Denis on 30 July 1769: 'It is impossible really to appreciate a play until it is performed on stage' ('On ne connaît bien une pièce que lorsqu'elle est sur les planches', D15783). Indeed, it was precisely the theatricality of his plays that led David Garrick to consider Voltaire to be France's greatest tragic poet because, unlike Racine, who, according to Garrick, said everything there was to say in his verse, Voltaire left something for the actor.[13]

Voltaire took a very practical approach to his work as a dramatist. Whenever possible, he followed closely the rehearsals of his plays and dispensed advice on acting, costumes and scenery. For example, he offered coaching to the actress Marie-Anne Dangeville, a precocious talent, who made her Comédie-Française debut in 1730, aged only 15. Voltaire entrusted her with the role of Tullie in his tragedy *Brutus* (1730), but she was not an immediate success. He wrote to her on 12 December 1730, the day after the premiere, carefully combining ecstatic praise with encouragement to do better in future: 'Remember not to rush anything, to bring everything to life, to introduce sighs into your declamation, and to leave long pauses' ('Souvenez-vous de ne rien précipiter, d'animer tout, de mêler des soupirs à votre déclamation, de mettre de grands temps', D387).

Captivated by theatre and theatrical performance ever since his youth,[14] wherever Voltaire set up home he also set up a private theatre, most notably at Cirey and at Ferney. During a visit to Cirey in February 1739, Léopold Desmarets recalled having played or rehearsed more than fifty acts of various plays and operas in the space of forty-eight hours (D1876). Voltaire was a born role-player, as his success in such private theatricals attests. Condorcet, for example, gives an account of Voltaire's performance as Cicero in the staging of his tragedy *Rome sauvée* at the home of the Duchesse Du Maine at Sceaux in June 1750: 'Never before, in any role, has an actor produced such a perfect illusion: it was as if he actually was the consul. This was not verse recited from memory, but a speech from the very soul of the orator' ('Jamais, dans aucun rôle, aucun acteur n'a porté si loin l'illusion: on croyait voir le consul. Ce n'étaient pas des vers récités de mémoire qu'on entendait, mais un discours sortant de l'âme de l'orateur').[15] In September 1772, a visiting Englishman, Thomas Orde, was able to sketch the 78-year-old Voltaire leaping around the stage of the Châtelaine theatre at Ferney in the role of Lusignan in *Zaïre* (fig. 4).[16] What is in evidence above all is Voltaire's ability to extend his sympathies and identify with a persona other than his own, and perhaps even his deep-seated need to play a role and to be other than himself. He seems to have fulfilled his own view of the ideal actor: the art of acting, he argues in his *Siècle de Louis XIV*, 'requires all the gifts of nature, great intelligence, hard work, a faultless memory, and above all that rare art of being able to transform oneself into the person you are performing' ('Cet art demande tous les dons de la nature, une grande intelligence, un travail assidu, une mémoire imperturbable, et surtout cet art si rare de se transformer en la personne qu'on représente').[17]

Voltaire's talent for adopting masks and playing roles was to serve him well not only as an actor, but also as a writer. It is this mobile, multi-faceted Voltaire who incessantly plays with masks throughout his works; and he does so all the better to express himself.

Theatricality

Voltaire presses the potential of role-playing into the service of intellectual exploration in many of his texts, beginning with his theatre. He experimented with the didactic potential of theatre, making tragedy in particular one of the weapons of the Enlightenment. Just a year after the success of *Zaïre*, Voltaire wrote in his *Lettre à un premier commis* (1733): 'I think of tragedy and comedy as lessons in virtue, reason and seemly conduct' ('Je regarde la tragédie et la comédie comme des leçons de vertu, de raison et de bienséance').[18] Since the seventeenth century, faced with the Church's

Fig. 4 *Le héros de Ferney au théâtre de Châtelaine*, engraving after a drawing from life by
Thomas Orde, 1772 (private collection)

view of the theatre as a force for moral corruption, dramatists had defended their plays by saying that they taught virtue and good behaviour. Seventeenth-century dramatists, however, did not claim that their plays taught reason. Voltaire alludes to the traditional defence of theatre, but in a subtly subversive way: his is a distinctly eighteenth-century conception of the theatre, and it opens the way for theatre to attack the status quo by encouraging in the audience the critical use of reason.

But a play is not the same as a philosophical treatise; in fact, Voltaire observes in his verse tale *Les Trois Manières* (1763), 'the theatre is better at instructing than any weighty tome' ('le théâtre instruit mieux que ne fait un gros livre').[19] And as he explains in the prefatory essay accompanying his tragedy *Sémiramis* (1746), 'the only difference between theatre proper and books on morality is that the instruction in tragedies comes entirely through the dramatic action' ('la seule différence qui soit entre le théâtre épuré et les livres de morale, c'est que l'instruction se trouve dans la tragédie toute en action').[20] Philosophical propaganda in the theatre must be theatrical.

In his plays, Voltaire creates dramatic and intellectual interest through debate: he sets characters in opposition to one another. He raises issues in the heat of the dramatic action which can give the audience, on subsequent reflection, pause for thought. He is alive above all to the need to write good drama that will seize and retain the audience's interest. Indeed, it is precisely this audience involvement – be it pity and fear in tragedy or laughter and amusement in comedy – that is the prerequisite for Voltaire's intellectual stimulus: by engaging the audience in a dramatic intrigue, he provokes them into thought.

The impact of ideas is dependent on theatrical structures. In a comedy, laughter at the expense of the fool ensures that the audience sides with the more right-thinking characters. This is the case, for example, in *La Femme qui a raison* (1748), where the right-thinking wife expresses views on luxury and money that are very close to those known to be Voltaire's, whereas the misguided husband offers a caricature of the views of Voltaire's contemporary Jean-Jacques Rousseau.[21] Similarly in a tragedy, the emotions of pity and fear determine how the audience reacts to the ideas raised, though the possibilities are potentially more complex. *Mérope* (1743) offers a case in point. Based on Greek mythology, it is a tragedy about the eponymous widowed Queen of Messenia, who avoids being usurped thanks to the reappearance of her long-lost son, Égisthe, who returns to kill the would-be usurper, the ambitious soldier Polyphonte. Polyphonte voices views which are intellectually tenable, but in the emotional climate of a theatrical performance, it is actually Mérope's emotional rejection of those views that wins the audience's sympathy and approval. In Act I, scene 3, for example, Polyphonte tries to persuade Mérope to marry him and hence lend him respectability as a ruler. Mérope reacts with horror to the suggestion that she should, in effect, betray her late husband and her son, who is the rightful ruler. She asks incredulously (lines 171–2):

> Would I hand over to you his mother and his kingdom,
> And place the crown on your head, you, a mere soldier?
>
> (Je mettrais en vos mains sa mère et son État,
> Et le bandeau des rois sur le front d'un soldat?)

Mérope clearly believes in hereditary rule: a mere soldier could not be king. Polyphonte replies with potent aphorisms (lines 173–6):

> A soldier such as I can justly lay claim
> To govern the state having fought in its defence.
> The first king was himself a fortunate soldier;
> He who serves his country well needs no ancestors.
>
> (Un soldat tel que moi peut justement prétendre
> A gouverner l'État quand il l'a su défendre.
> Le premier qui fut roi fut un soldat heureux;
> Qui sert bien son pays n'a pas besoin d'aïeux.)

These were some of the best-known lines of the play; indeed they were to become a popular Revolutionary battle-cry at the end of the century. They constitute, potentially at least, a powerfully subversive political message in a play written and performed in the monarchical society of eighteenth-century France.

But does Voltaire necessarily share Polyphonte's view? In the absence of any direct statement from him, it is difficult to be absolutely sure. If we consider the lines in their dramatic context, however, their impact changes. Voltaire is pitting a known violent tyrant against a distraught widow and mother with whom the audience has already been invited to sympathise in the first two scenes of the play. Mérope replies emotionally to Polyphonte, without taking on board the intellectual principles in his argument (lines 185–9):

> Is that the pledge, so pure and so sacred,
> That you swore to my husband and to me?
> The pledge that you owe to his betrayed spirit,
> To his pitiful widow, to his woe-begotten son,
> To the gods from whom he came and who gave him his power?
>
> (Est-ce là cette foi, si pure et si sacrée,
> Qu'à mon époux, à moi, votre bouche a jurée?
> La foi que vous devez à ses mânes trahis,
> A sa veuve éperdue, à son malheureux fils,
> A ces dieux dont il sort, et dont il tient l'empire?)[22]

Her response, expressed emotionally and emphatically, serves to increase the audience's sympathy for her, and Polyphonte's intellectual argument, by contrast, looks more and more like the bravado of a bullying tyrant. The result is that the explicit views of Polyphonte are rejected in favour of the unargued views of Mérope. The philosophical view which emerges from the dramatic action, then, is support for hereditary monarchy, not subversive questioning of it. But crucially this view is not expressed clearly or unambiguously; rather, it emerges from the play of conflicting ideas, from the drama of clashing characters. Debates give theatrical pleasure in Voltaire's plays; they also provide intellectual stimulation. At its best, Voltaire's theatre airs ideas rather than expresses them directly and didactically.

Theatricality beyond the theatre

If Voltaire writes 'philosophical' theatre throughout his life, he also writes 'theatrical' philosophical texts. His success in playing with ideas in his theatre parallels that in other genres, where he also exploits role-playing, masks, debate and dialogue for polemical ends. One such text is Voltaire's first major philosophical work, the *Lettres philosophiques* (1733–4), the product of his stay in England (1726–8), where he learnt English by going to the theatre, sitting with a copy of the play on his lap and following the action.[23] The I-persona in the first of the letters is seemingly an open-minded, inquisitive Frenchman, but he gradually starts to make fun of his Quaker interlocutor, first for his appearance and gestures, and then for his views on baptism: Voltaire effectively dons the mask of the traditional Catholic. Whereas the Frenchman ends up looking foolish for his unthinking adherence to social convention, the Quaker emerges as tolerant and peace-loving, a follower of natural religion. The art of the *philosophe* is that of the role-player as the authorial voice slips suggestively from the 'Frenchman' at the start of the letter to the 'Quaker' later on.[24]

Elsewhere in the *Lettres philosophiques* Voltaire seems to adopt a similarly English mask, praising England's good example and implicitly criticising France, such as the celebration of religious freedom in Letter 6. But he also adopts a more typically French mask, criticising, for example, the imperfection of English theatre in Letter 18. Voltaire wears different masks at different times in order to prompt readers to think through ideas for themselves, to view difficult questions from a variety of angles and to use their critical judgement: as the writer in Letter 8 puts it, addressing the reader directly having juxtaposed the legal condemnation of Charles I in England and the assassination of Henri IV in France: 'Weigh, I say, all these wicked attempts, and then judge' ('Pesez ces attentats et jugez').[25]

Voltaire was proud of his literary and intellectual cosmopolitanism. When in England, for instance, he seemingly feels fully English, or, as he puts it (in English) in a letter to his friend Des Alleurs on 11 April 1728: 'I think and write like a free Englishman' (D330). Similarly, on 23 April 1754 he writes to Mme Du Deffand from Colmar, apologising that he does not have anything interesting to send her: 'I had become English in London, now I am German in Germany. My chameleon's skin would become more colourful still if I were with you: your imagination would reignite my sluggish mind' ('J'étais devenu anglais à Londres, je suis allemand en Allemagne. Ma peau de caméléon prendrait des couleurs plus vives auprès de vous: votre imagination rallumerait la langueur de mon esprit', D5786). Voltaire the chameleon, like Voltaire the actor, is endlessly adaptable.

Something of this mutability can also be seen in the *Dictionnaire philosophique* (1769), a work teeming with masks. Voltaire's personal presence in the text seems strong: a speaking I-persona dominates more than half of the articles. But that 'I' actually changes suggestively from article to article. It seems most clearly to be Voltaire in an article such as 'Fausseté des vertus humaines', a biting attack on the Oratorian Jacques Esprit's *La Fausseté des vertus humaines* (1677–8), which ends with the writer declaring: 'I shall say no more about it, for I shall lose my temper' ('Je n'en dirai pas davantage, car je me mettrais en colère').[26] Elsewhere he adopts a mock-naïve stance, such as in the article 'Lois', where the I-persona seeks different people's views on the laws governing warfare, leading him to conclude: 'Having been thoroughly instructed . . . it appeared to me that most men have received enough common sense from nature to pass laws, but that not everybody has enough justice to make laws' ('Après avoir été bien instruit . . . il m'a paru que la plupart des hommes ont reçu de la nature assez de sens commun pour faire des lois; mais que tout le monde n'a pas assez de justice pour faire de bonnes lois').[27] If naivety here serves as a mask for ironic criticism, at other times Voltaire subversively dons the mask of the well-informed, seemingly good Christian, as in the article 'Credo', where the I-persona is proud of the fact that he says the Lord's Prayer every morning, though the creed he recites is conspicuously deist in tenor, stressing that God is the father of all humankind and that 'theological disputes are at once the world's most ridiculous farce and the most frightful scourge, immediately after war, pestilence, famine and the pox' ('les disputes théologiques sont à la fois la farce la plus ridicule et le fléau le plus affreux de la terre, immédiatement après la guerre, la peste, la famine et la vérole'): the mask of the good Christian gives voice to Voltaire's unorthodox views.[28]

But the polyphony of the *Dictionnaire philosophique* is more complex still, for eleven of the articles are in dialogue form: 'Catéchisme chinois',

'Catéchisme du curé', 'Catéchisme du Japonais', 'Catéchisme du jardinier', 'Dieu', 'Fraude', 'Idée', 'Liberté', 'Liberté de penser', 'Nécessaire' and 'Papisme'.[29] Some of these dialogues, such as 'Idée', follow a simple teacher–pupil dynamic, with helpful questions from the latter prompting the former into a clear exposition of characteristically Voltairean ideas. Others, however, are less didactic and more heuristic. 'Catéchisme chinois', for example, stages a meeting of apparently equally right-thinking minds: as they discuss topics as diverse as God, creation, morality, the soul and virtue, the two interlocutors, Cu-Su and Kou, both in some senses 'represent' Voltaire, with the result that the dialogue is less about the straightforward exposition of truth as its active exploration.

This use of dialogue for the purposes of polemic and intellectual exploration permeates Voltaire's writing in a number of other genres, too. Of the *contes*, for example, the last, *Histoire de Jenni* (1775), is perhaps the most polyphonic: focusing on the debate between Freind, the voice of reason who attacks atheism and defends deism, and Birton, the advocate of materialism who is ultimately converted to his opponent's cause, the *conte* is a good example of Voltaire's ability to speak both as himself and as his enemy. But perhaps Voltaire's most 'dialogic' texts are his thirty-one philosophical dialogues proper, written between 1751 and 1777 and therefore contemporaneous with his better-known *contes*.[30]

In some of his dialogues, Voltaire revels in the sheer theatrical fun of destroying systems of thought and encouraging irreverence in his readers. Such dialogues do not rely on the presence of a spokesperson for Voltaire with a lesson to teach; rather, Voltaire adopts the mask of one of his enemies, whose words and actions make him appear ridiculous. The *Relation du banissement des jésuites de la Chine* (1768), for example, stages a comic exchange between a Jesuit called Rigolet and the Chinese Emperor, the former trying to explain to the latter the biblical account of the birth of Jesus:

THE EMPEROR. — A God who's a carpenter! A God born of a woman! This is all marvellous stuff.

BROTHER RIGOLET. — Oh! Sire, she wasn't a woman, she was just a girl.
[. . .]

THE EMPEROR. — What? She was a virgin, and she had children?

BROTHER RIGOLET. — Absolutely. That's the best bit of the story: it was God who gave this girl a child.

THE EMPEROR. — I don't understand. You told me earlier that she was the mother of God. So God slept with his mother in order then to be born of her?

BROTHER RIGOLET. — You've got it, Your Majesty; divine grace is already at work.

(L'EMPEREUR.	– Un Dieu charpentier! un Dieu né d'une femme! tout ce que vous me dites est admirable.
FRÈRE RIGOLET.	– Oh! sire, elle n'était point femme, elle était fille.
[. . .]	
L'EMPEREUR.	– Quoi! elle était pucelle, et elle avait des enfants!
FRÈRE RIGOLET.	– Vraiment oui. C'est là le bon de l'affaire; ce fut Dieu qui fit un enfant à cette fille.
L'EMPEREUR.	– Je ne vous entends point. Vous me disiez tout à l'heure qu'elle était mère de Dieu. Dieu coucha donc avec sa mère pour naître ensuite d'elle?
FRÈRE RIGOLET.	– Vous y êtes, Sacrée Majesté, la grâce opère déjà.)[31]

Serious religious questions are treated in a comically playful way through dialogue. Neither voice is truly that of Voltaire. Rather, he wears now the mask of the ridiculous religious, now the mask of the naïve questioner. But the exchange gives expression, implicitly, ironically and theatrically, to Voltaire's distinctive brand of unorthodoxy.

Other dialogues are more straightforwardly didactic, such as the *Dialogue de Pégase et du vieillard* (1774), where the old man is quite transparently Voltaire, voicing his well-known criticisms of contemporary literature and philosophy. But others are more genuinely dialectical, such as the *Dialogues entre Lucrèce et Posidonius* (1756), a pair of dialogues of the dead in which the ancient world serves as the setting for a conspicuously contemporary philosophical debate. Voltaire makes Lucretius a spokesman for modern materialist atheism, while Posidonius, a Stoic philosopher, defends deism. Though in the course of the first dialogue Lucretius seems increasingly persuaded by Posidonius's arguments for the existence of God, the second dialogue, by contrast, about the nature of thought and the soul, is characterised more by doubt, and it ends with both interlocutors reaching the same impasse, namely ignorance, as Posidonius concedes: 'I do not claim to know any more about this than you do. Let us enlighten one another' ('Je ne prétends pas en savoir plus que vous. Éclairons-nous l'un l'autre').[32] The different voices in the text, heard together, speak of Voltaire's own uncertainties and inner debates.

Drama, debate and dialogue are fundamental to Voltaire's anti-systematic system of thought. For Voltaire, dialogue is not a dogmatic tool, but a form which allows him to air and explore ideas with a varying mixture of uncertainty and conviction. The wearing of masks through dialogue allows him to present thought processes in action and to prompt the reader to think. Significantly, sending Frederick a copy of his *Dialogue entre Marc-Aurèle et un récollet* in June 1751, Voltaire defines his aesthetics of dialogue with reference to the ancient model of Lucian: 'Lucian is ingenuous, he makes his readers think, and one is always tempted to add to his dialogues' ('Ce Lucian est naïf, il fait penser ses lecteurs, et on est toujours tenté d'ajouter à ses dialogues', D4486). Like Lucian, Voltaire opens up interpretative spaces in his texts, provoking the reader into active thought rather than passive acceptance of his ideas. As he puts it in the 1754 preface to his *Essai sur les mœurs*, 'whoever thinks makes other people think' ('qui pense fait penser').[33] Voltaire deals in the ebb and flow of ideas, not in dogmatic didacticism, and so it is unsurprising that he should write texts of a theatrical nature in which he dons different masks and in which different voices can be heard. Ultimately all the voices help his own voice of playful scepticism to resonate.

Voltaire wears many different masks within his texts; he also disguises himself richly on the title pages to his texts. No fan of publishing his texts anonymously, he very often attributes his works to others, not just out of a fear of official censorship and repression, but for ludic and polemical reasons too. He sometimes attributes his texts to other well-known writers, and his choices are always laden with meaning. Some of these writers are fellow *philosophes*. For instance, he uses the name of his freethinking English friend Lord Bolingbroke when publishing his powerfully unorthodox *Examen important de milord Bolingbroke, ou le Tombeau du fanatisme* in 1767, which, for good measure, he antedates to 1736, fifteen years before Bolingbroke's death. The text offers a thoroughgoing analysis of the implausibilities and inconsistencies in the Bible, and Voltaire exploits the voice of the (Anglican) Bolingbroke as a mask for his own criticisms of the Roman Catholic Church. The allonym distracts attention from Voltaire, and at the same time it attracts the attention of the knowing reader already familiar with the status and reputation of the supposed author: adopting another person's name is a safety device, but it also establishes a game of complicity.

Voltaire also writes in the name of enemies of the *philosophes*, donning their mask the better to unmask and mock them. For example, the Abbé Tamponet, an obscure and reactionary Sorbonne theologian who helped to have the *Encyclopédie* banned, is drafted in as the supposed translator of both *Les Questions de Zapata* (1767), in which the eponymous young Spanish theologian's sixty-seven questions to his teachers constitute a powerful critique of the Bible and the history of the Church, and *Les Lettres d'Amabed* (1769), a *conte historique* praising ancient Indian civilisation and calling into question decadent Christianity. The mask of orthodoxy amplifies Voltaire's seditious satire.

Voltaire also coins pseudonyms.[34] He attributes his poem *Le Russe à Paris* (1760) to one Ivan Alethof, supposedly the secretary to the Russian ambassador in Paris, but whose name is actually a suitably Russian-sounding version of the Greek word for 'truth' (*aletheia*). Echoing the satirical technique deployed so successfully by Montesquieu in his *Lettres persanes* (1721), Voltaire has his truth-telling foreigner comment with disarming bluntness on the sorry state of life in Paris, overrun by the enemies of free thought. Some of Voltaire's other pseudonyms are more prolific. In 1764, for example, Voltaire attributes a series of prose and verse *contes* to Guillaume Vadé, a fictional relative of Jean-Joseph Vadé, the author of scabrous verse and popular comic opera. Another imaginary relative is Jérôme Carré: Voltaire presents his theatrically innovative comedy *L'Écossaise* as Carré's translation of a play by the well-known English dramatist John Home (1722–1808); and Carré re-appears the following year as the supposed author of the anti-Shakespeare *Appel à toutes les nations de l'Europe* (1761), before being killed off, his death announced in 1769 in the *Discours historique et critique* preceding the tragedy *Les Guèbres*.

Conclusion

Voltaire's complex use of masks is part of his arsenal to elude the rigours of censorship: as the Marquis de Condorcet puts it, Voltaire aimed to avoid trouble by 'hiding his name' ('en cachant son nom') and 'masking his attacks' ('masquer ses attaques').[35] But there is more to Voltaire's use of masks. His role-playing is also a creative device in his battle against injustice and intolerance. It is a ludic mechanism, a game of mystification used to engage the reader ever more closely in the pursuit of meaning in his texts. The text becomes a stage on which the author plays a series of roles for the engaged reader, or rather, the spectator. Adopting a mask does not obscure Voltaire's voice, the voice of playful irreverence; rather, it sharpens it and gives it a greater range. If Voltaire wears a mask, it is the mask of the actors of ancient Athens, worn in order to amplify their voices.

To think about the place of the theatre in Voltaire's life and works is to identify the guiding principle of that life and many of those works. The Voltairean text is typically one in which the author is constantly playing a role, or a variety of roles: Voltaire the *philosophe* is also Voltaire the *homme de théâtre*. His writing is characterised by playful polyphony, as he invents voices and characters which from their different vantage points repeatedly reinforce his own characteristic preoccupations. Indeed, theatricality offers a key to understanding Voltaire's distinctive brand of irony, for polyphony allows him to say the opposite of what he means: he adopts a mask and puts forward a view that is not his own, all the better to make fun of that view and, at the same time, to ensure that his own stance of witty scepticism gets the best possible press. As one of Voltaire's (critical) contemporaries remarked:

This author is a real Proteus; you think you have managed to pin him down, but then he slips your grasp. One minute he is a Russian, the next a Quaker; one minute Guillaume Vadé, the next Jérôme Carré. But apart from the name, he is always the same character.

(Cet auteur est un vrai Protée; il vous échappe lorsque vous croyez le tenir. Tantôt c'est un Russe, tantôt un Quaker; ici c'est Guillaume Vadé, là Jérôme Carré mais au nom près, c'est toujours le même personnage.)[36]

NOTES

1. P. Valéry, 'Voltaire', in *Œuvres*, 2 vols., ed. J. Hytier (Paris: Gallimard, 1957–60), vol.1, p.522.
2. C. Villaret, *L'Esprit de Monsieur de Voltaire* (Paris: Prault, 1759), p.iii.
3. *Candide and Other Stories*, trans. R. Pearson (Oxford: Oxford University Press, 1990), p.302; *RC*, p.551.
4. See C. A. Collini, *Mon séjour auprès de Voltaire* (Paris: Léopold Collin, 1807), p.347.
5. *OCV*, vol.10, p.123.
6. See *OCV*, vol.1A, p.90; H. Lagrave, *Le Théâtre et le public à Paris de 1715 à 1750* (Paris: Klincksieck, 1972), pp.585, 597; and H. C. Lancaster, *French Tragedy in the Time of Louis XV and Voltaire, 1715–1774* (Baltimore, MD: Johns Hopkins University Press, 1950), pp.54–6.
7. See, for example, Voltaire's remarks on Corneille's *Théodore* and *Sertorius* in the *Commentaires sur Corneille* (*OCV*, vol.54, p.474, and vol.55, p.845).
8. See *OCV*, vol.8, pp.282–92, and Lancaster, *French Tragedy in the Time of Louis XV and Voltaire*, pp.140–7.
9. See S. Vance, 'History as Dramatic Reinforcement: Voltaire's Use of History in Four Tragedies Set in the Middle Ages', *SVEC*, 150 (1976), 7–31.
10. See R. Goulbourne, *Voltaire Comic Dramatist*, *SVEC*, 2006:03.
11. See *OCV*, vol.16, pp.45–7.
12. See P. Peyronnet, 'Voltaire comédien', *Revue d'histoire du théâtre*, 25 (1973), 262–74, and 'Voltaire "metteur en scène" de ses propres œuvres', *Revue d'histoire du théâtre*, 30 (1978), 38–54, and R. S. Ridgway, 'Voltaire as an actor', *Eighteenth-Century Studies*, 1 (1967–8), 261–76.
13. See Grimm, *Correspondance littéraire, philosophique et critique*, 16 vols., ed. M. Tourneux (Paris: Garnier, 1877–82), vol.6, p.321.
14. Writing to the Italian scholar Giovanni Bianchi in November 1761, Voltaire recalls that the best thing about his education at the Jesuit *collège* in Paris was 'their practice of getting the pupils to put on plays for their parents' ('l'usage de faire représenter des pièces par les pensionnaires, en présence de leurs parents', D10126).
15. Quoted in *OCV*, vol.31A, p.71.

16. See G. de Beer and A.-M. Rousseau, *Voltaire's British Visitors*, SVEC, 49 (1967), pp.168–70.
17. *OH*, p.1136.
18. *OCV*, vol.9, p.321.
19. Moland, vol.10, p.30.
20. *OCV*, vol.30A, p.164.
21. See *OCV*, vol.30A, pp.266–70.
22. Moland, vol.4, p.204.
23. See A.-M. Rousseau, *Voltaire et l'Angleterre*, SVEC, 145–7 (1976), pp.117–18.
24. See J. L. Epstein, 'Voltaire's Ventriloquism: Voices in the First *Lettre philosophique*', SVEC, 182 (1979), 219–35.
25. *Letters*, p.36; *LP*, vol.1, p.92.
26. *Philosophical Dictionary*, trans. T. Besterman (London: Penguin, 1972), p.205; *OCV*, vol.36, p.116.
27. *Philosophical Dictionary*, pp.285–6; *OCV*, vol.36, pp.317–18.
28. *Philosophical Dictionary*, p.161; *OCV*, vol.35, p.655.
29. See J.-M. Moureaux, 'Le dialogue dans le *Dictionnaire philosophique*', in *Voltaire et le 'Dictionnaire philosophique': leçons et questions*, ed. M.-H. Cotoni (Nice: Publications de la Faculté des Lettres, Arts et Sciences Humaines de Nice, 1995), pp.105–20.
30. As with theatre, Voltaire's first contact with philosophical dialogues seems to have been as a schoolboy at his Jesuit *collège*: see S. Pujol, *Le Dialogue d'idées au dix-huitième siècle*, SVEC, 2005:06, pp.21–4. On Voltaire's dialogues, see also the collection of articles in *Revue Voltaire*, 5 (2005).
31. Moland, vol.27, pp.5–6.
32. Moland, vol.24, p.68.
33. *EM*, vol.2, p.888.
34. See O. Ferret, '*Vade mecum, vade retro*: le recours au pseudonyme dans la démarche pamphlétaire voltairienne', *La Lettre clandestine*, 8 (1999), 65–82.
35. Condorcet, *Vie de Voltaire*, ed. E. Badinter (Paris: Quai Voltaire, 1994), p.112, 158. See also C. Lavigne, 'Les stratégies de Voltaire face à la censure', in *Censure, autocensure et art d'écrire de l'Antiquité à nos jours*, ed. J. Domenech (Brussels: Éditions Complexe, 2005), pp.165–82.
36. P.-H. Larcher, *Supplément à la Philosophie de l'histoire* (Amsterdam: Changuin, 1767), p.299, note 1.

7

GIANNI IOTTI

Voltaire as story-teller

Some years ago, a critic rightly denounced as 'almost scandalous' the fact that Voltaire had been studied far more as a thinker than as a writer.[1] Since then many studies on Voltaire's writing have appeared, yet the restrictive notion of literature inherited from the nineteenth century remains preponderant. If the *contes* and the tragedies seem 'naturally' to lend themselves to literary analysis, the same cannot be said for his other works, which continue to be studied from an essentially ideological perspective, with insufficient attention being paid to the formal qualities of the writing. The challenge is not so much to study the figures of writing, according to some outmoded notion of 'style', as to broaden the notion of literature, embracing rhetoric and history so as to come closer to the eighteenth century's understanding of literature.

Comedy of masks

It has been said that Voltaire 'thinks narratively'.[2] Even in the case of his philosophical or historical prose, his arguments are readily resolved into short narratives or dazzling anecdotes whereby the reasoning process takes a narrative (and emotional) turn. With Voltaire, arguments are first and foremost personae or masks, and this essential trait of his writing needs to be studied across all the literary genres which he practised. In fact, in studying Voltaire as a 'story-teller' (*conteur*), we should not limit ourselves to the texts traditionally characterised as *contes*. We need to look beyond to the large quantity of short texts situated on the frontiers of fiction and philosophical propaganda: the pamphlets, short dialogues, fables, allegories, philosophical fragments – the 'scraps' ('rogatons') as Voltaire called them – which multiplied in number from the 1760s, as the battle against *l'Infâme* intensified.

The game of masks which forms part of the structure of the narrative exists also in the very act of narrating. Apart from *Micromégas*, Voltaire published none of his *contes* under his own name: from the first, *Zadig*,

attributed to the Arabic poet Sadi, to the last, *Histoire de Jenni*, attributed to
'M. Sherloc, traduit par M. de la Caille', and including *Candide* ('traduit de
l'allemand de M. le docteur Ralph'), and *L'Ingénu* ('histoire véritable tirée
des manuscrits du P. Quesnel'). This game is not limited to the *contes*: think,
for example, of the collection of heterogeneous texts attributed to Guillaume
Vadé (*Contes de Guillaume Vadé*), to the *Dîner du comte de Boulainvilliers*
attributed to Saint-Hyacinthe, to the *Canonisation de Saint Cucufin, mise en
lumière par le sieur Aveline, bourgeois de Troyes*. Almost always these
pseudonyms are real names, chosen as much for reasons of polemical
strategy as for precaution. But the creation of such magic mirrors by this
'commander of spectacle'[3] is also an attempt to emphasise his own presence
at the heart of that spectacle. Whereas classical tradition required a narrator
to remain discreet, Voltaire dons a mask precisely so as to project better
onstage. At the same time, within the narration, the narrator employs
devices of ironic distancing (used earlier in the century by the French writer
Antoine Hamilton in such tales as *Le Bélier* or *Les Quatre Facardins*) such as
remarks that interrupt the action, throwaway asides, humorous comments
and so forth. While he stops short of the metafictional techniques of a
Laurence Sterne or a Denis Diderot, Voltaire manages in this way to disrupt
the illusion of the spectacle which he is creating, and so obtain the critical
complicity of the reader. For, as we are told in the preface to the *Dictionnaire philosophique*, 'the most useful books are those where the readers
themselves do half the work' ('les livres les plus utiles sont ceux dont les
lecteurs font eux-mêmes la moitié').[4]

Creating his *contes* and pseudo-fictions halfway between fantasy and
satire, Voltaire always insists on the idea that fiction must have a point: 'Isn't
a fiction which announces new and interesting truths a fine thing? . . . Those
fictions that are incoherent and thrown together, which are so common, are
they anything more than dreams?' ('Une fiction qui annonce des vérités
intéressantes et neuves n'est-elle pas une belle chose? . . . Et si elles [les fictions]
sont incohérentes, entassées sans choix, comme il y en a tant, sont-elles autre
chose que des rêves?').[5] Voltaire remains wedded to the notion of fiction as a
vehicle for intellectual truths. Condorcet, following in the footsteps of his
master, similarly stresses the 'simple truths' conveyed by the *conte*:

> The human race would be condemned to eternal error if, in order to free itself,
> it was obliged to study or meditate the proofs of truth. Luckily the natural
> precision of intelligence is all that is required for simple truths, and they are
> also the most necessary. What remains therefore is to find a way of attracting
> the attention of men who are lacking in application, and above all of fixing
> these truths in their memory. This is the great advantage of philosophical
> fictions, and in this Voltaire surpasses both his imitators and his models.

(Le genre humain serait condamné à d'éternelles erreurs si, pour l'en affranchir, il fallait étudier ou méditer les preuves de la vérité. Heureusement la justesse naturelle de l'esprit y peut suppléer pour les vérités simples qui sont aussi les plus nécessaires. Il suffit alors de trouver un moyen de fixer l'attention des hommes inappliqués, et surtout de graver ces vérités dans leur mémoire. Telle est la grande utilité des romans philosophiques, et le mérite de ceux de Voltaire, où il a surpassé également et ses imitateurs et ses modèles.)[6]

In the twentieth century, Paul Valéry continues to insist on this notion of the Voltairean *conte* as the sugaring of an ideological pill:

We have long known that literature is not only about the pure pleasure of reading ... under the cover of these pretexts and seductive forms, through pleasure and amusement, a critique of manners and laws, of the powerful and the powers-that-be insinuates itself, instilling poisons all the more pernicious for being so delicious.

(Depuis longtemps déjà on savait que la littérature peut s'employer à d'autres fins que le pur plaisir de la lecture ... sous le couvert de ces prétextes et de ces espèces séduisantes, et par le détour des agréments, et de l'amusement, la critique des mœurs, des lois, des puissants et des puissances s'y glisse, et insinue des venins d'autant plus pernicieux qu'ils sont plus délicieux à absorber.)[7]

Voltaire's debt to the ancient tradition of philosophical irony is evident. But it is still possible to question the received wisdom, inherited from Horace, about the need to combine 'instruction' and 'delight'.[8] Rather than identifying the twin factors of comic delight and moral lesson, we might instead examine more closely the relationship in these texts between 'buffoonery' and the 'seriousness of a profession of faith'.[9] It is of course with his overall ideological aim in mind that Voltaire, in his *contes* and *facéties*, has recourse to what are typically fictional and dramatic devices, embedding concepts in anecdotal material, creating characters and painting true theatrical scenes. Even so, when you look closely at the structure of these small essays in philosophical fiction, you see to what extent it is hard to separate the fiction from the strict economy of the argument. According to one critic, in the Voltairean *conte*,

fiction is no longer a pretext, it is the thought itself, bringing together both sides of the argument to which Voltaire is equally attached, representing life as he feels it, irreducibly diverse, sad, absurd, exalting, incoherent ... With Voltaire, the organisational principle of the *conte* is only apparently intellectual ... in reality, it is situated at a level where intelligence is no longer articulated in ideas but as an attitude, the response of a living organism to the questions posed by the existence of the world and of fellow man.

(la fiction n'est plus un prétexte, elle est la pensée même, rassemblant le pour et le contre auquel [Voltaire] est également attaché, représentant la vie telle qu'il la ressent, d'une diversité irréductible, triste, ridicule, exaltante, décousue ... Chez Voltaire le principe d'organisation du conte n'est intellectuel qu'en apparence ... en fait, il se situe à un niveau où l'intelligence ne s'articule plus en idées, mais est attitude de l'être, réponse d'un organisme vivant aux questions que pose l'existence du monde et des autres hommes.)[10]

In the case of Voltaire, the fictional mask remains firmly attached to the concept, so much so that it would be impossible to reduce the fiction to a mere argument without sacrificing an essential part of the meaning, just as in the interpretation of a metaphor, the meaning cannot be reduced to a mere 'translation' of the two elements being held in comparison.[11]

The quest for truth

From the beginning, Voltaire was strongly attracted to the form of the *conte*. Until around the 1760s, his tales dealt with philosophical problems such as the limits of human knowledge (*Micromégas*), fate (*Zadig*), the problem of evil (*Candide*). After that, with an occasional emphasis on the exotic and the supernatural, it is social and historical problems that come to the fore: the link between nature and civilisation, and the question of toleration in the reign of Louis XIV (*L'Ingénu*), the European political and cultural framework (*La Princesse de Babylone*), economic and scientific debate in the France of Louis XV (*L'Homme aux quarante écus*), questions of biblical criticism and ancient history (*Le Taureau blanc*), the problem of atheism (*Histoire de Jenni*). But at the heart of the Voltairean *conte* lies always the intractable confrontation between characters and the truths of the world, the problem of exercising virtue which, in the humanist tradition, ought to coincide with the acquisition of knowledge. We are talking here of knowledge reduced to its bare essentials. The world in which these heroes move is a world corrupted by fanaticism, ignorance and egotism, a world in which, in the little fable entitled *Éloge historique de la raison*, 'la Raison' ('Reason') and her daughter 'la Vérité' ('Truth') strive in vain to make mankind better and are obliged to go into hiding:

Reason and Truth appeared, they spoke; but they found so many evil people contradicting them, so many fools in the pay of the evil ones, so many selfish individuals occupied only with themselves and the present moment, with no interest in them or in their enemies, that they quietly went back to their hiding place.

(Elles [la Raison et la Vérité] parurent, elles parlèrent; mais elles trouvèrent tant de méchants intéressés à les contredire, tant d'imbéciles aux gages de ces méchants, tant d'indifférents uniquement occupés d'eux-mêmes et du moment présent, qui ne s'embarrassaient pas d'elles ni de leurs ennemis, qu'elles regagnèrent sagement leur asile.)[12]

When the narration assumes the form of a journey, as is often the case, the Voltairean protagonist, if he is not already a *philosophe* before his departure (like Micromégas or Zadig), achieves a state of doubt or wisdom at the end of his adventures, after suffering in both mind and body – a rationalist variation of the baroque and picaresque motif of *desengaño* ('disillusion'). So, after having foolishly adopted 'the ridiculous project of being perfectly wise' ('le projet insensé d' être parfaitement sage'),[13] and after undergoing a series of terrible setbacks including the loss of an eye, Memnon, hero of the *conte* of that name, ends up suspecting 'that our little earthly globe might just be the madhouse of the universe' ('que notre petit globe terraqué ne soit précisément les petites-maisons de l'univers').[14] To the genius who urges him to consider from on high 'the arrangement of the whole universe' ('l'arrangement de l'univers entier'), he replies in an afflicted tone: 'Ah! I shall only believe that . . . when I'm no longer blind in one eye' ('Ah! je ne croirai cela . . . que quand je ne serai plus borgne').[15] We find a similar form of disenchantment in the conclusion to the *Histoire des voyages de Scarmentado*, when the protagonist, having lived through prejudice, foolishness and violence, finds himself confined to a life as uneventful as it is demeaning:

> I went to plough the field of an old black woman, to keep my ears and my nose. I was bought after a year. I had seen all that is beautiful, good and admirable on earth: I resolved to stay at home. I married on the spot; I was cuckolded, and I saw that it was the sweetest state of life.
>
> (J'allai labourer le champ d'une vieille négresse pour conserver mes oreilles et mon nez. On me racheta au bout d'un an. J'avais vu tout ce qu'il y a de beau, de bon et d'admirable sur la terre: je résolus de ne plus voir que mes pénates. Je me mariai chez moi; je fus cocu, et je vis que c' était l'état le plus doux de la vie.)[16]

It is easy to see in this ending an anticipation of the disillusioned ethic of *Candide*: 'That is well said, replied Candide, but we must cultivate our garden' ('Cela est bien dit, répondit Candide, mais il faut cultiver notre jardin').[17] It is true that other Voltairean tales finish on a more optimistic note, for example *L'Ingénu*, the *Histoire de Jenni* or *L'Homme aux quarante écus*, in which a man with nothing at the start is metamorphosed into the rich and cultivated Monsieur André:

> How the good sense of M. André has been strengthened since he acquired a library! He lives with books as with men; he makes choices; and he is never taken in by names. What a pleasure to instruct oneself and perfect one's soul for one *écu*, and without leaving home! He congratulates himself on being born at a time when human reason is beginning to be perfected . . . Misery had weakened the springs in M. André's soul, well-being has made them elastic once again. There are a thousand Andrés in this world, men who, with one spin

of the wheel of fortune, could have become persons of real merit. Today he is familiar with the affairs of all Europe, and more than that, with the progress of the human spirit.

(Comme le bon sens de M. André s'est fortifié depuis qu'il a une bibliothèque! Il vit avec les livres comme avec les hommes; il choisit; et il n'est jamais la dupe des noms. Quel plaisir de s'instruire et d'agrandir son âme pour un écu, sans sortir de chez soi! Il se félicite d'être né dans un temps où la raison humaine commence à se perfectionner . . . La misère avait affaibli les ressorts de l' âme de M. André, le bien-être leur a rendu leur élasticité. Il y a mille Andrés dans le monde auxquels il n'a manqué qu'un tour de roue de la fortune pour en faire des hommes d'un vrai mérite. Il est aujourd'hui au fait de toutes les affaires de l'Europe, et surtout des progrès de l'esprit humain.)[18]

But even in narratives where the protagonist improves his lot and makes positive progress in his understanding, Voltaire still places in the foreground the chaos of the world, the muddle of the irrational, the weakness of man – except, that is, when he exacts unexpected revenge through laughter.

This approach fosters a plethora of caricatures and grotesque figures in which the writer's comic force is given full rein and his taste for creating fictions indulged to the full. Rather than the pure knowledge of things such as Adam could have known (to quote Malebranche), the eighteenth century prefers the model of knowledge by approximation.[19] In the context of Lockean empiricism, the eighteenth-century philosophical tale uses narrative as a progressive quest for the truth. The ideal universe attained by the avoidance of vice (the universe which Fénelon paints in his novel *Télémaque*) is replaced, in authors such as Jonathan Swift, Voltaire or Samuel Johnson, with a universe of hesitant progress and of knowledge gained with diffi-culty.[20] There is of course a close link between the fictional forms which emerge in the eighteenth century and the empirical notion of the subject which evolves on the basis of experience: the narrative form is 'in movement' (like Locke's ideas), and so reflects the process of evolution in heart and mind that the hero experiences in the course of his adventures. There is a clear link between the ideology of the Enlightenment and its fictional embodiment:

In mocking systems – the optimism of Leibniz, the fatalism attributed to Spinoza – they are fighting for more harmony between men. The reader will be shown the characters' formative experience. Argument is replaced by example. The philosophical tale is a miniature *Bildungsroman*.

(À railler les systèmes – l'optimisme de Leibniz, le fatalisme imputé à Spinoza – on luttera pour une meilleure harmonie entre les hommes. On exposera au lecteur l'*expérience formatrice* des personnages. L'argument sera remplacé par l'exemple. Le conte philosophique est un petit *Bildungsroman*.)[21]

The notion of transformation in the sense of the German (or English) *Bildungsroman* implies however an identity which was not previously present and which emerges only after a veritable ethical and social initiation. In Voltairean fiction, it is a question of making visible and conscious what was present in a virtual state before the beginning of the narrative, that is to say reason unaware of itself. Voltairean heroes make discoveries rather than conquests, they experiment more than they fight. This is why, for Voltaire, time tends to be identified with a space, narrative with a demonstration, adventure with a repertoire of ideological questions.[22] To be precise, Voltairean narratives exist in constant tension between philosophical and narrative models: Hercule in *L'Ingénu* or M. André in *L'Homme aux quarante écus* evolve in the course of the narrative more than do Micromégas, Zadig or Candide, but this evolution is inescapably part of a recurring pattern. This brings us to a fundamental problem concerning the *conte philosophique* as a genre. In one narrative universe, everything is determined by the protagonist's growth in self-knowledge. In Voltairean narrative, however, the dialectical progression between experience and (self-)knowledge is reduced to a mechanical repetition of the recognition of the world's disorder. In this way the hero learns to apply common sense or at least to question his initial naivety.

Reason and unreason

This synthesis between experience and knowledge proves to be highly problematic. A principal source of the comic in Voltaire lies in deflating characters' extraordinary experiences into ordinary ones, reducing – always with irony – the exceptional to the banal, the unacceptable to the normal. Voltaire delights in the repetition of inappropriate connections between disparate terms, affecting, as narrator, an absolute indifference to the resulting absurdities:

> Nothing presents a happier picture, he used to say, than a philosopher reading that great book which God put before our eyes. The truths he discovers are for him alone: he nourishes and elevates his soul, he lives in peace; he fears nothing from his fellow man, and his dear wife doesn't come and cut off his nose.
>
> (Rien n'est plus heureux, disait-il, qu'un philosophe qui lit dans ce grand livre que Dieu a mis sous nos yeux. Les vérités qu'il découvre sont à lui: il nourrit et il élève son âme, il vit tranquille; il ne craint rien des hommes, et sa tendre épouse ne vient point lui couper le nez. *Zadig*)[23]

> They sang devoutly very beautiful prayers, after which they burned all the guilty men on a slow flame; and the entire royal family seemed extremely edified.

(On chanta dévotement de très belles prières, après quoi on brûla à petit feu tous les coupables; de quoi toute la famille royale parut extrêmement édifiée. *Histoire des voyages de Scarmentado*)[24]

My dear young woman, replied Candide, when one is in love, jealous, and whipped by the Inquisition, one forgets oneself . . .
(Ma belle demoiselle, répondit Candide, quand on est amoureux, jaloux, et fouetté par l'Inquisition, on ne se connaît plus . . . *Candide*)[25]

He was gentle, charitable, modest; and was roasted in Valladolid, in the year of grace 1631. Pray for the soul of brother Zapata.
(Il fut doux, bienfaisant, modeste; et fut rôti à Valladolid, l'an de grâce 1631. Priez pour l'âme de frère Zapata. *Les Questions de Zapata*)[26]

You can see that a girl who is afraid of seeing her lover swallowed by a large fish and having her throat slit by her own father, needs to be amused; but try to amuse me in a way I like.
(Vous sentez qu'une fille qui craint de voir avaler son amant par un gros poisson, et d'avoir elle-même le cou coupé par son propre père, a besoin d'être amusée; mais tâchez de m'amuser selon mon goût. *Le Taureau blanc*)[27]

One might multiply such passages in which man's evil-doing and bizarre but familiar horrors are presented as part of an allegedly natural order: lopsided moral truths designed to make us smile. But deep down these episodes have a serious purpose: they express in their incongruity the dislocation of a world from which Providence is absent, in which human beings are credulous, betrayed by their fellow men, burned to death by fanatics, and threatened by those in power. 'I have seen so many extraordinary things', says the sceptic Martin in *Candide*, 'that there is nothing extraordinary left' ('J'ai tant vu de choses extraordinaires qu'il n'y a plus rien d'extraordinaire').[28] In a universe in which the distinction between the extraordinary and the ordinary is erased, in which anything can happen in the most 'normal' way, knowledge in the classical sense no longer seems possible. The prestigious classical form of the *maxime* which encapsulated a general moral truth disintegrates in Voltaire's hands to become a grotesque caricature profoundly at odds with reality. And it goes without saying that Voltaire has no time at all for that elaborated form of the absurd which provokes horror in the reader: the narrator's self-conscious casual attitude is a clue here to the stance of the author himself.

Since Voltaire regards reason as natural, his characters are, from the start, good reasoners, even if they are naïve and even if their development is, as we have said, less an apprenticeship in the world than a tragi-comic confrontation with the world's disorder. It remains a fact that the protagonists of Voltaire's short fictions change their views as the narrative progresses, and, above all, that the scene is littered with the symbols of despised and discarded tradition.

Voltaire, the self-styled 'great demolisher' ('grand démolisseur', D16372), holds that the construction of the future is predicated on the destruction of the past; or, to put it another way, the affirmation of truth becomes the incessant refutation of error. 'Truth is found in opposition: to speak the truth is first, and always, for Voltaire, to criticise error, to leaf through the comic chapters of the novel of the human mind' ('*La vérité se pose en s'opposant*: dire la vérité, c'est d'abord – et toujours – pour Voltaire, critiquer l'erreur, feuilleter les chapitres bouffons du roman de l'esprit').[29] Like Bayle, but using grotesque narration instead of philosophical comment, Voltaire constantly examines the false in order to find the true. If only to ridicule tradition, he has to represent it, lend it life and speech. The caricaturing of the adversary and the sarcastic depiction of error are two essential features of Voltairean fiction. Without this aggressive insistence, there would be no literary fabulation: Voltaire is a narrator to the extent that he constantly brings the past back to life – in order to destroy it. Literature has in any case always had a tendency to recreate the things that reason and convention have left behind, either to poke fun, or to lament their passing, or (given the ambivalence of any ironic denial) to poke fun and lament both at once.

So in a pamphlet such as *Conformez-vous aux temps*, in which he celebrates the irresistible onward march of modern times, Voltaire begins with a short anecdote about a representative of times past. The man in question is M. de Montampui, rector of the Sorbonne, who, because he is afraid to be seen going to the theatre, dresses up as a woman, and ends up in prison.[30] To our delight, truth is triumphantly asserted by means of the systematic exposition of anti-truth. More than that, the present tale even arouses some sympathy for the pathetic old man who lacked the good sense just to indulge his passion for the theatre. It is here that Voltaire reveals himself a great comedian, in the tradition of Molière and of Pascal's *Lettres provinciales* (written to satirise the Jesuits). He is more indebted to Pascal as polemicist than we might guess just from reading the twenty-fifth of the *Lettres philosophiques*. We may, for example, be shocked by the moral laxity of Sanchez as quoted in the ninth *Provinciale*: 'One may swear . . . that one has not done something, even if one has actually done it, by knowing in one's own mind that one didn't do it on a certain day, or before one was born, or in some other similar circumstance' ('On peut jurer . . . qu'on n'a pas fait une chose, quoiqu'on l'ait faite effectivement, en entendant en soi-même qu'on ne l'a pas faite un certain jour, ou avant qu'on fût né, ou en sous-entendant quelque autre circonstance pareille').[31] Yet it is hard not to be impressed by the imperturbable narcissism shown by Pascal's Jesuits. This is of course the paradox of any parodic discourse: it ends up conferring on the object of parody an ambiguous power and a hidden strength.

Voltaire does not limit himself to fictionalising ideas, he goes out of his way to emphasise the contrary of what he thinks and wants us to think. By finding reason where none exists, by giving voice to fanatics, imbeciles, obtuse or even intelligent clerics, he ends up according the adversary a certain importance in the reader's mind, and in this he reveals himself as a great writer. As readers of these short works, we do not simply imbibe an ideological message. On the contrary, our attention is held by the details, the tics, the absurdities of these ridiculous characters. Even their stupidity can, briefly, fascinate us. In other words, jokes accompany irony, and the militant use of defamiliarisation is in part mitigated by sheer linguistic bravura. In keeping with Freud's theory of the joke, we are led despite ourselves to understand the motivations of these grotesque characters, to admire the cunning and energy with which they pursue their aims, and even, momentarily, to feel sorry for them. We must recognise that Voltairean writing explodes the limits of pure demonstration.[32] How could one define Pangloss simply as a caricature of Leibnizian Optimism? How could one reduce the adventures of the Ingénu in Brittany merely to a series of clashes between common sense and Christian prejudice? And in the dialogue between Freind and Birton in the *Histoire de Jenni*, how could one focus only on the defence of deism and ignore the act of seduction?

It is not meaningful to speak of these narratives as being either more 'philosophical' or more 'fictional'. (A close link between narration and 'ideas' is found in all eighteenth-century French fiction, in such novels as Marivaux's *La Vie de Marianne*, Crébillon's *Les Égarements du cœur et de l'esprit*, or Sade's *Justine*, as much as in 'philosophical novels' such as Montesquieu's *Lettres persanes*, Rousseau's *La Nouvelle Héloïse* or Diderot's *Jacques le fataliste*.) Despite the evident ideological content of Voltaire's tales, we as readers are drawn into identifying with characters and situations, even though the author runs counter to the trend of contemporary French fiction in rejecting the 'realistic' depiction of social behaviour and psychology (as we find in the novels of Prévost, Marivaux or Rousseau). His highly stylised fictional universe – created through parody, the grotesque, the absurd, the marvellous, the sentimental – aims at constructing a paradoxical image of civilisation and human life which constantly challenges us to make sense of the fiction. Of course it is difficult to 'believe' in Voltaire's fictional world in the way one believes in Stendhal's or Flaubert's fictional worlds. To an extent, his rambling philosophers, his stupid and evil clerics, his fabled heroes 'are nothing but signs. As in algebra, the signs can be positive or negative.'[33] Yet it would be wrong to labour this point and reduce Voltairean characters purely to their demonstrative and satirical functions, to the status of 'puppets', and so ignore their fictional substance.[34] Fiction cannot be confined within the limits of mimesis.

The dramatisation of ideas

From this perspective, the problem is less about claiming a fictional quality (which one?) for Voltaire's prose than about recognising its fundamental preference for the narration and concrete realisation of ethical and intellectual ideas. This process of fictionalisation depends on the ludic representation of ideas far more than on the imitation of actions and emotions for parodic and polemical ends. In the *Relation du jésuite Berthier*, the evil influence of the (Jesuit) *Journal de Trévoux* is transmuted into toxic fumes, cured with the application of 'a page of the *Encyclopédie* in white wine, to purge the humours of the heavy bile' ('une page de l'*Encyclopédie* dans du vin blanc, pour remettre en mouvement les humeurs de la bile épaissie').[35] Or, in the short pamphlet *De l'horrible danger de la lecture* (*On the Hideous Danger of Reading*), there is the threat that the mufti Joussouf-Chéribi makes against 'any idea which might present itself in writing or speech at the city gates' and his order that 'the said idea, bound hands and feet' should be brought to him, 'so that we may inflict on it such punishment as may please us' ('toute idée qui se présenterait par écrit ou de bouche aux portes de la ville . . . ladite idée pieds et poings liés . . . pour lui être infligé par nous tel châtiment qu'il nous plaira').[36] This passage is deliciously ambivalent: the image in which the fanatic's obscurantist lunacy is expressed conveys a rational denunciation of fanaticism, and at the same time accords readers the secret pleasure of a momentary regression to childlike (irrational) logic which elsewhere they, like the author, would be inclined to mock.

Some literary genres were identified in this period with the ignorance of primitive ages, and the ironical borrowing by the *philosophes* of such models as the oriental or fantastic tale and of other parodic forms of narration, contributed, paradoxically, to the survival of those literary forms. More than the other *philosophes* (Fontenelle in particular), Voltaire is inclined to see in the fables of the Ancients a naïve form of truth,[37] and he himself relishes 'allegorical' discourse. 'Voltaire's *contes philosophiques*', writes Roger Pearson, 'are modern allegories which, by seeking never to pull the wool of fiction over our eyes, promote the cause of reason and clear-sightedness.'[38] Allegory remains in any case suspect in the eighteenth century. The *philosophes* regard it as a dangerous distortion of clear meaning, a mode of discourse redolent of religious thinking.[39] As a historian, Voltaire also mistrusts allegorisation, too tied to biblical interpretation.[40] But as a

story-teller, he advocates the strategic use of allegory. As the Huron in
L'Ingénu remarks: 'Ah! if we need fables, at least let these fables be the
emblem of truth! I love the fables of the *philosophes*, I laugh at those of
children, and I hate those of impostors' ('Ah! s'il nous faut des fables, que ces
fables soient du moins l'emblème de la vérité! J'aime les fables des philosophes, je ris de celles des enfants, et je hais celles des imposteurs').[41] The
Princess Amaside in *Le Taureau blanc* is of the same view:

> I require a story to be essentially plausible, and not always sounding like the
> account of a dream. I prefer it to be neither trivial nor far-fetched. I particularly
> like the ones which, from beneath the veil of the plot, reveal to the experienced
> eye some subtle truths that will escape the common herd. I am tired of suns and
> moons that old women do as they please with, and mountains that dance, and
> rivers that flow back to their source, and dead people coming back to life. But,
> worst of all, when this sort of nonsense is written in an inflated and incom-
> prehensible style, I find it dreadfully tiresome.[42]
>
> (Je veux qu'un conte soit fondé sur la vraisemblance, et qu'il ne ressemble
> pas toujours à un rêve. Je désire qu'il n'ait rien de trivial ni d'extravagant. Je
> voudrais surtout que, sous le voile de la fable, il laissât entrevoir aux yeux
> exercés quelque vérité fine qui échappe au vulgaire. Je suis lasse du soleil et de
> la lune dont une vieille dispose à son gré, et des montagnes qui dansent et des
> fleuves qui remontent à leur source, et des morts qui ressuscitent; mais surtout,
> quand ces fadaises sont écrites d'un style ampoulé et inintelligible, cela me
> dégoûte horriblement.)[43]

Voltaire uses 'the veil of fable' only on condition that it conceals 'some subtle
truths'. His incursion into the irrational world of allegory is no exercise in
satire but a ludic display.

Finally, this ludic display of narrative material works both by accumu-
lation and concentration. Voltaire's prose is built on the mismatched
multiplication of subjects and styles: pagan and biblical mythology, oriental
exoticism and fictional adventure, bourgeois realism and historical recon-
struction, scientific knowledge and literary polemics, modern and ancient,
satire and celebration, ordinary and extraordinary – in Voltaire's writing,
everything is topsy-turvy. This amazingly rich polemical confusion needs to
be seen in the context of the providentially ordered world of the theologians
and historians.[44] Voltairean narrative also functions through concision, the
vertiginous elimination of causal conjunctions and other words suggesting
the subjective inflexion of the speaker'.[45] Voltaire endlessly parodies earlier
philosophical models, he deforms myths and ancient tales, he tells new
stories using ironically the expression of the past – this re-use of earlier
languages is perhaps his most typical stylistic trait. Voltaire, an admirer of
traditional literary forms, appropriates them inappropriately, undermining

them with excessive concision. This 'searchlight device', as Erich Auerbach called it, is a constant of Voltairean prose: it 'consists in overilluminating one small part of an extensive complex, while everything else which might explain, derive, and possibly counterbalance the thing emphasized is left in the dark; so that apparently the truth is stated, for what is said cannot be denied; and yet everything is falsified'.[46]

Conclusion

Voltaire, in other words, is a great parasite. His language feeds off the language of his enemy as much as it devours it. We find in Voltairean narrative an interweaving of reason and unreason, irony and enchantment, which has long haunted European literature. At the end of the nineteenth century, Anatole France, a true descendant of Voltaire, wrote: 'In vain we try to be reasonable and love only the truth, there are moments when ordinary reality no longer satisfies us and we long to escape nature. We know perfectly well that it is impossible, but we do not desire it any the less' ('On a beau être raisonnable et n'aimer que le vrai, il y a des heures où la réalité commune ne nous contente plus et où l'on voudrait sortir de la nature. Nous savons bien que c'est impossible, mais nous ne le souhaitons pas moins').[47] In the eighteenth century, of course, things present themselves differently. Yet Fontenelle, even as he denies it, refers to the same propensity when he suggests that 'the human mind and the false are in close sympathy' ('l'esprit humain et le faux sympathisent extrêmement').[48] In Voltaire's ironically constructed plots, the irrational is conjured up only to be denied. Enlightenment rationalism does not simply reject the past; its relish for the re-telling of tales means that it enters into a compact with the past. To quote Jean Goldzink:

It is precisely the assumption and elaboration of this contradiction between the story told by our great-great-great-grandmothers and the tale according to Locke, the ironical and grating co-existence of fable and reason, superstition and enlightenment, which is at the heart of the Voltairean tale. Let us be clear: *Voltaire's novels seem to reflect in their most intimate structure the fundamental contradiction of the eighteenth century, generated out of the opposition of past and future.* Fable is in no way the *cloak* of truth, but one half of that CONTRADICTION which energises Voltairean fiction.

(*Le cœur du conte voltairien, c'est précisément la prise en charge et la mise en forme de cette contradiction* entre le conte raconté aux quadrisaïeules de nos grand'mères et le conte d'après Locke, c'est la coexistence ironique et grinçante de la fable et de la raison, des superstitions et des lumières. Soyons clair: *les romans voltairiens semblent refléter, dans leur structure la plus intime la contradiction centrale du XVIIIème siècle, travaillée par l'affrontement du passé et de l'avenir.* La fable n'y est nullement le *voile* de la vérité, mais l'un des deux termes de la CONTRADICTION qui fait vivre le roman voltairien.)[49]

translated by Nicholas Cronk

NOTES

1. J.-M. Moureaux, 'Voltaire: l'écrivain', *Revue d'histoire littéraire de la France*, 79 (1979), 331–50 (p.350).
2. R. Pearson, *The Fables of Reason: A Study of Voltaire's 'contes philosophiques'* (Oxford: Clarendon Press, 1993), p.5.
3. R. Pomeau, 'Voltaire conteur: masques et visages', *L'Information littéraire*, 13 (1961), 3.
4. OCV, vol.35, p.284.
5. Article 'Fiction', *Questions sur l'Encyclopédie* (Moland, vol.19, p.121).
6. Condorcet, *Vie de Voltaire* (Paris: Quai Voltaire, 1994), p.93.
7. P. Valéry, *Variété*, in *Œuvres*, Bibliothèque de la Pléiade (Paris: Gallimard), vol.1 (1957), p.527.
8. Horace, *Ars poetica*, verses 333–46.
9. Terms taken from the introduction of Voltaire, *Facéties*, ed. J. Macary (Paris: L'Harmattan, 1998), pp.34–5.
10. H. Coulet, *Le Roman jusqu'à la Révolution* (Paris: Colin, 1967), vol.1, p.396.
11. See M. Black, 'Metaphor', *Proceedings of the Aristotelian Society*, 55 (1954), 25–47, and 'More about Metaphor', in *Metaphor and Thought*, ed. A. Ortony (Cambridge: Cambridge University Press, 1979), pp.19–43.
12. RC, p.569.
13. RC, p.125.
14. RC, p.129.
15. RC, p.130.
16. RC, p.142.
17. RC, p.233.
18. RC, p.469.
19. See P. Gay, *The Enlightenment: An Interpretation. The Rise of Modern Paganism* (New York: Norton, 1995), p.141.
20. See F. M. Keener, *The Chain of Becoming: The Philosophical Tale, the Novel, and a Neglected Realism of the Enlightenment: Swift, Montesquieu, Voltaire, Johnson, and Austen* (New York: Columbia University Press, 1983), pp.28–31.
21. Y. Belaval, 'Le conte philosophique', in *The Age of Enlightenment: Studies Presented to Theodore Besterman* (Edinburgh: Oliver and Boyd, 1967), p.310.
22. See J. Dagen, *L'Histoire de l'esprit humain dans la pensée française de Fontenelle à Condorcet* (Paris: Klincksieck, 1977), p.309.
23. RC, p.62.
24. RC, p.137.
25. RC, p.164.
26. *Mél.*, p.948.
27. RC, p.554.

28. *RC*, p.200.
29. J. Goldzink, *Roman et idéologie dans 'Candide'* (Paris: Centre d'études et de recherches marxistes, 1971), p.20. Emphasis in the original.
30. *Mél.*, p.709.
31. Pascal, *Œuvres complètes*, Bibliothèque de la Pléiade (Paris: Gallimard, 1954), p.760.
32. See S. R. Suleiman, *Authoritarian Fictions: The Ideological Novel as a Literary Genre* (New York: Columbia University Press, 1983), p.206.
33. J. Scherer, '"L'univers en raccourci": quelques ambitions du roman voltairien', *SVEC*, 179 (1979), 117–42 (p.124–5).
34. See D. A. Bonneville, *Voltaire and the Form of the Novel*, *SVEC*, 158 (1976), pp.13–18.
35. *Mél.*, p.339.
36. *Mél.*, p.714.
37. See the article 'Fables', *Dictionnaire philosophique* (*OCV*, vol.36, pp.99–104).
38. Pearson, *The Fables of Reason*, p.14.
39. See, for example, Dumarsais, *Des Tropes ou des différents sens et autres écrits* (Paris: Flammarion, 1988), p.150.
40. See *EM*, vol.1, pp.173–4.
41. *RC*, p.318.
42. *Candide and Other Stories*, trans. R. Pearson, Oxford World's Classics (Oxford: Oxford University Press, 1990) p.304.
43. *RC*, pp.553–4.
44. See G. Lanson, *L'Art de la prose* (Paris: Éditions de la Table ronde, 1996), p.207.
45. See B. E. Schwarzbach, *Voltaire's Old Testament Criticism* (Geneva: Droz, 1971), p.176.
46. E. Auerbach, *Mimesis: The Representation of Reality in Western Literature*, trans. W. R. Trask (Princeton, NJ: Princeton University Press, 1953), p.404.
47. A. France, *La Vie littéraire*, 1ère série (Paris: Calmann Lévy, 1889), p.117.
48. Fontenelle, *Nouveaux Dialogues des morts*, in *Œuvres* (Paris: Brunet, 1752), vol.1, p.26.
49. Goldzink, *Roman et idéologie dans 'Candide'*, p.39–40. Emphasis in the original.

8

PHILIP STEWART

Candide

Candide, ou l'Optimisme was an instant best-seller: within the year of its publication early in 1759 there were dozens of pirated editions, and its popularity has never lagged in the two and a half intervening centuries. As *Candide* is for many readers their first introduction to the Enlightenment, one is entitled to ask, among other things, what kind of image of the Enlightenment it projects, and how representative it can be thought to be. As is characteristic of Voltaire's method during his Geneva and Ferney years, he published *Candide* anonymously, pretending to know nothing about it. His friends and even, no doubt, many public officials knew this was a feint. The addendum 'Translated from the German of Dr Ralph' is a typical cover, reinforcing the fictional pretence that the work was of foreign origin.

Ideas

Along with the announced theme of 'Optimism',[1] Voltaire picks up on several other key terms commonly linked with the philosophy of Gottfried Wilhelm Leibniz (1646–1716), notably *raison suffisante* and *harmonie préétablie*. These both appear, for example, in D'Alembert's *Discours préliminaire* to the *Encyclopédie* in 1751, and relate to Leibniz's resolution of the problem of theodicy, the existence of evil in a divinely created universe (his *Essais de théodicée* had appeared in 1710). It was not in God's power, he reasoned, to create a *perfect* world, but among *possible* worlds, he created the best – a notion which Voltaire mocks with the expression 'the best of all possible worlds' ('le meilleur des mondes possibles') – or, for that matter, of all possible chateaux, or of all possible barons' daughters. In *Zadig*, ten years earlier, Voltaire had himself sketched such a tentative Leibnizian conclusion.

By mid-century, however, Leibniz's argument had largely been conflated in the public mind with Alexander Pope's own version of Optimism as expressed notably in his *Essay on Man* (1733):

> All nature is but art, unknown to thee;
> All chance, direction, which thou canst not see;

All discord, harmony not understood;
All partial evil, universal good.
And, spite of pride, in erring reason's spite,
One truth is clear, *Whatever is, is right.*

(Epistle I)

Pope's point is broadly providential: in the larger scheme of things, which man cannot fathom, all is necessarily good insofar as it must exist for some purpose: 'God sends not ill, if rightly understood.' That it is foolhardy and presumptuous to doubt the wisdom of God is fundamentally a lesson that goes back to Job. Voltaire deliberately satirises this vision in the oversimplification of Pangloss's deduction: 'the more individual misfortunes there are, the more all is well' ('plus il y a de malheurs particuliers, et plus tout est bien', chap.4). While Candide's own experiences cannot directly refute the proposition that partial ills are necessary components of a universal good, over time they come to make that explanation sound unfeeling and arrogant.

The treatment of Optimism in *Candide* is clearly foreshadowed in Voltaire's *Poème sur le désastre de Lisbonne*, subtitled 'or examination of the axiom that all is well' ('ou examen de cet axiome: tout est bien'). The terrible earthquake and tidal wave that struck Lisbon on 1 November 1755 leads Voltaire to deny angrily that any of the conventional moral explanations could justify or explain human suffering on such a scale: to impute any fault to the victims, to suggest that there is any correlation between guilt and 'acts of God', is an offence to human reason and suffering. The fictional role of the Portuguese Inquisition in *Candide* (chap.6) is of course related to the assumption that the Lisbon earthquake was a divine punishment for human sins. The poem, like *Candide*, is less a formal philosophical refutation of providential reasoning than an insistence on the moral bankruptcy of a sort of Optimism that comforts no one and changes nothing for the better. As the preface to the poem states, the author admires Pope but insists that, since suffering is an all-too-present reality, 'the expression *All is well*, taken in an absolute sense and without a future hope, is but an insult to our life's suffering' ('le mot *Tout est bien*, pris dans un sens absolu et sans l'espérance d'un avenir, n'est qu'une insulte aux douleurs de notre vie').

Jean-Jacques Rousseau, who reacted forcefully to the poem in a long letter to Voltaire which was later published, concedes that the existence of a benevolent providence cannot be proved, but for his part he falls back on inner persuasion: 'I feel it, I believe it, I desire it, I hope for it, and I will defend it to my last breath' ('Je la sens, je la crois, je la veux, je l'espère, et je la défendrai jusqu'à mon dernier soupir', D6973). Since Voltaire, in acknowledging this letter, abstained from responding to its arguments,

Rousseau later claimed that the true reply was none other than *Candide* itself.[2] Most scholars, however, have doubted that Voltaire had Rousseau so specifically in mind.

That these questions were actively debated at the time is indicated by the fact that the Berlin Academy proposed 'Optimism' as subject for its essay contest in 1755 – some months before Lisbon – with specific reference to Pope's proposition, which it translated as 'Tout est bien' ('all is well').[3] In this context, one more easily understands the repetition of this mantra in *Candide*: 'tout est bien' occurs seven times in *Candide*, in addition to six minor variations such as 'tout est au mieux' ('all's for the best').

In fact, the philosophical terminology in *Candide* extends well beyond Leibniz and Pope, to Descartes (systematic reasoning, chains of cause and effect, cosmology) and Thomas Hobbes (themes of war of every man against every man, and liberty and determinism) among others. Pangloss himself has conflated all these philosophical strains into an apparently seamless, rosy view, amusingly styled *métaphysico-théologo-cosmolonigologie*, to which he adheres come what may: 'I am a philosopher. It would not do for me to go back on what I said before, what with Leibniz not being able to be wrong, and pre-established harmony being the finest thing in the world, not to mention the *plenum* and *materia subtilis*' ('je suis philosophe: il ne me convient pas de me dédire, Leibniz ne pouvant pas avoir tort, et l'harmonie pré-établie étant d'ailleurs la plus belle chose du monde, aussi bien que le plein et la matière subtile').[4] And such terms fill the head of his pupil: 'There is no effect without a cause, replied Candide humbly. Everything is connected in a chain of necessity, and has all been arranged for the best' ('Il n'y a point d'effet sans cause, répondit modestement Candide, tout est enchaîné nécessairement et arrangé pour le mieux', chap. 3). Pangloss couches his bastard theodicy in slogans that make it obviously illogical, inappropriate, even ludicrous to the reader. But Pangloss is also very simply a *fatalist*, in both the providential (God does everything for a purpose) and the material and mechanical (all effects follow from necessary causes) senses. Either way, he concludes – another of his tireless refrains – that everything must be as it is and could not be otherwise. Pangloss can never take action to repel evil in the world because he has already decided that nothing in it is mutable. A true fatalist would be utterly passive, and such is the tendency of Pangloss's disciple: Candide just lets things happen to him, from chapter 1, when he lets Cunégonde take the amorous initiative, to all but the last page.

Candide, a Latinate name despite the pseudo-Germanic context, connotes, in the dictionaries of the time, candour, sincerity, purity of soul and love of truth. Our Candide is, of course, naïve – so much so that for a long time, though he acknowledges grief and joy, he is impervious to any logical inferences that might be drawn from them. To the young and inexperienced, the local is the measure of all things. Buffeted by alternating ups and downs, Candide is a sort of *picaro*, less gifted and more passive than Zadig, a Job without tragic grandeur – in fact a virtually comic Job. Though he is constantly on the move, he is never quite sure where he will be going next. And because his are the wanderings of exile, his vast geographical trajectory never comes full circle, ending up in Turkey rather than in Westphalia where he started.

At the outset, everything thus seems to be a part of a coherent system, but one that turns out to be provincially myopic. Pangloss himself is, of course, incorrigible. Alone he persists to the end in his attempt to confer ultimate meaning on every experience; but by that point everyone else has tuned out. Pangloss dismisses human woes, his own included, as ephemeral and insignificant; the only difference between him and a *pessimistic* fatalist is that he chooses *a priori* to qualify everything as good. Like the other characters, he is essentially modelled on the stock figures of the *commedia dell'arte* – today's equivalent would be a cartoon character – who forever reverts to his personal reflex, unfazed by reiterated calamities; or at best any learning acquired is short-lived, with the same patented tics resurfacing at the beginning of each new episode. Pangloss is nevertheless the appropriate foil for Voltaire's anti-optimist jests. There is no formal disproof of the argument, and Martin's 'tout est mal' ('all is evil') is not a preferable alternative; but what *Candide* purports to demonstrate is that anyone who goes through life excusing all evil with a moronic nostrum like 'Whatever is, is right' is making an ass of himself.

Voltaire's famously short, paratactic sentences expose Candide to a large number of relatively disconnected events which leave his moral compass in perpetual vertigo. Though he keeps looking for 'necessary causes and effects', he finds it all but impossible to link disparate events together. Indeed all perception of causality seems hopelessly short-term. 'The bayonet too was the sufficient cause of the death of a few thousand' ('La baïonnette fut aussi la raison suffisante de la mort de quelques milliers d'hommes', chap.3): cannons and swords kill, and there is little explanation of the purposes behind such facts. Each *Te Deum* ordered up by rival kings embodies the presumption of elevating such limited causes to the grandeur of providential design. Violence is random in its choice of victims. Everything seems in a way cyclical as violence begets violence. All power is transient; usurpers in turn are usurped (for example, the six dispossessed kings in chapter 26). If the good of the 'whole' is the justification of particular evil, in *Candide* the whole does not look very good either.

Intertexts

Voltaire's tales are often referred to as *contes philosophiques*, but in fact Voltaire generally eschews both the word *conte* (tale) and *roman* (novel) in favour of *histoire* (story). 'Once upon a time in Westphalia . . .' ('Il y avait en Westphalie . . .') is a formula that immediately frames *Candide* as a sort of fairy tale, though it does not truly answer to that description either. For in *Candide* there is nothing supernatural, which is not to say the story is credible. *Candide* owes much to centuries-old traditions of comic fiction or what in the mode of parody was called 'burlesque', from *Le Roman de Renart* to *Till Eulenspiegel*, the *Decameron* to *Don Quixote*, *Francion*, *Tom Jones* and *Shamela*. Voltaire was thoroughly familiar with the mock-epic, especially Ludovico Ariosto's *Orlando furioso*, a famous sixteenth-century parody of Matteo Maria Boiardo's *Orlando innamorato*, and practised the genre himself in *La Pucelle d'Orléans*, a typical burlesque or 'travesty' both of high legend in general and of a particular work, namely Jean Chapelain's pompous *La Pucelle ou la France libérée* (1656). And one easily recognises in *Candide* aspects of the oriental tale, in the lineage of Antoine Galland's *Arabian Nights* (1704–16) and the tales of Hamilton, Crébillon and Diderot.

Like many of these, *Candide* is largely a parody *of novels themselves*, and in particular the 'heroic' novels or 'romances' characteristic of the seventeenth century, one of the last avatars of which was Prévost's multi-volume novels published between 1728 and 1740: *Mémoires et aventures d'un homme de qualité* (1728–31), *Le Philosophe anglais* (1732–39), and *Le Doyen de Killerine* (1735–40). Of the second of these, there are especially strong resonances in *Candide*, so much so that one might call it the very prototype of the sort of work Voltaire mimics: for example, Mme Riding and Cécile turn up years after they were thought to have been eaten by savages, just as Cunégonde and Pangloss die only to resurface – and Cunégonde's brother twice. *Candide* includes in ironic form all the principal attributes and peripeteia of romance, or, as his own critic puts it in one of Voltaire's 1761 additions to the text, 'those situations you can find in any novel' ('ces situations qu'on trouve dans tous les romans', chap.22). The very third sentence of *Candide* – 'The older servants of the household suspected that he was the son of the baron's sister by a kind and upright gentleman of the neighbourhood, a man whom this lady had consistently refused to marry' ('Les anciens domestiques de la maison soupçonnaient qu'il était fils de la sœur de monsieur le baron, et d'un bon et honnête gentilhomme du voisinage, que cette demoiselle ne voulut jamais épouser') – would instantly have been recognised by many readers as a take-off on the genealogy of

Tom Jones,[5] who like Candide is raised at the manor house alongside the master's own son.

From start to finish, the text of *Candide* is laced with humorous allusions of this sort that need not necessarily be interpreted at each juncture as carrying a specific message. There are echoes of other satirico-philosophical tales, which footnotes to modern editions often point out, but the number is limitless: the very multiplicity of reference throughout the story doubtless counts, along with the uncertain equilibrium between comedy and tragedy, among Voltaire's most original contributions to short prose fiction. The opening characterisation of the baron's scraggly pack of dogs which he calls hounds (*la meute*), not to mention the compact summary of Pangloss's philosophy, is the stuff of burlesque, and already provides clues to the reader of the appropriate reading mode, as does the constant wordplay, for example Cunégonde's 'desire for knowledge' ('désir d'être savante'), where the suggestion is of knowledge both carnal and intellectual.

Next to the garden at the end of the story, the sojourn in Eldorado is doubtless the most discussed passage in *Candide*. Obviously it represents a sort of pseudo-utopia, not satirical but not a serious model either, inasmuch as it sets forth no political theory. Its most notable feature, aside from its ironic banalisation of conventional symbols of value such as precious metal and stones, is its deistic religion, devoid of priests: 'What! You mean you have no monks to teach and dispute and govern and intrigue and burn people who don't agree with them?' exclaims Candide ('Quoi! Vous n'avez point de moines qui enseignent, qui disputent, qui gouvernent, qui cabalent, et qui font brûler les gens qui ne sont pas de leur avis?', chap.18). The reader must grasp (this may be less evident today) that Candide's question reduces to a matter of 'opinion' what in Christian orthodoxy (which was after all the state religion in France) was a domain of unique and exclusive truth. Subversive twists of this sort, embodying the essentially relativist doctrine which the story implies, are countless.

Many commentators have stressed Voltaire's borrowings from Garcilaso de la Vega's *Histoire des Incas*, and André Morize even declares it to be the direct source of the entire Eldorado episode.[6] In particular, he cites such details as the gigantic bird 'contour' ('condor') – which in fact Voltaire could as well have found elsewhere, even in the *Dictionnaire de Trévoux*.[7] Richard Brooks points to several other specifics, including the savage 'Oreillons', with 'a propensity for nudity, sodomy with monkeys, cannibalism, and use of elementary weapons like arrows, clubs, and stone hatchets'.[8] Some have strained to explain every possible detail in *Candide* by reference to specific sources, and no one has carried the process further than Morize.

But there is much futility in such diligent pursuit of the tale's presumed 'sources', for it is obvious that anything mentioned in the story must be something that the author has encountered somewhere, directly or otherwise; there will always be more sources to be ferreted out, with dubious gain. Thus, for example, the inaccessible mountains and other obstacles, rivers and gorges resemble Garcilaso's description of Peru and Muzu.[9] But for that there are several other precedents, including the Nopande kingdom sealed away high in the mountains in books 13–14 of the aforementioned *Philosophe anglais*. With his 'red sheep' Voltaire likely had in mind the llama – or was it the *guanaco* which is described by Garcilaso as reddish-brown ('de couleur baye'), which Brooks states the Spaniards called by the name sheep;[10] that would still not explain why their colour is referred to in chap.20 as scarlet ('un rouge éclatant').[11]

The city of gold does of course relate to the Peruvian histories, but even here we should not overlook a precedent that no one ever mentions, namely the New Jerusalem of the Apocalypse, another spectacular city paved with gold and encrusted with jewels. René Pomeau glosses the sentence 'I certainly have no right to keep strangers from leaving' ('je n'ai pas assurément le droit de retenir des étrangers', chap.18) as an allusion to Frederick II's 'tyranny' in detaining Voltaire in Prussia in 1753,[12] never thinking it is equally reminiscent of the prince of the Nopandes refusing to let Mme Riding leave his kingdom. The trouble with being over-concerned with Voltaire's sources is that there are too many and too few. A text like *Candide* is so over-determined that the quest is never over; the endless 'sources' usually tell us little that is significant at the risk of overlooking others at the same time that could be just as meaningful.

Experience

It may be more important to stress, firstly, that Candide leaves Eldorado of his own accord, not disillusioned with it but determined nevertheless to pursue his own quest for Cunégonde;[13] and secondly, that the riches he carries away with him will sustain him until the end of the story, even though radically reduced from a hundred treasure-laden sheep to just one: 'There was more joy in Candide at finding this one sheep than there had been sorrow at losing an hundredfold all laden with large Eldorado diamonds' ('Candide eut plus de joie de retrouver ce mouton qu'il n'avait été affligé d'en perdre cent tous chargés de gros diamants d'Eldorado', chap.20) – indubitably an allusion to the biblical parable of the lost sheep in Matthew 18. (Voltaire's polemical writings from *Candide* on frequently use the Bible as a foil.) But there is no real 'lesson' to draw from Eldorado; Candide's happiness there is no more a function of merit or providence than his happiness or unhappiness anywhere else.

In fact, Voltaire hardly disagrees with Rousseau about 'moral' evil, which is man's doing,[14] witness Jacques's reply to Pangloss in chapter 4:

> Men must surely have corrupted nature some, he would say, for they were not born wolves, and yet wolves they have become; God gave them neither twenty-four pounders nor bayonets, and they have made bayonets and twenty-four pounders in order to destroy each other.
>
> (Il faut bien, disait-il, que les hommes aient un peu corrompu la nature, car ils ne sont point nés loups, et il sont devenus loups; Dieu ne leur a donné ni canon de vingt-quatre, ni baïonnettes, et ils se sont fait des baïonnettes et des canons pour se détruire.)

Virtually all of the violence and suffering in *Candide*, aside from the Lisbon earthquake and pestilence, is consciously perpetrated on human beings by other human beings. Not that the specific source matters much in the story, where most people are, when it comes to justice and compassion, nearly as unfeeling as Nature herself. There is a vast repertory of human vices delivered by Candide in chapter 21: men are murderers, liars, avaricious, and so on; they all pretty much boil down to a brutal combination of intolerance and amoral self-interest.

For however long it takes for things really to register upon the hero's consciousness, Candide's story is about accumulated experience, most of it bad. As early as chapter 13, Candide wishes he could see Pangloss again in order to raise 'some objections' to the 'admirable things' he would have to say about 'physical and moral evil' ('le mal physique et le mal moral'). And at the conclusion of chapter 17 he is prepared to deny the original myth: 'And whatever Maître Pangloss might have said, I often observed that everything went rather badly in Westphalia' ('Et, quoi qu'en dît maître Pangloss, je me suis souvent aperçu que tout allait assez mal en Westphalie'). The Quest devolves into the gradual demythification of everything, and most especially of deceitful consolations. To be an Optimist is fundamentally an attempt to deny the sordid details of human life. As Voltaire wrote to a friend in 1756, 'Optimism is dismaying. It is a cruel philosophy under a consoling name' ('L'optimisme est désespérant. C'est une philosophie cruelle sous un nom consolant', D6738).

By this time Candide has in fact long since rejected the Optimist premise, though of course he has no explanation to put in its place. He has also developed more than a little cynicism about even the broader philosophical notion of 'nature': facing consumption by cannibals, he wonders what Pangloss would think if he could see this manifestation of 'pure nature' ('la pure nature', chap.16); and Cacambo expresses the harsh general lesson that 'the laws of nature teach us to kill our neighbour' ('le droit naturel nous enseigne à tuer notre prochain', chap.16). It is true that, once delivered from the immediate quandary, Candide tries as usual to recuperate his positive attitude; he frequently bounces back when things suddenly seem to be going swimmingly. But ultimately he revolts against his master's philosophy:

> 'Oh Pangloss', cried Candide, 'this is an abomination you never thought of; that's enough, I must finally give up on your Optimism'. 'What's Optimism?' asked Cacambo. 'I'm afraid to say,' said Candide, 'that it's a mania for insisting that all is well when things are going badly.'
>
> (Ô Pangloss! s'écria Candide, tu n'avais pas deviné cette abomination; c'en est fait, il faudra qu'à la fin je renonce à ton optimisme. Qu'est-ce qu'optimisme? disait Cacambo. Hélas! dit Candide, c'est la rage de soutenir que tout est bien quand on est mal.)[15]

As Voltaire was to say in his article 'Enthousiasme' in the *Dictionnaire philosophique*, 'reason consists in always seeing things as they are' ('la raison consiste à voir toujours les choses comme elles sont').[16]

At length, Candide is even tempted by Martin's contrarian pessimism ('tout est mal'), though he himself doesn't go quite that far. Martin is the counterpoint of Pangloss: everything is bad, even when things seem to be getting better (like all prophets, he is often wrong). The evidence, according to Martin, allows one to draw a conclusion diametrically opposed to a beneficent God: the world must instead have been abandoned to 'some malign being' ('quelque être malfaisant', chap.20). Nevertheless, as late as chapter 22, Candide is still characterised as an innocent, and the proof is that he still blabs too much, thereby constantly alerting predators to his vulnerability and inviting new troubles.

Towards the end, the pace of the action slows, and Candide, reunited though disappointingly with Cunégonde, and in the utter absence of any providential conclusion, settles with his reassembled band in a relatively protected environment near Constantinople. There is no longer any theory behind it: the garden is a refuge, not a family nor a social model. Candide accepts that the metaphysical order is inaccessible to reason and cannot be expressed. There is room in the garden for all, even the bad metaphysicians, with the exception of Cunégonde's incorrigible brother.

The crux of the final transition is that, in the initial stage, only Cacambo is put to work, while the other seven become seriously bored. Then the group visits a Turkish family of five who are living pretty decently on just a few acres, with even some luxuries, by labouring collectively, inspired by the largely negative goal of holding at bay the three plagues of man: ennui, vice and want. This to Candide is an illumination; and coming soon after, his concluding verdict, 'we must cultivate our garden' ('il faut cultiver notre jardin') has a new meaning: he has moved from the seigneurial manner of owning a property that is worked by slaves or sharecropped, and engaged in the principle of collective labour that includes each and every member.

That Cunégonde, initially described as 'of a high complexion, fresh, chubby, and toothsome' ('haute en couleur, fraîche, grasse, appétissante') – in other words sensuously plump – has turned ugly is the main symbol of Candide's lowered expectations. But there are some satisfactions even in the absence of absolute happiness. In an atmosphere of toleration, eschewing all religious and national prejudices, Candide is adamant that metaphysical reasoning is futile because it attempts to explain too much. Candide himself is not a reasoner: he has always left the philosophising to others, except on those occasions when he tried to make some sense of it in terms of his experience, and failed. Over Pangloss's irrepressible prattle, Candide chooses benign ignorance.[17] But some positive, practical form of action is still possible.

Even Pangloss by now has mellowed; he is no longer quite so categorical, though he goes on reciting his old dogmas because he cannot contemplate the void they would leave if he were to abandon them. In the final paragraph he puts the best face he still can on pre-established harmony – without all the calamities Candide has undergone, he says, 'you wouldn't be here now eating candied citron and pistachio nuts' ('vous ne mangeriez pas ici des cédrats confits et des pistaches', chap.30) – but Candide cuts him short. His causal chain, although in a sense irrefutable, cannot be said to prove anything at all. As for final causes, it is the dervish who has the last word: 'When his Highness sends a ship to Egypt, does he worry whether the mice on board are comfortable or not?' ('Quand Sa Hautesse envoie un vaisseau en Égypte, s'embarrasse-t-elle si les souris qui sont dans le vaisseau sont à leur aise ou non?', chap.30). Voltaire's own response to the problem of theodicy was, similarly, to confirm the deistic conviction that while God exists, he has no relationship to us and we can never know his designs. Suffering exists not because it is deserved, nor because God allows or is unable to prevent it, but because God, like his universe, is oblivious to it. If there is a purpose in anything, it is inaccessible to human reason.

Biography

For as long as strict literary history held full sway in the study of literature, *Candide* was read solely as an allegory of its author's life and mood, which was supposed to have become progressively darker in the wake of the Lisbon earthquake. Candide's acquisition of a garden was assumed to allegorise

Voltaire's installation at Les Délices in 1755 with its attendant, though disabused, 'garden' of limited pleasures. Hence, Voltaire's putative gloom was supposed to have propelled the narrative in an ever downward spiral toward the constricted, 'pessimistic' conclusion which Candide is presumed to be expressing at the end; the whole story was designed to culminate with an almost rigorous logic that necessarily summarises the meaning of the whole.[18] As Morize put it, it is Voltaire in person who utters Candide's last line.

Now there is little doubt that the tale contains many asides which intimates of Voltaire would readily have recognised as having some relevance to his own situation. He also was following closely, and with consternation, the beginnings of the Seven Years War; the king of the Bulgars in *Candide* is undoubtedly an allusion to Frederick II of Prussia. But while all frames of reference in the story, philosophical as well as world-historical, were indeed current in 1759, most other episodes would be hard to correlate with anything very specific in Voltaire's life or even in contemporary history.

It is also true that in his correspondence, in the period at Les Délices, Voltaire often referred to himself as a 'gardener' and to the delight he was taking in his 'gardens'; no one has shown this more conclusively than Geoffrey Murray.[19] To him, *Candide* is written, like Voltaire's letters, in a 'language of connivance':[20] Voltaire played many roles, just as he used many pseudonyms, which could be understood in more or less coded fashion by various circles of initiates. There are also repeated echoes of *Candide* in Voltaire's letters in the two or three years preceding its publication, which inform us among other things that many phrases that might appear wittily spontaneous were in fact used repeatedly by Voltaire over a period of time. But this fact hardly means that the story is encrypted specially for the cognoscenti and is incomprehensible to anyone not possessing this key.

Finally some critics reacted against this narrowly biographical tradition by proposing a strictly 'literary' reading of *Candide*, detaching it from the notion that the protagonist is a mere foil and stand-in for the author. Candide now became a *character*, not a person; and it was *he*, not Voltaire, who voices the conclusion. The trend began with an elegant dismantling of many conventional readings by Jean Sareil in his *Essai sur 'Candide'*. Roy Wolper in turn opposed the 'limited vision' of Candide the character to Voltaire's broader one as author: as he saw it, the only thing one can properly conclude from the protagonist's small world at the end of the story is that it suits him. And were one to draw attention to the delights of such refinements as pistachios, Wolper replies that while epicurianism may be a solution for Candide's now much-contracted mind, such was not the case with respect to Voltaire himself.[21]

Some scholars expressed shock to hear it propounded that *Candide* could be considered as something other than a direct expression of its author; it represented to Lester Crocker, for one, a bewildering 'displacement of the ground of interpretation from ideological content, or from external (biographical) evidence' in the direction of 'an esthetic question, point of view'. He countered that even if Voltaire's mentality and Candide's are two different things, they merge in the conclusion, where the author's ironical treatment of his protagonist ceases and 'the underlying seriousness surfaces'. Nevertheless, in essence Crocker partially adopts the character-oriented reading, and formulates a conclusion that should satisfy both schools: 'The essential point is that Candide has given up the way of self-delusion and has learned how to live in a modestly constructive fashion.'[22]

In a way, this debate illustrates a familiar sort of conflict in literary interpretation, insofar as virtually any work can be read both as autonomous artefact – as if its origin were unknown, in what in the mid-twentieth century was called a 'new critical' mode – or as one document among others on the life and thought of the author (or his times). This is largely a question of interpretative attitude. In the first case you try to forget Voltaire and con-centrate on the individual text; in the second you bind them together as tightly as you can.

This schema is, however, more complex in practice. No one would con-tend that *Candide* can be thoroughly understood without certain historical references: Lisbon, the execution of Admiral Byng, the Incan conquest; and any editor would be remiss who did not provide some assistance in the form of footnotes to readers whom such allusions might elude. On the other hand, it should be possible to read any text without pointing constantly at this or that personal fact about the author. But where to draw the line? Are not even certain aspects of Voltaire's personal experience (his ill-fated stay at the Prussian court, the public debate over theodicy, his Swiss 'garden', etc.) also 'historically' pertinent references? In other words, the categories are not wholly distinct, and a question of relative judgement must ultimately influence their admixture.

On the other hand, there seems to be little justification for treating Can-dide as a simple mouthpiece for Voltaire, because, to put it simply, Voltaire never talked the way Candide does, nor could Candide have written *Can-dide*. The narrative voice, which keeps considerable ironic distance from the protagonist, is the controlling one in this story, where none of the characters can be said to possess much psychological depth or complexity. But it does not state precisely what the moral of the story is. For *Candide* does not come down to a single lesson, but rather seems to incorporate a general one, which is that experience does not confer on life the meaning we would like to give it, whereas grand theories do not mesh with the events of real life.

Though today theodicy as such does not appear to us as a really central theme of Enlightenment thought, it does relate to the crucial principle of critical reasoning, which is very central indeed. And *Candide* embodies, if only indirectly, two of Voltaire's most cherished moral themes. One is, very simply: do not inflict suffering on others. Now that would appear to be an age-old Christian adage, but because it has been perverted by fanaticism, it must be coupled to the second, which is that of toleration. Though Pangloss may be a fool and Martin a crank, there is room for them in the garden. But not for the baron, who is himself intolerant. *Candide* teaches, but does not preach, that no one owns the truth.

NOTES

1. The term 'Optimism' is here capitalised when it describes a philosophical position, to distinguish this from the more familiar modern sense of 'optimism' as meaning simply 'hopefulness about the future'.
2. *Confessions*, book 9 (*Œuvres complètes*, vol.1, Paris: Pléiade, pp.429–30).
3. See the Morize edition of *Candide* (Paris: Didier, [1913] 1957), pp.xxviii–xxix. The winning essay by A. F. Reinhard, published that same year, carried the highly explicit title: *Le Système de Pope sur la perfection du monde comparé avec celui de M. de Leibniz, avec un examen de l'optimisme.*
4. End of chap.28. This is the sole actual mention of either Pope or Leibniz in the text.
5. H. Fielding, *A History of Tom Jones, A Foundling* (1749).
6. Note 1, pp.73–4, in his edition.
7. Supplement of 1752, article 'CONDOR ou CONDUR'.
8. R. A. Brooks, 'Voltaire and Garcilaso de la Vega', *SVEC*, 30 (1964), 189–204 (pp.194–5).
9. Brooks, 'Voltaire and Garcilaso de la Vega', p.198.
10. Brooks, 'Voltaire and Garcilaso de la Vega', p.199.
11. For other possible sources for them, see P. Flobert, 'Voltaire et les moutons rouges', in *Missions et démarches de la critique: Mélanges offerts au professeur J. A. Vier* (Paris: Klincksieck, 1973), pp.487–9.
12. *OCV*, vol.48, p.192, note 13.
13. Again, like Madame Riding in *Le Philosophe anglais*, who leaves the Nopandes only in order to continue her search for Axminster, Cleveland and Fanny.
14. He ironises at the distinction, however: there are in *Candide* four instances of the expression 'le mal moral et le mal physique'.
15. Chap.19. This passage represents in fact the only instances of the word 'optimisme' in the text of *Candide*.
16. *OCV*, vol.36, p.60.
17. See P. Naudin, 'Candide ou le bonheur du non-savoir', in *Missions et démarches de la critique: mélanges offerts au professeur J. A. Vier* (Paris: Klincksieck, 1973), 624–39 (p.633).

18. See notes on p.223 and 224 of the Morize edition.
19. G. Murray, *Voltaire's 'Candide': The Protean Gardener, 1755–1762*, SVEC, 69 (1970).
20. Murray, *Voltaire's 'Candide'*, pp.16–17.
21. R. S. Wolper, 'Candide, Gull in the Garden?', *Eighteenth-Century Studies*, 3 (1969), 265–77 (p.268, 275).
22. L. G. Crocker, 'Professor Wolper's Interpretation of *Candide*', *Eighteenth-Century Studies*, 5 (1971), 145–51 (pp.146–7).

9

CATHERINE VOLPILHAC-AUGER

Voltaire and history

To think today of 'Voltaire historian' might seem odd, so far have his historical works fallen from critical fashion in the last fifty years. His *Histoire
de Charles XII*, his *Siècle de Louis XIV*, his *Essai sur les mœurs* and his
Histoire de l'empire de Russie sous Pierre le Grand are all little more than
titles for most modern readers, who regard them as works that are at best
old-fashioned, at worst obsolete. At most Voltaire might be credited with a
talent for elegant popularisation, forced into playing into the hands of
authority when he wrote the history of the 1741 war, becoming an 'official'
historian, set on a path that was certainly prestigious (since, just as history
painting was at the top of the hierarchy of the visual arts, so history and
tragedy were the most elevated of the literary genres), but which at the same
time caused him to turn his back on the fundamental issues at stake in a
career dedicated to the most fervent form of philosophical militancy: the
historian has to be impartial, but Voltaire cannot and even must not be. And
so specialists of Voltaire or of Enlightenment thought, not finding them to
their taste, seem destined to remain indifferent to Voltaire's historical
writings.[1] Everything seems to conspire to ensure that this part of his output,
covering several thousand pages, should be confined to dusty libraries.
Requiescant in pace?

However, it is clear that this sweeping conclusion – contradicted by the
scholarly studies of J. H. Brumfitt, F. Diaz and J.-M. Moureaux, among
others[2] – takes no account of what his historical works meant for Voltaire
himself and for his contemporaries. These are complex works in which he
developed his essential ideas, and which in turn provided these ideas with an
unrivalled vehicle for their diffusion. Without the influence of Voltaire,
Gibbon would have conceived quite differently his *Decline and Fall of the
Roman Empire*. The *Essai sur les mœurs* is one of the most characteristic
works of the French Enlightenment, testing out one of the founding principles of Voltaire's thought: that the human spirit does not develop in an
uninterrupted way, but rather needs to find some nourishment to enable
reason to grow. Thus the events of history (*res gestae*) are the ideal vantage

point for anyone seeking to understand the functioning and the ebb and flow of the human spirit and to understand humanity, with all its strengths and above all weaknesses, even when it is horrific. And writing history (*res scriptae*) – that is, proper history, not the chronicles that Voltaire so abhorred and which he incessantly denounces as hagiographical compilations of useless details[3] – is the best proof of the existence of reason, which is both the subject and the object of history. This reflexivity is the cornerstone of Voltaire's historiography, and this too needs to be seen in context, at a time when the writing of history was a major cultural activity and when it followed strict rules, which Voltaire enjoyed deftly playing with. This can best be seen by considering both his historical works themselves and the numerous theoretical works he wrote, usually to justify himself (his works were the subject of countless virulent attacks), but also to proclaim the dignity of history and the duties of the historian, as in the *Encyclopédie* article 'Histoire', published in 1765 but written as early as 1756.[4] What better stage could there be for Voltaire to establish himself as the champion of the kind of 'philosophical history' that was ushered in with the Enlightenment?

The art of writing history

In order to guarantee a readership (which was large in the eighteenth and nineteenth centuries, judging by the number of editions of the *Siècle de Louis XIV* and of *Charles XII*), and so to become a means of shaping public opinion, which was its natural vocation,[5] the historical narrative was embellished with the ornaments of literature: it was not so much about instructing and pleasing as two separate goals as about ensuring that these two elements mutually reinforced each other. Indeed it is worth remembering that history in the eighteenth century was considered to be an integral part of *belles lettres*, and Voltaire would have been highly amused to see it being promoted in the nineteenth century to the status of a science. In the eighteenth century, critics and scholars (such as those in the Académie des inscriptions) provided readers with a piecemeal and technical knowledge of Antiquity in the form of learned essays and books on carefully circumscribed topics. This subject matter, far from having to be 'popularised', as we might say today,[6] had to be transformed by the historian's art, which consisted not in addressing the sources (which was the task of the scholar),[7] but in exploiting earlier works: the historian's task was to make otherwise difficult material interesting. Modern history involved reducing the available material: 'It is therefore all about creating a properly proportioned body out of all these scattered limbs and painting in their true colours, but with one brushstroke, what Larrey, Lamberti, Roussel and so many others falsify at length in volume after volume' ('Il ne s'agit donc que de former un corps bien proportionné à tous ces membres épars et de peindre avec des couleurs vraies, mais d'un trait, ce que Larrey, Lamberti, Roussel, etc., etc., falsifient et délayent dans des volumes').[8] The ultimate aim was to be read by a demanding public. And to achieve that, it was obviously not enough simply to romanticise, or to compose perfectly balanced sentences or even to give a clear structure to the narrative, as has often been said, on account of a letter to d'Argenson of 26 January 1740 (D2148), in which Voltaire remarked that 'what is needed in a history, as in a play, is a beginning, a middle and an end' ('Il faut dans une histoire, comme dans une pièce de théâtre, exposition, nœud et dénouement'). History had to be seen therefore to be true, or accurate; it had to maintain the reader's interest by revealing the links between a sequence of events; and it had to tell only what was worth telling, so as to instruct the reader and not simply to prick his curiosity. Voltaire makes the distinction in his *Nouvelles considérations sur l'histoire* (1744):

> [H]aving read three or four thousand descriptions of battles and the tenor of several hundred treatises, I realised that I had essentially learned very little. All I learned about was events. I know nothing more about the French and the Saracens by knowing about the battle of Charles Martel than I do about the Tartars and the Turks by knowing that Tamerlan defeated Bajazet.
>
> (après avoir lu trois ou quatre mille descriptions de batailles, et la teneur de quelques centaines de traités, j'ai trouvé que je n'étais guère plus instruit au fond. Je n'apprenais là que des événements. Je ne connais pas plus les Français et les Sarrasins par la bataille de Charles Martel, que je ne connais les Tartares et les Turcs par la victoire que Tamerlan remporta sur Bajazet.)[9]

These principles may seem elementary, but sometimes they were in fact contradictory and a careful balance between them had to be struck.

The historian had first and foremost to forsake the fantastic, be it large or small, and the seductive charm of anecdotes invented as need dictated, such as 'the story of a Spanish nobleman who burnt down his house in Madrid because the treacherous Bourbon had spent the night there'; for 'Bourbon's constable never went to Spain, and in any case it was characteristic of Spanish nobility to protect the French who were persecuted in their own country' ('l'historiette d'un grand d'Espagne qui brûla sa maison à Madrid parce que le traître Bourbon y avait couché . . . Le connétable de Bourbon n'alla jamais en Espagne, et d'ailleurs la grandeur espagnole consista toujours à protéger les Français persécutés dans leur patrie).[10] In just one sentence, then, Voltaire denounces both an attack on factual truth and the 'spirit of the time'. This concept is important, for Voltaire's aim is both to define this very spirit and to use it as a distinguishing criterion. This concept also allows us to revise the traditional view of Voltaire's short-sighted rationalism: for he refuses to believe anything which seems to him to go beyond the realms of human nature, such as Nero's finely honed cruelty[11] – human nature, held to be universal, would in this way be nothing more than what an eighteenth-century bourgeois Frenchman chose to make of it. Voltaire does not downplay the human potential for cruelty, but believes that the eyewitness or the historian who happily recounts such facts – in this case, Tacitus – can rightly be suspected of being gullible or biased, which was a remarkable attitude at a time when all his contemporaries revered Tacitus and almost unquestioningly repeated everything of his they read.[12] Nevertheless, Voltaire often exploits for his own ends a nation's capacity to believe the unbelievable: 'Even if this adventure is untrue, it is nevertheless certain that it was believed as if it were something quite ordinary, and this belief in itself is testimony to the barbarity of the time' ('Si cette aventure n'est pas vraie, il est du moins prouvé qu'elle a été crue comme une chose ordinaire, et cette opinion même atteste la barbarie du temps').[13] Shifting the reader's interest away from events (wars, royal marriages, treaties) and towards the realm of 'opinion', and judging eyewitness and historical accounts according to the criteria of this critical history of the spirit, rather than adopting or rejecting them all together, was without doubt one of the key innovations introduced by Voltaire's historiography. He also broke with the common practice of seventeenth- and eighteenth-century historians in denouncing the ancient historians, who had hitherto been seen as indisputable models: for Voltaire, nothing was more suspect than ancient history, with its miracles and absurdities, despite the reputation enjoyed by, for example, Livy and Plutarch. Charles Rollin, the respected author of a history of the ancient world which started to appear in 1730, is the object of countless sarcastic remarks by Voltaire, who ridicules him for having used uncritically some rather dubious sources.

Modern critics also tend to underestimate the originality of Voltaire's determination to decentre history by tearing the reader away from himself, or rather from the mirror formed by the founding accounts of his own nation or religion. The *Essai sur les mœurs* opens with a series of 'exotic' chapters which have nothing really 'historical' about them at all, but which do have an emblematic function: they simply point out the remarkable antiquity and intellectual wealth of China, India and Persia, which were ignored at the time by scornful Europeans. There could be no better way for Voltaire of highlighting what he always saw as the weakness of his great predecessor, Jacques-Bénigne Bossuet, who, in his *Discours sur l'histoire universelle* (1681), was interested solely in 'God's chosen people' ('peuples élus de Dieu') and in their enemies, according to a Christian-centred perspective derived from the principle of providentialist causality, which formed the guiding thread of his apologetic history: men were simply doing God's will, namely ensuring the triumph of Christianity. Of course, Voltaire's determination to decentre history bore relatively little fruit, with the *Essai* still focusing mainly on Europe, if only because of the limitations imposed by the material available to him; but by offering the reader a kind of history which confronted him with 'the Other' rather than simply offering a means of identification, he sketched out a way of renewing history-writing in early modern France.

If history was to be useful, it also had to focus on what was essential. When Voltaire writes, he draws on a mass of useless and dry details, mercilessly leaving out those which strike him as superfluous or gratuitous, or which seem false or uncertain, the historian's real task being to choose, not to copy: the historian has to be properly 'critical', and so ancient history, which was highly suspect, was necessarily considered to be inferior to modern history.[14] Voltaire makes the point repeatedly, and frequent false claims not to mention something while actually mentioning it allow him, by dint of the telling contrasts they create, to point up his own rigorous approach. He also rejects the traditional 'ornaments' of history, such as portraits and harangues,[15] then seen as artificial. He denounces anecdotes, not just because they are highly likely to be fictitious, but also, as he says in the preface to the *Histoire de l'empire de Russie*, because they blur the distinction between private life and public life:

> If a public man's failing, his secret vice that you are trying to expose, has influenced public affairs, causing the loss of a battle, interfering with the country's finances or causing the citizens to suffer, you must talk about it: it is your duty to get to the bottom of this hidden little motive which has led to such major events; other than that, you must say nothing.
>
> (Si cette faiblesse d'un homme public, si ce vice secret que vous cherchez à faire connaître, a influé sur les affaires publiques, s'il a fait perdre une bataille, dérangé les finances de l'Etat, rendu les citoyens malheureux, vous devez en parler: votre devoir est de démêler ce petit ressort caché qui a produit de grands événements; hors de là vous devez vous taire.)[16]

The author of the *Anecdotes sur Louis XIV* and the *Anecdotes sur le czar Pierre le Grand* (1748) sticks rigidly to this position, as he does even in chapters 25–8 of the *Siècle de Louis XIV*, entitled 'Particularités et anecdotes' – how anecdotes are used could almost be a way of distinguishing between good and bad history, the latter marred by bias and sometimes even calumny. However, the author of the *Siècle de Louis XIV* is also able to speak of 'an unparalleled event' ('un événement qui n'a point d'exemple'),[17]

CATHERINE VOLPILHAC-AUGER

the story of the man in the iron mask, the mysterious prisoner who pops up furtively in Louis XIV's shadow, hinting at some greater affair of state. Bound both to say nothing and to tell the truth, the historian's only option is deftly to suggest to the reader what he should think.[18]

Of course, Voltaire is also proud of his ability to seek out new information that he can use against his enemies: memoirs, reliable eyewitness accounts, hitherto unknown documents and so on, but only in the case of contemporary history involving major public figures (Louis XIV, Charles XII, Peter the Great): the discretion, if not the obsequious obedience of courtiers, reason of state and the inattention of those who were too closely involved in public affairs and did not realise the full extent of what was at stake, all resulted in the misrepresentation of the subject matter. In such cases the investigation has to be laid bare and the evidence marshalled, not in the footnotes and glosses so typical of scholarly works,[19] but in proper discussions where Voltaire can deal out references and authorities, refusing to be caught out. Thus to the 380 pages of the *Histoire de Charles XII* proper Voltaire adds some 110 pages of supplementary documents and additional texts, making up a kind of preface like *Le Pyrrhonisme de l'histoire* (1768), as well as an 'Avis important', an 'Autre avis' and 'Réponses' to the *Remarques* addressed publicly to Voltaire by the learned critic La Motraye shortly after the 1731 publication, all of which appear in the different editions of the work and which demonstrate the extent to which this was a living work.

Philosophical history

Voltaire's insistence on this point is not simply the product of some vindictive temperament: to call into question his honour (and his originality) as a historian was to threaten his status as a *philosophe*, or freethinker. History had become an integral part of philosophy, presented not simply as a narrative account, but also as a mode of interpretation: history had to provide the principle of the intelligibility of the facts presented, their having already been tested by the criterion of reason, as we have seen. The causal explanations offered by historians up to the time of Montesquieu's *Considérations sur les causes de la grandeur des Romains et de leur décadence* (1734) were essentially concerned with the psychological (or what the eighteenth century would call 'moral') study of individuals and crowds, the conduct of the latter being governed by simple principles: they are uncontrollable until they are subjugated by a ruler. Thus princes, great captains, queens and royal favourites were traditionally the primary concern of history: they alone, by dint of their status, deserved attention; the inner workings of their characters, at once extraordinary and fully human, were sufficient to explain wars, alliances, successes and failures. History therefore contributed to a 'closed' anthropology: all human attitudes having been listed, identified and classified, all that remained to be done was to relate human behaviour to one or more of these character types.[20] History, then, was a branch of moral analysis, albeit possibly coloured by politics when it came to understanding the motives and machinations of princes. Material factors (such as the invention of a weapon or a natural phenomenon) could of course play a role, but only as accessories or unforeseen obstacles.

In 1734, Montesquieu, turning this hierarchy of causes on its head, rejected heroic figures, even individuals, and instead put at the heart of his system the institutions and the very spirit of Rome: not concerned with reducing everything to one single cause, he was interested instead in how all the relevant factors (material, institutional, human) converged or clashed. The nature of history-writing had changed completely, though the reading public did not yet realise just how significant this change was, not least because Montesquieu was no historian: if he used history, it was as a means of studying politics, not as an end in itself. It was to fall to Voltaire, as a true historian, to develop this new approach and to sell it to readers, and above all to reshape it in line with the principles he had sketched out as early as 1731 in the *Histoire de Charles XII*. Indeed, Voltaire did not adopt Montesquieu's interpretative principle, such was the importance he attached in his history of the human spirit to those in a position to further that spirit and above all to carry the majority of the public with them. Enlightened monarchs or 'great men' (but not conquerors or 'heroes') occupied a significant place in this system, as suggested by the very titles of his major works, devoted to those figures who had profoundly shaped the destiny of their peoples and even of the world. If Charles XII is presented as an enigmatic figure, as we shall see later, the man who set off from a small northern country to conquer Poland and then take on the whole of Russia, and who, following his defeat at Poltava, took refuge with the Turks from whom he finally made his escape before dying a hero's death at the age of 36, is a source above all of surprise. But it is admiration that Peter I inspires, a figure whom Voltaire idealises, capable of dragging Russia out of its quasi-feudal state, of breaking the resistance of a particularly backward-looking clergy and of opening up his country towards Europe by founding a new capital, St Petersburg.[21] But the great man *par excellence*, after Alexander the Great,[22] was Louis XIV: 'I have sought simply to present the characteristic features of the century of Louis XIV, the changes brought about right across the administration, in the mind and spirit of men, and, in short, what sets this fine century apart from all others' ('Je n'ai cherché qu'à mettre sous les yeux ce qui peut caractériser le siècle de Louis XIV, les changements faits dans toutes les parties de l'administration, dans l'esprit et dans les mœurs des hommes, et en un mot ce qui distingue ce beau siècle de tous les autres').[23] Louis XIV, known as 'Louis the Great', earned his name by championing 'the arts and the progress of the human spirit' ('les arts et les progrès de l'esprit humain'),[24] which were only able to prosper in the way they did thanks to the support given to them by an extraordinary personality. In this respect, Louis XIV ranked alongside Philip, Alexander, Caesar, Augustus and the Medici family, under all of whom arts and literature flourished: the century of Louis XIV was the last of 'those four ages defined by their great talents' ('ces quatre âges distingués par les grands talents'), 'perhaps that one of the four which came the closest to being perfect' ('peut- être celui des quatre qui approche le plus de la perfection').[25] In other words, although he was appointed historiographer by Louis XV in 1745, Voltaire was no simple champion of the French monarchy, at a time when Louis XIV still came in for severe criticism. Rather, he aimed to write a history of humanity, seen through the person who had brought it to the peak of its achievement; and it is for this reason that, having mentioned the military campaigns, he turns his attention to the internal government of France, including justice, trade, the navy, sciences, the arts and so on.

Voltaire nevertheless comes close to the kind of philosophical history sketched out by Montesquieu when he focuses, like him, on the multiplicity and complexity of causes, which are examined in depth, thanks to the historian's discernment, political insight and understanding of events, both great and small, and of mentalities. Though he may devote a lot of space to individual characters, Voltaire is far from reducing history to contingency, even when he delights in condensing events, making a bowl of water, for instance, the cause of France's salvation in the War of Spanish Succession:

A few pairs of unusual gloves that she [the Duchess of Marlborough] refused to give to the Queen, and a bowl of water that before her very eyes she spilt, accidentally on purpose, on Mrs Masham's dress, changed the face of Europe. People turned bitter: the brother of the new royal favourite asked the Duke for a regiment of his own; the Duke said no; the Queen gave it to him. The Tories seized on this to free the Queen from her domestic slavery, to weaken the power of the Duke of Marlborough, to change the ministry, to create peace ... If the Duchess had been willing to be a little more flexible, her reign would have continued.

(Quelques paires de gants d'une façon singulière qu'elle [la duchesse de Marlborough] refusa à la reine, une jatte d'eau qu'elle laissa tomber en sa présence, par une méprise affectée, sur la robe de Mme Masham, changèrent la face de l'Europe. Les esprits s'aigrirent: le frère de la nouvelle favorite demande au duc un régiment; le duc le refuse, et la reine le donne. Les torys saisirent cette conjoncture pour tirer la reine de cet esclavage domestique, pour abaisser la puissance du duc de Marlborough, changer le ministère, faire la paix . . . Si le caractère de la duchesse eût pu admettre quelque souplesse, elle eût régné encore.)[26]

The art of the story-teller or the letter-writer should not be confused with a proper theory of history, such as it emerges from the whole body of Voltaire's historical writings, where he also has to avoid overwhelming his reader with details, identifying instead the major trends[27] and maintaining the 'thread' of the story, such as the clash between Empire and Church in medieval Europe, if he is to stand any chance of being read and understood.

In this way, Voltaire succeeds in formulating, albeit somewhat belatedly, a 'philosophy of history', which is in fact the title of a work in which he offers a kind of summation of the themes he has explored hitherto: he dismisses the whole of ancient history (including in particular the Bible), which he does by going back to the beginning and writing simultaneously the history of the human race and the history of history in a series of short articles, recalling his technique in the *Dictionnaire philosophique*. He does this in 1765, when history emerges as a key element in his campaign to *Écraser l'Infâme*, and so becomes part of Voltaire's 'philosophy'. Followed up by sharp rebuttals of his critics, including *La Défense de mon oncle* (Voltaire attributed *La Philosophie de l'histoire* to one Abbé Bazin, whose memory is then defended by his supposed nephew), and actively hunted down by the police, *La Philosophie de l'histoire* works as a kind of demonstration of Voltaire's philosophical method and of the lessons to be drawn from it, complete with lashings of sarcasm. But are such militancy and fury actually compatible with the impartiality of the historian? Voltaire always positions himself on the side of reason and denounces his enemies, whatever form they may take. The history of the human spirit is also the history of prejudice and error, which must always be resisted (since they are still a threat in the present) with logical arguments and implacable irony. Standing up against those who have been in authority (religious, political, military) for too long,[28] Voltaire is not the defender of the *philosophes*; rather, he is the judge who condemns in the name of Reason.

Forms and works

How does Voltaire come at history? Why and how does he appropriate tried-and-tested literary forms? And what is his trajectory? When he first tries his hand at the genre with the *Histoire de Charles XII* in 1731, he is known above all as a poet who has breathed new life into tragedy and epic poetry, and France is still waiting for a historian worthy of the name. The next forty years will see him so shaping his career as to ensure that he makes a name for himself in this domain too, exploiting successively and increasingly the different prevailing forms of history-writing.

He starts by writing an 'individual history', a genre that is more accessible than a 'general history' and certainly more so than a 'universal history',[29] but infinitely superior to biography. In fact, *Charles XII* bears no relation whatsoever to the little-respected genre of 'lives', a form which Voltaire will exploit only once in his *Vie de Molière* (1734, published in 1739), which is in reality more akin to a biographical introduction to the dramatist's works. Voltaire concentrates on one period in the sovereign's life (following his accession to the throne), without having to go into the kind of detail or private affairs which are typical of biography, and without having to give the 'key' to understanding the individual in question. He soon grows in confidence, undertaking around 1740 a *Nouveau plan d'une histoire de l'esprit humain* (published in 1745), an individual history, limited to a precise subject but considerable enough to enable it to lay claim to being a general history, as the title indicates (and Voltaire's titles, as we shall see, repay particular attention). It is at this point that his historical output takes on its true shape, thanks again to his decision to work in a 'mixed' genre, the *Siècle de Louis XIV*, which he defines as early as 1738 in his famous letter to the Abbé Dubos which serves as a preface to his *Essai sur le siècle de Louis XIV*: the work is neither the 'life of this prince' ('la vie de ce prince'), for this will be the subject of his *Anecdotes sur Louis XIV* in 1748, nor the 'annals of his reign' ('les annales de son règne'), for that would smack of a commissioned work, which is precisely what his *Annales de l'Empire* will be in 1753. Instead, the work is a 'history of the human spirit, drawn from the most glorious century of the human spirit' ('histoire de l'esprit humain, puisée dans le siècle le plus glorieux de l'esprit humain'), completed in 1751, and thus an 'individual history', insofar as it is limited in time and subject matter, but also a 'general' history, since it aims to identify the 'spirit' of an entire nation. So, for Voltaire, the project has a peculiarly double focus:

> This work is divided into chapters. About twenty of these are devoted to general history: these are twenty depictions of the great events of the time . . . Woe betide details . . . What characterises the century, what caused revolutions, what will be important one hundred years from now: that is what I want to write about today.
>
> There is one chapter on Louis XIV's private life; two on the major changes made in the administration of the kingdom, in trade and in finance; two on the government of the church . . .; five or six on the history of the arts.

(Cet ouvrage est divisé en chapitres. Il y en a vingt environ destinés à l'histoire générale: ce sont vingt tableaux des grands événements du temps . . . Malheur aux détails . . . Ce qui caractérise le siècle, ce qui a causé des révolutions, ce qui sera important dans cent années, c'est là ce que je veux écrire aujourd'hui.

Il y a un chapitre pour la vie privée de Louis XIV; deux pour les grands changements faits dans la police du royaume, dans le commerce, dans les finances; deux pour le gouvernement ecclésiastique . . .; cinq ou six pour l'histoire des arts.)[30]

The *Siècle* has to be read in the light of this distinction: thus the famous phrase 'Woe betide details', so often quoted to decry Voltaire as a historian, in fact only applies to the broad 'depictions', and not to the portraits or to the subtle way in which the private life of a prince can be revealed to the public.

The *Histoire de l'empire de Russie sous Pierre le Grand* (1763), foreshadowed by the *Anecdotes sur le czar Pierre le Grand* (1748), and undertaken at the behest of the Russian government, enacts a similar broadening of focus: 'The history of Charles XII was amusing, that of Peter I is instructive' ('L'histoire de Charles XII était amusante, celle de Pierre Ier est instructive'), says Voltaire in the foreword,[31] since what he wishes to celebrate is the tsar's civilising work. If this work does not have the same scope as that of the *Siècle* and does not enjoy the same success, it is also because in the meantime Voltaire channelled his efforts into another project, begun in the 1740s and to which he now returns, becoming the *Abrégé de l'histoire universelle* (1753), and subsequently the *Essai sur l'histoire universelle* (1754) and finally his *Essai sur l'histoire générale et sur les mœurs et l'esprit des nations depuis Charlemagne jusqu'à nos jours* (1756). This is ultimately a modest title, clearly chosen in reaction to all those who would see in him a victim of excessive ambition,[32] but which does not disguise the scope of the project, which will actually continue to grow. In fact the project goes on to incorporate both the *Siècle* and subsequently the more modest *Précis du siècle de Louis XV* (1768), which allows Voltaire to perform his role as royal historiographer. And, most significantly of all, the project is topped off in 1765 with *La Philosophie de l'histoire*, which in 1769 becomes the 'Discours préliminaire' to the whole work, thus constituting its introduction, defining its philosophical significance and linking the progress of the human race, since its origins, to the history of the world from Charlemagne to the present day. Nothing escapes the attention of Voltaire historian, who can in the *Essai* indulge in playing with the rules of the genre, wilfully exploiting irony, even jokes and sarcasm, and practising in all his works the consummate art of story-telling, constantly intervening in the first person to show his indignation or his satisfaction. Some of his contemporaries, including Gabriel Bonnot de Mably, who were used to the neutral 'middle style' that was alone judged to be suitable in history, criticised him sharply for his style. But they forgot that rather than just being historical works, they were first and foremost works by Voltaire.

Most surprising of all is the fact that the image which still persists today of both Charles XII and Louis XIV is one that owes much to Voltaire. Our view is shaped by his historical writings – even if we do not know them. It is the ultimate Voltairean paradox that the very success of the historian is to be forgotten.

translated by Russell Goulbourne

NOTES

1. See, for example, the article 'Histoire' in the *Dictionnaire des lettres françaises: Le XVIIIe siècle*, ed. Cardinal G. Grente, revised F. Moureau (Paris: Fayard, 1995), pp.598–600.
2. J. H. Brumfitt, *Voltaire Historian* (Oxford: Oxford University Press, 1958); F. Diaz, *Voltaire storico* (Turin: Einaudi, 1958); and J.-M. Moureaux's introduction to his edition of *La Défense de mon oncle*, OCV, vol.64, pp.3–164.
3. See, for example, the 'Avant-propos' of the *Essai sur les mœurs*: 'Almost every town today has its own true or false history, fuller and more detailed than that of Alexander. The annals of one single monastic order contain more volumes than those of the Roman Empire' ('Presque chaque ville a aujourd'hui son histoire vraie ou fausse, plus ample, plus détaillée que celle d'Alexandre. Les seules annales d'un ordre monastique contiennent plus de volumes que celles de l'Empire romain', *EM*, vol.1, pp.195–6).
4. OCV, vol.33, pp.164–86. Voltaire was adamant that he would write this article.
5. See F. Lotterie, *Progrès et perfectibilité: Un dilemme des Lumières françaises (1755–1814)*, SVEC, 2006:04.
6. This is the interpretation proposed by G. Gusdorf in *L'Avènement des sciences humaines au siècle des Lumières* (Paris: Payot, 1973), p.374.
7. J.-M. Moureaux notes that Voltaire often uses second-hand sources rather than the Greek or Latin originals (*OCV*, vol.64, p.60).
8. Voltaire's letter to the Abbé Dubos of 30 October 1738, reproduced in *OH*, p.606.
9. Moland, vol.16, p.139. See also the edition of this work by G. Abbattista at www.eliohs.unifi.it/testi/700/voltaire/nouvconsid.html.
10. *EM*, vol.2, p.184.
11. See *Le Pyrrhonisme de l'histoire* (1768), in *Histoire de Charles XII* (OCV, vol.4, pp.567–78).
12. See C. Volpilhac-Auger, *Tacite en France de Montesquieu à Chateaubriand*, SVEC, 313 (1993).

13. *EM*, vol.1, p.139 (the adventure in question concerns Brunehaut, Queen of France, judged and punished by her people); see also *EM*, vol.1, p.518.

14. Ancient history is also infinitely less useful than modern history, which has the further advantage of being derived more from reason than from memory, as Voltaire points out in the *Remarques sur l'histoire* of 1741 (Moland, vol.16, pp.134–7).

15. See article 7 of the preface to the *Histoire de l'empire de Russie sous Pierre le Grand* (*OCV*, vol.46, pp.404–5). On harangues in history-writing, see *Des voix dans l'histoire: La parole et ses représentations dans le récit historique, XVII*ᵉ–*XIX*ᵉ *siècles*, ed. C. Volpilhac-Auger (forthcoming).

16. *OCV*, vol.46, p.402. See also the *Encyclopédie* article 'Histoire' (*OCV*, vol.33, p.183).

17. *OH*, p.895.

18. See also the *Questions sur l'Encyclopédie*, article 'Ana, anecdotes' (*OCV*, vol.38, pp.281–322). On this question, see C. Volpilhac-Auger, 'L'historien et ses masques: Voltaire théoricien de l'anecdote', in *L'Histoire en miettes*, ed. C. Poulouin and C. Dornier, *Elseneur*, 19 (2004), 216–29.

19. See A. Grafton, *The Footnote: A Curious History* (Cambridge, MA: Harvard University Press, 1999).

20. See L. Van Delft, *Nature humaine et caractères à l'Âge classique* (Paris: Presses Universitaires de France, 1993), part 1.

21. See J. R. Iverson, 'La guerre, le grand homme et l'histoire: l'*Histoire de l'empire de Russie*', in *Voltaire et ses combats*, ed. U. Kölving and C. Mervaud (Oxford: Voltaire Foundation, 1997), vol.2, pp.1413–22.

22. See K. E. Khristodoulou, 'Alexandre le Grand chez Voltaire', in *Voltaire et ses combats*, ed. Kölving and Mervaud, 1423–34.

23. Voltaire's letter to the Maréchal de Belle-Isle of 4 August 1752 (D4966).

24. *Le Siècle de Louis XIV*, 'Avertissement, 1752' (Moland, vol.23, p.558).

25. *Le Siècle de Louis XIV*, chap.1 (*OH*, pp.617–18).

26. *Le Siècle de Louis XIV*, chap.22 (*OH*, p.871). Compare Voltaire's letter to Frederick II of Prussia on 5 August 1738 (D1574): 'If the Duchess of Marlborough had not spilt a bowl of water in front of Lady Masham, and a few drops on Queen Anne, Queen Anne would not have thrown herself at the Torys and would not have given France the peace which it needed to survive' ('Si la duchesse de Marlborough n'avait pas jeté l'eau d'une jatte au nez de milady Masham, et quelques gouttes sur la reine Anne, la reine Anne ne se fût point jetée entre les bras des Torys et n'eût point donné à la France une paix sans laquelle la France ne pouvait plus se soutenir').

27. See, for example, chapter 11 of the *Essai sur les mœurs* which treats the causes of the fall of the Roman Empire: 'Two misfortunes finally destroyed this great giant: the barbarians and religious disputes' ('Deux fléaux détruisirent enfin ce grand colosse: les barbares, et les disputes de religion', *EM*, vol.1, p.303).

28. See G. Benrekassa, *La Politique et sa mémoire: Le politique et l'historique dans la pensée des Lumières* (Paris: Payot, 1983), chap.3.

29. On these distinctions, see the second 'entretien' of Mably's *De la manière d'écrire l'histoire* (1783), ed. G. Bartalozzi and R. Minuti, at www.eliohs.unifi.it/testi/700/mably/ecrire.html.

30. *OH*, p.605.
31. *OCV*, vol.46, p.414.
32. Compare the *Lettre civile et honnête à l'auteur malhonnête de la 'Critique de l'histoire universelle' de M. de Voltaire qui n'a jamais fait d'histoire universelle* (1760). On this, see C. Volpilhac-Auger, 'Mably–Voltaire, match nul? Mably lecteur de l'*Essai sur les mœurs*', *Revue Voltaire*, 5 (2005), 235–48.

10

CHRISTIANE MERVAUD

Voltaire's correspondence

Voltaire's correspondence is arguably his masterpiece. No one would now suggest, as scholars once did, that 'it is to be read, not to be studied';[1] nonetheless the study of the correspondence poses many problems, for each single letter needs to be analysed with respect to its date and to the relationship between author and addressee. Generalisations are therefore unsafe, but this enormous corpus of letters remains at the heart of current research into Voltaire.[2]

The creation of the corpus

The great novelty of the Kehl edition (1784–9), the first edition of Voltaire's complete works published after his death in 1778, was that it was the first to include correspondence (some 4,500 letters in all); in the view of the editors, the presence of the letters in the edition was designed to show that 'the greatest of writers was also the best of men' ('le plus grand des écrivains fut aussi le meilleur des hommes'):[3] behind the marketing publicity for the edition lay an evident concern with the great man's posthumous reputation. The correspondence has figured in every complete edition of Voltaire's works ever since. The Beuchot edition, in the early nineteenth century, brought together 7,500 letters, and the tally had reached 10,000 in the Moland edition by the end of the century. The standard edition of reference is now that of Theodore Besterman, whose 'definitive edition', which includes letters written to Voltaire and also selected letters by third parties about Voltaire, reaches a total of 21,222, of which over 15,000 are by Voltaire himself.[4]

The very first letter, signed 'Zozo', is dated 29 December 1704 (though its authenticity has been questioned), while the last message dates from 26 May 1778: spread over seventy years, and with 1,800 correspondents, this corpus of letters is remarkable in every sense. In any year, new letters come to light, and the corpus continues to grow: the last letter which Frederick II wrote to

Voltaire, dated 15 April 1778, has recently been published, as has the correspondence of Voltaire's last secretary, Jean-Louis Wagnière;[5] the publication is awaited of other letters in library collections in Paris, Geneva and New York. On the other hand, some letters need to be excluded from the corpus: recent research has shown that 42 letters written from Berlin to Mme Denis are in fact 'epistolary pseudo-memoirs', composed by Voltaire after his return from Prussia as part of a (never-published) epistolary novel 'Paméla'.[6]

The corpus may be enormous, yet the losses are equally immense. Of the correspondence between Voltaire and Mme Du Châtelet, only fragments survive. Did Du Châtelet's husband perhaps burn the eight volumes of letters alluded to by one contemporary?[7] And what of the genuine letters which Voltaire wrote to his niece from Berlin? Were they destroyed in order to make way for the rewritten 'Paméla'? The letters constantly reveal the traces of other letters lost or destroyed, and there are gaps even in the exchanges with Voltaire's most prestigious correspondents, as witness the recent discovery of a letter from Voltaire to Frederick II dating from 1777.[8] Some letters were knowingly destroyed, as when Voltaire alleges that he has burned ninety-four anonymous letters that he has received (D14254). But on a brighter note, Louis XVI's order that Voltaire's papers should be seized after his death was never carried out.[9]

Even though editors no longer subscribe to the policy of the Kehl edition which (with a few exceptions) published only letters by Voltaire, the fact remains that Voltaire's correspondence is predominantly single-voiced. We have, for example, 1,202 letters from Voltaire to the Comte d'Argental, but only 41 of his replies; 559 letters to 'brother' Damilaville, yet only 18 in the other direction. Voltaire clearly did not keep all the letters he received. The Kehl editors exacerbated this imbalance, making enquiries across Europe in order to contact people who had received letters from Voltaire (in the *Courier de l'Europe* of 7 July 1780 they undertook to return all letters submitted to them). Another imponderable factor concerns the working practices of the Kehl editors, since they claim in the edition to have made cuts which it is now hard for us to evaluate: 'We have not printed all the letters we have collected: we have rejected those which tell us nothing about the author or his works, which, containing no judgements on men, affairs or books, could have held no interest' ('On n'a pas imprimé toutes les lettres qu'on a pu recueillir: on a supprimé celles qui, n'apprenant rien sur l'auteur, ni sur ses ouvrages, qui, ne renfermant aucun jugement sur les hommes, sur les affaires ou sur les livres, n'auraient pu avoir d'intérêt').[10] As we can see from the mutilations suffered by the correspondence between Voltaire and Frederick, early editors were liable to correct the text or delete a line, even a paragraph, for reasons of propriety, personal circumstance or political pressure.[11] The Besterman edition, which lists manuscripts (and where appropriate, printed editions), dates the letters, and provides editorial and explanatory notes, marks a significant advance over its predecessors. Progress in the two centuries since the Kehl edition has been qualitative as well as quantitative.

Variations in theme and form

The sheer volume of the correspondence makes it unique – Voltaire himself claimed in 1761 to be 'crushed by a correspondence stretching from Pondicherry to Rome' ('accablé d'une correspondance qui s'étend de Pondichéry jusqu'à Rome', D9542). It grows with the years: 11 letters in 1717; 16 in 1727; 162 in 1737; 101 in 1747; 436 in 1757; 844 in 1767; and 655 in 1777, when Voltaire is in his 80s. It is no surprise that the volume of letters should increase as Voltaire reaches middle age, at a time in his life when he is exiled from the capital and separated from his friends; but there is no slowing down in his old age. The overall impression is one of an astonishing 'presence' in the world. This multi-faceted mass of texts, with no unity of purpose, evolves over nearly 70 years. Some correspondents disappear, to be replaced by others. Some are life-long companions, such as Thiriot, whose presence in the correspondence begins in 1716 and lasts until his death in 1772, or the Comte d'Argental, present from 1724 until 1778. Others, like the Genevan painter Jean Huber, make a brief but dazzling appearance. There are the 'star' turns, where a sequence of letters in each direction allows us to follow Voltaire's dialogue with Frederick II, or Catherine II, or D'Alembert, or Mme Du Deffand. But out of these 1,800 correspondents, there are many obscure names too. Would we know the identities of the business managers of the Duke of Württemberg if Voltaire had not had a dispute with them about the repayment of his loans?

Ephemeral and aleatory, the correspondence is dominated by the affairs of the moment: the travails of life at court, when Voltaire is trying his chances at Versailles, or the pangs of the fugitive from Frankfurt after the appearance of the *Abrégé de l'histoire universelle*, but also the joys of settling at Les Délices and of overseeing the works at Ferney, or of following various judicial affairs. If the letters of a single day often share a family resemblance, other letters fit into long series, as when Voltaire orchestrates a campaign of denials following the scandal unleashed by the publication of the *Dictionnaire philosophique*.

There is a whole range of texts, from the utilitarian *billet* dashed off in a rush, to the carefully worked letters, some of them intended for publication.

When in England, Voltaire writes some of his letters in English; when held prisoner at Frankfurt, he addresses the city council in Latin; and he composes love letters to his niece in Italian. This use of other languages is explained in part by circumstances and by his wish for discretion, but it also reflects a certain linguistic specialisation, in which one can discern a reverence for the elite nature of Latin, a fondness for English, and sheer pleasure in using 'la lingua d'amore' (D3277). He wrote just one letter in German, during the Frankfurt episode (D5352), but he also amused himself by putting his secretary's name to a letter written in crude Swiss dialect (D13537).

The article 'Poste' in the *Questions sur l'Encyclopédie* emphasises the usefulness of the institution, 'the link in all business dealings and negotiations' ('le lien de toutes les affaires, de toutes les négociations'),[12] but this fine invention can be undermined. The censors are active, and in Prussia Voltaire is rightly suspicious: when in 1743 he is charged by the French government with an official mission at the court of Frederick, he writes and receives messages in code. When writing to men of business or to his publishers, especially Gabriel Cramer, Voltaire writes with business-like concision: 'Notes lead to conversation' ('Billets font conversation', D5164), and 'short letters and long friendships, that's my motto' (courtes lettres et longues amitiés, telle est ma devise', D466). With close friends he may not stand on epistolary ceremony, but he is never casual. The *billet* encourages in him brevity of thought and epigrammatic turns of phrase. The correspondence between Voltaire and the Comtesse de Bentinck, though made up of many short *billets*, has nonetheless all the trappings of epistolary art, including the requisite shafts of wit and finely turned compliments.[13]

Voltaire's correspondence, in common with others of its time, includes many letters containing verse, and some which even alternate between verse and prose, on the model of the *Voyage de Bachaumont et de Chapelle*. The Kehl edition collects the 'Lettres en vers et en prose' into one volume (volume 15), an editorial choice reflecting the prestige of poetry in this period. Voltaire had from an early age been part of this poetic culture, and he remained always faithful to it. From one poet to another, verse is expected, and poetic emulation is a key feature of his correspondence with Frederick, or with Cideville, a great lover of 'poetic bonbons' ('bonbons poétiques', D2209). Since 'good poetry is to good prose what dance is to a simple noble walk' ('la bonne poésie est à la bonne prose ce que la danse est à une simple démarche noble'),[14] so a compliment or an expression of thanks made in verse rings changes on the usual civilities.

We do not have a complete typology of Voltaire's letters, and more research remains to be done into the various epistolary genres. An important study of the early letters up to 1733, shows how the young Voltaire was deeply schooled in the traditions of letter-writing, and how he very quickly adapted and renewed the received models, forging in the process a wholly original voice.[15] Voltaire had, of course, to write letters of consolation, recommendation, thanks, advice, acknowledgement, praise, in addition to letters containing requests, complaints, excuses, denials; informal letters sit alongside official ones, letters of love and friendship alongside those of pure formality: the virtuosity of such a letter-writer explodes the carefully contrived categories of the literary theorist.

The Voltairean hallmark is a sign of concealment, and he makes frequent use of pseudonyms. This is sometimes for reasons of prudence: in 1754, 'Mme Daurade' designates Mme Denis, 'Cernin' Frederick II, and 'the imbecile abbé Godin' Louis XV.[16] Similar precautions are required during the Seven Years War when Voltaire, in correspondence with the Duchesse de Saxe-Gotha, is involved in obscure negotiations between the courts of Berlin and Versailles. More often, the use of pseudonyms is part of a society game. At the start of a letter from Voltaire to Condorcet, 'the butterfly *philosophe*, and much more *philosophe* than butterfly' ('Papillon philosophe, et beaucoup plus philosophe que papillon', D19617) refers, for the initiated, to Mme de Saint-Julien. Voltaire uses code names: D'Alembert is nicknamed 'brother Protagoras' ('frère Protagoras'), Diderot 'Tonpla' (from 'Platon', Plato), and the Abbé Morellet, 'Mords-les' ('Bite-them'). The d'Argentals are habitually referred to as his 'guardian angels' ('mes anges'), while the 'ox-tiger' ('le bœuf-tigre') designates Chancellor Pasquier. A whole sequence of letters to D'Alembert contain variations on a La Fontaine fable, 'The monkey and the cat' ('Le singe et le chat').[17]

Voltaire's letters embrace philosophical dissertations for the edification of the royal prince of Prussia, politico-military discussions during the Seven Years War, meditations on the meaning of life addressed to Mme Du Deffand, literary criticism and letters of philosophical camaraderie; and alongside these there are orders for food and wine, financial dealings and rebukes to publishers. Voltaire injects life into the most formal letter as into the briefest *billet*. However diverse these various missives, they share a certain indefinable tempo, characterised by an abrupt opening, an unexpected quotation, an aphoristic expression, and a cunning final turn of phrase. The reader can never remain indifferent to letters that dispense with the initial formalities and immediately establish the writer's presence: 'Ah! Madame, Madame, what have you done?' ('Ah! madame, madame, qu'avez-vous fait?', D13078) begins Voltaire as he reproaches Mme Du Deffand for her indiscretions. The index of quotations provided by the Besterman edition (volume 134) is testimony to the range of Voltaire's learning. The most frequently cited work by far is the Bible, and biblical references are subject to playful manipulation.[18] Brilliant and lapidary formulae abound in these letters, with maxims on all manner of subjects.[19] Voltaire has no equal in the art of signing off a letter so that the final point carries weight, and while he is perfectly familiar with epistolary protocol, he gives a personal and idiosyncratic twist to the standard conventions. Hence the numerous permutations of his signature: 'the old invalid V.' ('le vieux malade V.', D20735), 'the unworthy Capuchin' ('le capucin indigne', D16001), 'Christmoque' (D11060). The slogan 'Écrasez l'Infâme' ('Crush the despicable'), reduced to 'Ecrlinf' or even just 'E.L.', is an encoded sign of recognition and a rallying cry in his letters to Damilaville, the 'brother' who served as Voltaire's factotum and intermediary.[20] And Voltaire jokily deflates ceremony when he writes to the king of Prussia: 'I place myself at Your Majesty's feet. De profundis. V.' ('Je me mets aux pieds de Votre Majesté. De profundis. V.', D20393).

Documenting a life

In addition to their thematic and stylistic interest, Voltaire's letters also have evident documentary value. Described by his biographers as a 'document of the first importance' ('document capital') or as an 'exceptional instrument' ('instrument exceptionnel'), the correspondence provides the basis for understanding a man who, adulated and attacked in equal measure by his contemporaries, was a prime witness of the eighteenth century.

The correspondence furnishes both the account of a life and the chronicle of a century, the two being inseparable.[21] The letters give us a ringside seat from which to observe the unfolding of a life, with its daily preoccupations, with all its agitations and tensions, its successes and setbacks, its hopes and disappointments, its friendships and feuds. Certainly the letters afford an insight both fragmentary and partisan. It is important to avoid too positivist a reading and to bear in mind that any one letter presents us with a reality filtered and distorted through the prism of an individual shaping his or her language for the benefit of a particular correspondent. But, even if they do need to be deciphered, the letters nonetheless provide us with irreplaceable documentation.

What would we know of Voltaire without his letters? He wrote no *Confessions*, and his *Mémoires pour servir à la vie de M. de Voltaire*, written on the classical model, is no autobiography in the modern sense. His contemporaries have left numerous accounts of the man they found beguiling, but Voltaire's letters take us to the heart of the matter. How would we understand his decision to stay three years in Berlin, were it not for what the correspondence reveals about Frederick's seductive invitations and Voltaire's difficulties in France? How else could we imagine life at Les

Délices and at Ferney? The accounts left by visitors tell us about outward appearances. But it is in his letters that Voltaire reveals himself in all his vibrant dynamism.

Voltaire assumes many roles: the courtier, failing to make a success at Versailles; the informal negotiator between Frederick and the Duc de Choiseul during the Seven Years War; the lawyer, fighting judicial campaigns in favour of the victims of intolerance. No one is more active in the affairs of his time, no one quicker to have his say on the events of the moment. Thus the whole history of the period is refracted through this correspondence. Voltaire always sought out the company of the great and powerful. During the Ferney years, he corresponded with both Frederick II, king of Prussia, and with his rival, Catherine II of Russia, as well as with other highly placed figures – Choiseul, the virtual prime minister of France, the Duc de Richelieu, even Malesherbes. His connections extend to London, Vienna, Poland, Sweden, even the Vatican, and they make him, among other things, a privileged political commentator: he comments ironically, in verse and prose, on the invasion of Silesia by a peace-loving prince, and he provides immediate reaction to such events as the reversal of alliances, the French loss of Louisiana and of 'a few acres of snow' ('quelques arpents de neige') in Canada, the 'crusades' of Catherine against Polish dissidents or against the Turks, the partitioning of Poland, or the internal troubles of the republic of Geneva. Alongside these international events, Voltaire is much taken up with with internal French politics, changes of government, the fall of Choiseul, the arrival in power of Maupeou and the dissolution of the Parlement de Paris, the accession of Louis XVI, the country's financial difficulties. He is equally alert to religious politics, in particular the expulsion of the Jesuits, and to the doings of the judicial system as they were relayed in the daily news.

In these letters we breathe the very air of the eighteenth century, yet it would still not be true to say, as early editors did, that they reveal 'the man himself'. The correspondence does not tell us everything. Some of the most important events, such as the Hirschell affair,[22] are carefully concealed from view, while other moments emerge with great vividness, like the dramatic events of 1 March 1768, the subject in one biography of an entire chapter:[23] Mme Denis sides with Jean-François de La Harpe when he is accused of stealing a manuscript from Voltaire, and after a row, she secretly leaves Ferney for Paris; Voltaire, who only the day before had thrown his niece out, is in despair, but he recovers sufficient sang-froid to tell his friends about the arrival of his niece in the capital, writing fifteen letters in the space of one day.

Referring to Desnoiresterres's pioneering nineteenth-century biography of Voltaire, René Pomeau comments that this work does not deal with 'the *philosophe* who thinks, the writer who conceives, elaborates and composes' ('le philosophe qui pense, l'écrivain qui conçoit, élabore et rédige').[24] This aspect of the writer is amply revealed in the correspondence. Voltaire has plenty to say about the status of the writer and the world of the book trade. His trials and tribulations with the authorities, his various difficulties with his publishers, his ruses to overcome various obstacles, all reflect the different facets of the writer's life. We similarly find echoes of the successes and fiascos of the literary world, the polemics of the time, the diverse campaigns against the *philosophes*; various antagonists crop up in the letters – Jean-Baptiste Rousseau, Fréron, La Beaumelle, Crébillon père, the despised Jean-Jacques Rousseau – as well as allies such as La Harpe, and 'brothers' D'Alembert and Damilaville who relay messages to Diderot.[25]

Voltaire, in exile from the capital, still wants to be a presence in Parisian theatre, and the correspondence is brimming with allusions to the theatrical life of the period. The letters take us backstage at the Comédie-Française and reveal the capricious moods and rivalries of the actors. The triumvirate made up of d'Argental, Pont de Veyle and Thiriot propose corrections and help him have his plays performed; the actual performance of many a tragedy is thus replicated by an epistolary performance, and one equally rich in *coups de théâtre* and verbal sallies.

The references in the letters to works in preparation, to works being printed, to published works enjoying success and scandal, all bear witness to abundant intellectual activity. For the scholar studying or editing a work, the letters provide essential information, sometimes providing a sort of diary of a work's progress. What has been called 'this capturing, from the inside, of the moment of creation, of development, of meaning' ('cette saisie sur le vif, et comme de l'intérieur, de sa création, de son évolution, de sa signification')[26] exists in varying degrees. Voltaire rarely records for us the process of correcting his works, except in the case of the theatre, nor does he reveal his sources, which we have to guess by other means. Allusions to his own works are generally aimed at giving them publicity. It is rare for us to get right inside the writer's laboratory. On the subject of his *contes*, Voltaire maintains a complete silence, leaving critics to sift through the most meagre references. Certain parallels in theme and expression have been noticed, for example, between *Candide* and some of the letters – but which came first? In this utilitarian perspective, the letters can often be mined for useful facts. But they also demand to be read in a more integrated way if we want to understand Voltaire's thought in all its diversity.

Voltaire is open to every aspect of the world around him, and the letters speak of physics (especially in the Cirey years) and of natural sciences (in the need to combat materialism), of medicine and of economy, of literature and the fine arts, of politics and religion, of metaphysics and theology, sometimes education, and even, rather oddly, of military tactics (when in 1757 he proposes to Versailles and then to Catherine II a new model of tank). With fragments from various letters, one could easily piece together a tract on history, or on the status of the writer, a treatise on aesthetics or poetics or Enlightenment philosophy; the collected maxims of this *moraliste* would constitute a work of moral philosophy. Voltaire's fight against *l'Infâme*, pivotal to his whole philosophy, cannot be studied without reference to the correspondence, the workshop in which Voltaire's ideas and convictions are forged, and also the place where, stone by stone, a new church is constructed.[27] The letters are a launch pad for ideas, a sounding board, a place for experiment, a space for dialogue. *L'Infâme*, an emotional reality as much as a concept, enjoys an epistolary existence far greater than the slogan *Écrasez l'Infâme*. *L'Infâme* represents for Voltaire a combination of fanaticism and superstition, and it is in denouncing *l'Infâme*, as the campaigns to energise public opinion celebrate him as a righter of wrongs, that he fulfils his dream of becoming an apostle. This battle against *l'Infâme*, and notwithstanding the very real divisions within the *philosophes*' camp, consecrates the patriarch of Ferney as the figurehead of the Enlightenment. The correspondence does not merely bear witness to this campaign; it is its very incarnation.

The letter as tool

Voltaire never tires of repeating that he does not write for writing's sake, which would be a waste of his time and that of others; he writes for a purpose.[28] His letters are not primarily concerned with the social niceties, with keeping in touch for form's sake or with pouring out his feelings. On the contrary, they form part of a concerted programme in which each letter targets a particular addressee whose opinion or collaboration is solicited for that project. This is writing tailored to the reader's expectations.

Voltaire adheres to the golden rule of epistolary exchange, namely that one should adapt the message to the reader. He knows intimately the art of pleasing different correspondents and deploys a range of varied tones and styles. In letters to important people he exhibits a consummate art of flattery, relieved with just a hint of impertinence; the reconciliation between Voltaire and Frederick was brought about through the calculated use of comedy.[29] For an exchange to have any chance of lasting, the correspondent needs to be capable of holding his or her own. Voltaire and Frederick, despite their argument, collaborate in a theatrical *pas de deux*, as, in the course of their exchanges, they confront points of view and share together in an intellectual adventure. Voltaire enjoyed correspondents worthy of him, in particular Mme Du Deffand, for whom he goes to great lengths. These two virtuoso artists perform a dazzling sparring match, each with an assigned role, the Marquise conveying boredom and trenchant pessimism, the *philosophe* extolling the bracing virtues of hard work and unremitting activity. Another exceptional set of exchanges is that between the two men of letters, Voltaire and D'Alembert.

Voltaire's practice of letter-writing might be characterised as optimistic in the sense that he is undeterred by the difficulties of carrying on a dialogue at a distance, and by the traps and distortions inherent in all writing. His 'chameleon's soul' adapts to all comers, and he is equally at ease whether communicating with his sovereign or a distant relation, with a society lady or a banker, with a fellow *philosophe* or a cleric. Even if he on occasion complains of a correspondence which 'eats up time' ('emporte le temps', D9352), Voltaire remains generous. He never gives the impression to a correspondent that he or she might be bothersome, even when he is replying to some unknown person angling to receive an autograph from the master. Until the very end, the correspondence resonates with an appetite for life and a desire to communicate; it is always predicated on a respect for the other.

From his correspondents, Voltaire expects that they observe certain unspoken rules, principally that of confidentiality. He was betrayed, unpardonably so, by Frederick. On 17 August 1743, the king sent to Paris 'a part of a letter by Voltaire', with the instruction 'to have it sent to the Bishop of Mirepoix by an indirect means'; his aim was so to compromise Voltaire in France that he would have no other option than to come to Prussia (D2813). The king then dispatched an extract entitled 'some Voltaire sayings', including a sentence taken from one of the philosopher's letters and some insulting verses which he himself had forged. The hoax was so crude that no one apart from 'the ass of Mirepoix' was taken in.[30] Voltaire protested in the name of 'literary decency' against the publication of his private letters, condemning the appearance of the *Lettres secrètes de M. de Voltaire* in 1765 and the *Lettres de M. de Voltaire à ses amis du Parnasse* in 1766. There are other instances besides of letters circulating without Voltaire's agreement.

There are important distinctions to be drawn between letters that are strictly private and those intended more or less for public consumption. When Voltaire writes to Mme Du Deffand, for example, he knows that his letters will be enjoyed in her fashionable circle, hence their tone of seeming spontaneity held in check by a contrived theatricality. Damilaville is no more than the notional addressee of a good number of letters, and through his good offices Voltaire is able to engage in dialogue one of the 'brothers', or indeed the 'dear brothers', as a group. Thus the letter to Damilaville dated 4 October 1763 contains messages for both Diderot and Helvétius (D11445); in other letters, entire paragraphs are intended for D'Alembert (D11475, D14213). The letter of 14 April 1762, announcing the news of the death sentence passed on Calas, avoids any ambiguity in being addressed to 'my dear brothers' ('mes chers frères', D10406). These letters to Damilaville who played the role of intermediary ensured Voltaire a delegated presence in Paris. Damilaville diffused the letters, and Grimm used them as an argument for promoting his *Correspondance littéraire*.[31] In certain correspondences, licensed indiscretion can form part of the epistolary contract. Epistolary threesomes can sometimes resolve difficult situations by allowing a deferred dialogue between two people who do not wish to converse directly. It was under the aegis of the Margravine of Bayreuth that Voltaire and Frederick communicated with each other from January 1757 to October 1758, and, as both of them recognised, this recourse to a third party transformed the tenor of their exchanges.[32] Voltaire himself served as post-box between Choiseul and the King of Prussia, for some undercover negotiations.[33] The letter lends itself to a variety of strategies, with or without the consent of the addressee.

The authorial construction of a self-image is a rich theme in the correspondence. In place of direct emotional outpourings, we find a series of filtered, sometimes masked images of the self. We enjoy the discipline of the worldly writer scorning anything crude or clumsy, the refined politeness of a man of society, the impertinence of a mind keen to demystify, the pleasure of a writing demanding to be read between the lines. The image of the correspondent invites the letter-writer in his turn to invent a stylised image of himself. In the plethora of changing images, there are certain constants, for Voltaire cannot always reinvent himself: obliged to repeat himself, his approach to the world follows paths which, if not identical, are at least similar.

In the theatrical world of the correspondence, one role which is permanently Voltaire's is that of the invalid, 'always with one foot in the coffin, and the other doing a dance' ('toujours un pied dans le cercueil, et l'autre faisant des gambades', D414). His obsession with death becomes more insistent as the years pass, but Voltaire defies 'the grim reaper' ('la camarde', D19136), joking that the 'De profundis are at my backside' ('les De profundis me battent les fesses', D19624). In a more general way, Voltaire adopts postures and tries out roles, that of the farmer, that of the patriarch, that of the old hermit reuniting the brothers. His skirmishing manoeuvres in his campaigns of denial alternate with his offensive tactics in his campaigns of combat. At one moment he engineers our connivance in his game-playing, at another he takes the moral high ground, defending the fate of a victim of the judicial system and of religious fanaticism. Truly horrified by the La Barre affair, he styles himself the 'Don Quixote of all the broken and hanged men' ('le Don Quichotte de tous les roués et les pendus', D13453).[34]

The correspondence, this mass of heterogeneous and unfinished texts, can be read in many different ways. Yet each letter, each fragment of the whole, bears the mark of a consummate stylist and a penetrating mind; each letter affords us the immediate pleasure unique to great writing.

translated by Nicholas Cronk

NOTES

1. R. Naves, *Voltaire: L'homme et l'œuvre* (Paris: Boivin, 1942), p.97.
2. See M.-H. Cotoni, 'État présent des travaux sur la correspondance de Voltaire', *SVEC*, 320 (1994), 283–310. See also the brief selection of Voltaire's letters translated into English: *Select Letters of Voltaire*, trans. T. Besterman (London: Nelson, 1963).
3. G. and M. von Prochwitz, *Beaumarchais et le Courier de l'Europe: Documents inédits ou peu connus*, SVEC, 273–4 (1990), no. 285.
4. *Correspondence and Related Documents*, OCV, vols 85–135. The version of Besterman's edition which appears in the Bibliothèque de la Pléiade includes only letters written by Voltaire, and numbers 15,284 letters (*Correspondance*, 13 vols, ed. T. Besterman, Paris, Gallimard, 1963–93).
5. C. Mervaud, 'Un inédit de Frédéric II: sa dernière lettre à Voltaire, 15 avril 1778 (D21157)', *Revue Voltaire*, 5 (2005), 9–29; C. Paillard (ed.), *Jean-Louis Wagnière ou les deux morts de Voltaire* (Saint-Malo: Cristel, 2005).
6. See A. Magnan, *Dossier en Prusse (1750–1753)*, SVEC, 144 (1986), and *L'Affaire Paméla: Lettres de Monsieur de Voltaire à Madame Denis, de Berlin* (Paris: Méditerranée, 2004). This thesis builds on a suggestion of J. Nivat, 'Quelques énigmes de la correspondance de Voltaire', *Revue d'histoire littéraire de la France*, 53 (1953), 439–63.
7. See D app.26.
8. M.-H. Cotoni, 'Une lettre oubliée de Voltaire à Frédéric II', SVEC, 341 (1996), 165–7. See also C. Mervaud, *Voltaire et Frédéric II: Une dramaturgie des Lumières*, SVEC, 234 (1985), 544–63.
9. See D19031, D19033–6.
10. Kehl edition, vol.52, p.ii.
11. See Mervaud, *Voltaire et Frédéric II*, pp.541–3.
12. Moland, vol.20, p.257.
13. See F. Deloffre and J. Cormier (eds), *Voltaire et sa grande amie: Correspondance complète de Voltaire et de Mme Bentinck (1740–1778)* (Oxford: Voltaire Foundation, 2003).
14. *OH*, p.1187.
15. G. Haroche-Bouzinac, *Voltaire dans ses lettres de jeunesse (1711–1733): La formation d'un épistolier au XVIIIᵉ siècle* (Paris: Klincksieck, 1992).
16. See D5500, D5503 and D5529.

17. See D. Dawson, *Voltaire's Correspondence: An Epistolary Novel* (New York: Peter Lang, 1994), chap.5.

18. See F. Bessire, *La Bible dans la correspondance de Voltaire*, SVEC, 367 (1999).

19. See R. Roche, *Voltaire en sa correspondance: Approche thématique de l'homme et de l'œuvre par sa correspondance*, 8 vols (Bordeaux: L'Escampette, 1995–9).

20. See C. Mervaud, 'La logique du combat contre l'infâme: la correspondance de Voltaire et de "frère Damilaville"', *Raison présente*, 112 (1994), 3–25.

21. See J.-M. Moureaux, 'La correspondance de Voltaire: du document au monument?', *Revue internationale de philosophie*, 187 (1994), 77–91.

22. Voltaire apparently tried to speculate on bonds issued by the bank of Saxony which were sold at less than par and could be redeemed at face value only by Prussian subjects. He became involved in a damaging lawsuit with the Jewish businessmen, Hirschell father and son, whom he had employed as agents in this transaction.

23. T. Besterman, *Voltaire* (Oxford: Blackwell, 1969), chap.38.

24. VST, vol.1, p.xiii.

25. See J.-M. Moureaux, 'La place de Diderot dans la correspondance de Voltaire: une présence d'absence', *SVEC*, 242 (1986), 169–217.

26. J. Hellegouarc'h (ed.), *Voltaire: Correspondance choisie* (Paris: Livre de poche, 1997), p.xiv.

27. See J.-M. Moureaux, 'Voltaire apôtre: de la parodie au mimétisme', *Poétique*, 66 (1986), 159–77.

28. See D10863, D15139 and D17006.

29. Mervaud, *Voltaire et Frédéric II*, pp.391–418.

30. Mervaud, *Voltaire et Frédéric II*, pp.143–4.

31. See É. Lizé, *Voltaire, Grimm et la 'Correspondance littéraire'*, SVEC, 180 (1979).

32. Mervaud, *Voltaire et Frédéric II*, pp.265–95.

33. Mervaud, *Voltaire et Frédéric II*, pp.324–58.

34. See C. Mervaud, 'Voltaire et le *Cri du sang innocent*: l'affaire La Barre dans sa correspondance', *L'Infini*, 25 (1989), 135–45.

II

OLIVIER FERRET

Voltaire: pamphlets and polemic

Twenty-two chapters and almost four hundred pages *in octavo*: this is what it takes Sabatier de Castres to enumerate, in chronological order, the enemies with whom Voltaire clashed between the 1730s and 1768. Published in 1771, his brochure, which he presents ironically as the 'portrait' of Voltaire's 'mind', describes a literary career punctuated by a series of quarrels: as the title of the 1802 edition indicates, Voltaire's was a 'polemical life'.[1] Seen in this admittedly not entirely impartial way, the whole of Voltaire's life and works could be said to be polemical. It would be impossible to conjure these up in their entirety in just a few pages, so I shall instead focus on the characteristic features of some of those texts which have often been called 'facéties' or, more commonly, 'pamphlets'.[2]

The pamphlet is a double-edged sword, for Voltaire presumably ran the risk, by responding to a particular enemy, of giving that person a notoriety which his own works alone would never have earned him: La Beaumelle, the Marquis de Pompignan, Fréron and many others are only known today, surely, because of their noisy quarrels with Voltaire. So why does Voltaire resort to writing pamphlets? The strategy is in fact only paradoxical if we take for granted the longevity of his pamphlets. We need, therefore, to consider their reception from the very time of their composition. Their longevity is beyond doubt, particularly in the light of recent criticism which, by interrogating the notion of literarity, has contributed to a comprehensive re-evaluation of the literary hierarchy, an idea inherited from a view of literary history as a history of masterpieces, made up of 'great' and 'minor' texts.[3] Despite their strong referential basis, I would argue that Voltaire's pamphlets can still be read today and even offer us a rare way into a kind of laboratory in which new literary forms take shape. As far as the topicality of their composition is concerned, which in turn raises the question of how Voltaire himself perceived these texts, it is less easy to judge: it is not at all clear that in writing these pamphlets Voltaire intended to establish them as a body of works; on the contrary, it is even quite probable that he saw them

167

initially as ephemeral works invested with an immediate pragmatic aim, *hic et nunc*, whose function needs to be understood in rhetorical terms. With the development of the periodical press and the emergence of public opinion in the eighteenth century, Voltaire's recourse to the pamphlet could be linked to the creation of his media image, the orchestration of pamphlet campaigns in a sense prefiguring the press campaigns that were made possible during the Revolution by the establishment of freedom of the press in France. The pamphlet is in fact the site of the creation of a twofold image: the image of an enemy, on the one hand, who is represented in a grotesque and even odious way, and, on the other hand, the image, inversely polarised, that Voltaire wants to create of himself as a man of letters and a freethinking *philosophe*. I shall consider here, then, the scope that the pamphlet has for creating such images, highlighting in this way the main features of the genre, and I shall examine the public which the pamphlets aimed to reach.

Voltaire's campaign against Pompignan

The pamphlet campaign targeting Jean-Jacques Lefranc de Pompignan between 1760 and 1763 allows us to consider how, while playing with a variety of forms, Voltaire manages never to weary his public but instead to keep their attention focused on an enemy whom he treats somewhat like a literary character, endowing him with new features which serve to heighten the satire; and also how, ultimately, Voltaire silences his enemy, just as in learned controversies the aim was to leave one's opponent speechless. Pompignan started the quarrel in a dramatic way.[4] Elected to the Académie Française in 1759, on 10 March 1760 Pompignan delivered his acceptance speech, which quickly turned into a diatribe. It is not enough, he explains, simply to want to be a man of letters, let alone a *philosophe*: the works of the vain glories of the century bear 'the imprint of a degenerate literature, a corrupt morality and a pompous philosophy which undermines both the Crown and the Church' ('l'empreinte d'une littérature dépravée, d'une morale corrompue, et d'une philosophie altière, qui sape également le trône et l'autel'). Certain historians, he goes on to say, clearly alluding to Voltaire, also make a living by presenting 'maliciously falsified facts, invented anecdotes and satirical attacks on the most sacred things and on the most sound maxims of government' ('des faits malignement déguisés, des anecdotes imaginaires, des traits satiriques contre les choses les plus saintes, et contre les maximes les plus saines du gouvernement').[5] Voltaire's reply takes the form of *Les Quand*, each paragraph of which begins with the conjunction 'When' (hence the title) and which condemns his enemy by quoting word for word from his speech, while at the same time exonerating the *philosophes* of the charges levelled at them:

> When one is honoured with being received into a respectable company of men of letters, one's reception speech must not be a satire of men of letters: this is to insult both the company and the general public . . . When one gives one of those speeches before an academy that people talk about for a day or two, and which is even presented before the king, it is to do a disservice to one's fellow citizens to dare to say in that speech that contemporary philosophy undermines the foundations of the Crown and the Church.
>
> (Quand on a l'honneur d'être reçu dans une compagnie respectable d'hommes de lettres, il ne faut pas que la harangue de réception soit une satire contre les gens de lettres: c'est insulter la compagnie et le public . . . Quand on prononce devant une académie un de ces discours dont on parle un jour ou deux, et que même quelquefois on porte aux pieds du trône, c'est être coupable envers ses concitoyens d'oser dire dans ce discours, que la philosophie de nos jours sape les fondements du trône et de l'autel.)[6]

Not content simply to reply by writing more pamphlets of the same kind, Pompignan decided to write his self-defence in the form of a memoir addressed to the king, in which he takes it upon himself to declare that 'the whole universe' ('tout l'univers') needs to know that not only the king but also the queen and the entire royal family have 'appeared to take an interest' ('paru s'occuper') in his reception speech, 'not as if it were some passing or indifferent novelty, but as a work which was not unworthy of the particular attention of sovereigns' ('non comme d'une nouveauté passagère ou indifférente, mais comme d'une production qui n'était pas indigne de l'attention particulière des souverains').[7] This was enough to stir Voltaire's imagination again. Following the trend set by *Les Quand*, which had inspired the Abbé Morellet's *Les Si* and *Les Pourquoi*, Voltaire wrote *Les Qui*, *Les Quoi*, *Les Pour*, *Les Que*, *Les Oui* and *Les Non*, which he gathered under the title of *Assemblée des monosyllabes* and published in the *Recueil des facéties parisiennes*,[8] to be followed in 1761 by *Les Car* and *Les Ah! Ah!*[9] While dealing with Pompignan 'particle by particle' ('par les particules'), as Morellet puts it,[10] Voltaire also wrote a number of verse satires: *Le Pauvre Diable*, *Le Russe à Paris* and *La Vanité*.[11] He even wrote in journalistic vein: his *Extrait des nouvelles à la main de la ville de Montauban en Quercy* recounts the supposed amazement and distress of Pompignan's family on finding out about the *Mémoire présenté au roi*, some parts of which they consider to have been written by 'a madman' ('une tête attaquée').[12] Not content with reprimanding Pompignan, Voltaire also wrote songs about him, including the 'Chanson en l'honneur de maître Lefranc de Pompignan' in 1761 and, two years later, the 'Hymne chanté au village de Pompignan accompagné par des bourdons de M. de Pompignan, sur l'air de Béchamel'.¹³ Thus the attack on Pompignan lasted from 1760 to 1763, and Voltaire used every means at his disposal. Anything and everything could be used to make people laugh at the 'Moses of Montauban', including the unfortunate comparison that Dupré de Saint-Maur had made in his reply to Pompignan's acceptance speech: if Jean-Jacques Lefranc de Pompignan is Moses, then his brother, the Bishop of Le Puy, is Aaron. From this point on, in Voltaire's hands, Jean-Jacques and Jean-George share the shameful limelight.¹⁴ Voltaire also refers to Jean-Jacques's earlier tragedy, *Didon*: writing a *Fragment d'une lettre sur Didon*, he shows that Pompignan is just as bad at writing plays as he is at translating the Psalms and writing poetry.¹⁵ Over the years, Pompignan's every move will be satirised, including the consecration of the church he has built in his village, recounted in 1763 in the *Lettre de M. de l'Écluse chirurgien-dentiste, seigneur du Tilloy près de Montargis, à M. son curé*, or in the *Relation du voyage de M. le marquis Lefranc de Pompignan depuis Pompignan jusqu'à Fontainebleau adressée au procureur fiscal du village de Pompignan*. In the course of this pamphlet campaign, a kind of tendentious biography takes shape from one text to another, a biography that Voltaire, writing in the guise of his secretary, sums up in the letter he writes to Pompignan's secretary at the beginning of 1764. 'Here', he explains, 'is what M. de Voltaire knows about M. Lefranc de Pompignan':

1. Quite bad poetry;
2. His speech at the Académie, in which he insults all men of letters;
3. A *Mémoire au roi*, in which he tells His Majesty that he has a fine library at Pompignan-lez-Montauban;
4. The description of a fine feast he gave at Pompignan, of the procession in which he walked behind a young Jesuit, accompanied by the local drones, and of the great meal for twenty-six, which was the talk of all the province;
5. A fine sermon he wrote, in which he says that he is with the stars in the firmament, while the preachers of Paris and all men of letters are wallowing in the mud at his feet.

(Voici tout ce que M. de Voltaire connaît de M. Lefranc de Pompignan:

1. D'assez mauvais vers;
2. Son discours à l'Académie, dans lequel il insulte tous les gens de lettres;
3. Un *Mémoire au roi*, dans lequel il dit à Sa Majesté qu'il a une belle bibliothèque à Pompignan-lez-Montauban;
4. La description d'une belle fête qu'il donna dans Pompignan, de la procession dans laquelle il marchait derrière un jeune jésuite, accompagné des bourdons du pays, et d'un grand repas de vingt-six couverts, dont il a été parlé dans toute la province;

5. Un beau sermon de sa composition, dans lequel il dit qu'il est avec les étoiles dans le firmament, tandis que les prédicateurs de Paris et tous les gens de lettres sont à ses pieds dans la fange.)[16]

In this series of pamphlets, Voltaire presents his enemy in a whole series of different guises, usually as grotesque as possible and always liable to damage his reputation, using polemical strategies deriving from what Simon-Nicolas-Henri Linguet calls 'the art of fruitful slander' ('l'art de calomnier avec fruit').[17] Pompignan's style is, in Voltaire's hands, ridiculous, his arguments absurd and his principles odious: in short, Voltaire, not shy of making *ad hominem* attacks, knowingly makes Pompignan's life the reflection of his works, and vice versa. Profiting from the scope for imprecision that comes from anonymous and pseudonymous publication, Voltaire, like the hero of Vladimir Nabokov's *Despair*, becomes the past master of 'light-hearted, inspired lying'.[18]

Rhetoric and genre

This much was well known by the royal officials responsible for policing booksellers, a role they performed with some leniency. The limits imposed by defamation were the concern not so much of the censors as of the law courts: legislation outlawed the writing and publishing of 'defamatory pamphlets'; those responsible for overseeing booksellers could refer to the law and justify their first concern to regulate the circulation of printed matter in an attempt to control it. As long as an author did not tackle, in an openly critical way, political or religious questions – which were still highly sensitive issues under a divinely ordained monarchy – then a lot was tolerated, in particular polemical texts about writers of all colours. Successive 'directeurs de la librairie' (heads of the government department controlling the book-trade) in the second half of the century maintained a position of impartiality vis-à-vis literary quarrels, judging that an author could legitimately exercise his right of reply. Numerous pamphlets were published, then, with permission which was 'tacit' but nevertheless entirely official. Voltaire's pamphlets, though his works were closely monitored, were no exception.

This much was well known by the readers of pamphlets, too: far from being the gullible victims of slander, as the virtuous opponents of these 'defamatory pamphlets' would claim, they were rather people of 'bad faith', in Jean-Paul Sartre's sense of the term, who, in an act of denial, would, while fully aware that all pamphlets contained their fair share of falsehoods, establish nevertheless a kind of malign pact with the author, allowing them to pretend to ignore the existence of these falsehoods. For his part the author had to foster and maintain this complicity, making it acceptable while keeping his attacks within the confines of 'good taste'. With the notable exception of certain particularly unpleasant texts attacking Jean-Jacques Rousseau,[19] Voltaire's success derives from the fact that he took care to be amusing rather than odious.

The formal diversity of the texts written in the campaign against Pompignan is an essential ploy, found again in a number of Voltaire's other pamphlets: in 1767, *Les Honnêtetés littéraires*, which, in addition to Nonnotte and others, attacks La Beaumelle, Pompignan, Fréron and Charles Palissot de Montenoy, is made up of a number of chapters based on a variety of different genres;[20] Voltaire's use of lists was already in evidence as early as 1738 during his quarrel with the Abbé Desfontaines (*Le Préservatif*), as was, the following year, the potential of the legal statement (*Mémoire du sieur de Voltaire*);[21] Voltaire's numerous confrontations with Fréron give rise to a series of anecdotes (*Anecdotes sur Fréron*) as well as a comedy (*L'Écossaise*).[22] It is clear that polemics can also inform works in other well-established genres, as demonstrated by several of Voltaire's short stories: *La Princesse de Babylone* ends with an invocation to the Muses which provides the context for a new salvo against the 'loathsome Coger, professor of gossip at the collège Mazarin' ('le détestable Coger, professeur de bavarderie au collège Mazarin'), the 'pedant Larcher' ('le pédant Larcher'), 'Master Aliboron, known as Fréron, hitherto a so-called Jesuit' ('maître Aliboron, dit Fréron, ci-devant soi-disant jésuite') and 'the worthy son of Fr Desfontaines' ('digne fils du prêtre Desfontaines'), Abraham Chaumeix and 'sieur Riballier';[23] Jean-Jacques Rousseau is taken to task in *L'Homme aux quarante écus*;[24] Candide's time in Paris sees him coming across a 'fat pig' ('gros cochon') of a 'hack', that is 'someone who churns out articles by the dozen, a Fréron' ('un faiseur de feuilles, un Fréron').[25] Once pamphlet-like attacks are found outside the confines of pamphlets proper, it becomes difficult to say with any certainty what the precise characteristics of the pamphlet genre are.

The rhetorical function of the texts therefore prompts us to see in Voltaire's works a more wide-ranging kind of pamphlet-writing which allows him to construct both a negative image of his enemies and a positive image of himself. In 1753 La Beaumelle published an annotated edition of the *Siècle de Louis XIV*, complete with a large number of polemical 'remarks' directed against Voltaire; equally aggressive were C.-F. Nonnotte's *Les Erreurs de Voltaire*, published in 1762, with an enlarged version appearing in 1766. But the criticisms that La Beaumelle – the 'novelist' responsible for the *Mémoires de Madame de Maintenon* – levels at the author of the *Siècle de Louis XIV* and the 'errors' that Nonnotte claims to unearth in the *Essai sur les mœurs* all give Voltaire the opportunity, in particular in *Les Honnêtetés littéraires*, to depict himself as an impartial and philosophical historian. The arguments he has with the editors of the *Observations sur les écrits modernes* and *L'Année littéraire* – 'that worm born out of Desfontaines's arse' ('ce vermisseau né du cul de Desfontaines'), to quote the memorable phrase in *Le Pauvre Diable*[26] – allow him to mount a defence of the figure of the writer and to distinguish the latter from the 'hack', while at the same time no doubt expressing a certain anxiety about the readership enjoyed by these press organs, with their constant onslaught on the *philosophes*. The pamphlets also contribute to the positive image of the *philosophes*, in contrast to the reactionary figures of the anti-*philosophes*, and this becomes yet more systematic from the 1760s, when Voltaire is christened by one of his enemies the 'oracle of the new freethinkers' ('l'oracle des nouveaux philosophes').[27] More than contributions to mere personal quarrels, then, these pamphlets engage with the interests of an entire group. Hence the lessons of the campaign against Pompignan: in part, since the polemic has its origins at the very heart of the Académie Française, Voltaire wants to lead the counter-attack as a fellow member of an organisation so emblematic of intellectual power but in which the *philosophes* are by no means in the majority;[28] and also, by ridiculing Pompignan, Voltaire wants to limit the danger posed by a figure who, with the support of the devout clan at Versailles, wishes to be, together with his brother, the Bishop of Le Puy, tutor to the king's children. For Voltaire, this influence of the anti-*philosophes* over the future ruler of France, were it ever to be exercised, would bring dangerously close the prospect of a political regime yet more hostile towards the *philosophes* than that of Louis XV. He writes to D'Alembert in 1761, observing that they should 'prevent Pompignan from causing harm by showing how much harm he wants to cause' ('Mettons-le hors d'état de nuire en faisant voir combien il veut nuire', D10080); and in 1763 he concludes a letter to Damilaville: 'This man wants to do us harm, but he will succeed only in making us glad' ('Cet homme voudrait nuire, et il ne fera que nous réjouir', D11121). In terms of media image-making, ridicule kills, and what is at stake is all the more important since the literary quarrels, far from being the sign simply of the touchy nature of writers, actually impinge upon religion and politics. The *philosophes* seemed to have won a victory when the king's eldest son, one of Pompignan's most faithful supporters, apparently quoted back at Pompignan the last line of *La Vanité*, one of the most humiliating ever aimed at him by Voltaire, thus signalling his utter failure: 'And our friend Pompignan thinks he is something special!' ('Et l'ami Pompignan pense être quelque chose!').[29]

The public sphere

Defining what is at stake in the decision to write pamphlets therefore involves identifying the power relations at work in a strategy aimed at assuming intellectual power in the institutional field and, more broadly, in the literary public sphere. Roland Barthes may be right to claim that Voltaire had 'the unusual pleasure . . . of having to struggle in a world where strength and stupidity were constantly on the same side' ('le bonheur singulier . . . d'avoir à combattre dans un monde où force et bêtise étaient continûment du même bord').[30] It is nevertheless true that this 'world', even if it seems progressively to be won over to the cause of the *philosophes* – and this is also the result of Voltaire's offensive, and the pamphlets are part of this undertaking – is far from being pacified, as these very pamphlets demonstrate. Moreover, we can get a better sense of their significance by considering the public to which they were addressed. Voltaire's unique geographical situation, based in Ferney from 1759 onwards, is well known: it explains the way in which the pamphlets were distributed, usually being printed by the Cramer publishers in Geneva before being transported to Paris via a network of correspondents. Voltaire's correspondence thus allows us to follow when and how texts were sent to certain privileged recipients: Frederick II in particular, who received most of the texts; men of the world (such as the Comte d'Argental) who mix in influential circles (be it directly or indirectly, the minister Choiseul knew about much of the production of pamphlets); people who frequent the salons (Mme Du Deffand, Mme Geoffrin, the Marquis d'Agence); close friends (Mme de Fontaine, Mme Denis); and last but not least, those whom Voltaire calls his 'brothers',[31] both in Paris (Thiriot, D'Alembert, Damilaville, Mme d'Épinay – and, through her, Grimm, editor of the *Correspondance littéraire*) and in the provinces (Charles Bordes, in Lyon). The 'brothers' thus play a crucial role in the circulation of texts in Paris both in philosophical circles and in the world of booksellers (a number of pamphlets are reprinted by Robin, Merlin and, from 1766 onwards, Lacombe, who almost becomes Voltaire's 'official' publisher in Paris). It also seems to have been possible, as the role of Bordes in this distribution network suggests, for texts to be made available to the reading public in the provinces, though the evidence for this is largely lacking. The circulation of Voltaire's pamphlets is part of a twofold strategy. Firstly, it is about ensuring the good will, if not the complicity, of those in power: the tactic is part of Voltaire's underlying aim to win over the elites and polite society more generally.[32] However, although the great often thought first and foremost about their own interests and displayed a particularly keen awareness of what distinguished them from men of letters, including Voltaire, the patriarch of Ferney nevertheless realised that 'opinion governs the world; but it is the wise who ultimately shape it' ('l'opinion gouverne le monde; mais ce sont les sages qui à la longue dirigent cette opinion').[33] And this is why, secondly, numerous pamphlets allude to the judgements to be made by 'the public' on the quarrels presented to them for their assessment. This 'public' is certainly a vague category, and one, moreover, in a state of flux, but it also prefigures what we might call, in the light of the work of Jürgen Habermas and historians of cultural practices, public opinion.[34]

Voltaire is, moreover, a past master in the art of using the resources of the periodical press. It is true that in the world of eighteenth-century journalism, the *philosophes* were far from enjoying a position of strength: faced with Fréron's *L'Année littéraire*, with its large audience, they could only really count on the *Journal encyclopédique* and the *Correspondance littéraire*, which, although distributed to a limited readership in manuscript form, nevertheless played a strategic role. (The *Mercure de France*, although at one time edited by Jean-François Marmontel, can hardly be considered a vehicle for the discourse of the *philosophes*.) Voltaire, who saw clearly what was at stake in the development of the press, appears eager, when about to launch a pamphlet, to start spreading rumours about it, to arouse interest in it and, in short, to control its reception. Thus the periodical press is an effective vehicle for spreading the word about his pamphlets, the existence of which they often refer to and the most striking parts of which they sometimes quote. In terms of a pamphlet strategy, if it is vital that a pamphlet should have a definite impact and that the power of the text be prolonged and increased by the texts to which it in turn gives rise, then victory has surely been secured once the deadliest attacks on one's enemy start being repeated by others. The essential thing is that everyone should talk about pamphlets.

But why can we still talk about them today? And are Voltaire's pamphlets of any interest beyond the confines of the history of ideas or the history of the disputes that went on in what we might call the eighteenth-century 'republic of letters'? The allusions that these topical texts contain are to a large extent lost on the reader who has no access to the circumstances of their composition: this is true both for the modern reader and for certain eighteenth-century readers. That this is the case is demonstrated by the way in which some of these pamphlets were reprinted in collections: the editors furnish them with forewords and footnotes, providing, in embryonic form, a kind of critical edition, which is also, in a sense, what contemporary and subsequent editions of the complete works of Voltaire try to do, right up to and including the edition currently being produced in Oxford by the Voltaire Foundation, albeit in a more systematic way. That said, the aim is not the same now: modern editors are concerned not with trying to prolong the ability of the text to harm those whom it targets, but with trying to give the reader those elements which make the text fully readable. However little we may know about those things referred to in the footnotes, these pamphlets, which practise the art of polite insult, provide access to entertaining and neglected aspects of Voltaire's œuvre. If Voltaire appears to be more innovative when writing in those forms which are the least codified or the least prized in the hierarchy of literary genres,[35] he is absolutely free when he is writing what he calls his 'little pies' ('petits pâtés'), 'bits of old rubbish' ('rogatons') and other 'loads of bollocks' ('couillonneries'). It is in such works that his imagination runs wild, new forms take shape and a new style is created, all of which influence the rest of his work.

translated by Russell Goulbourne

NOTES

1. [A. Sabatier de Castres], *Tableau philosophique de l'esprit de M. de Voltaire, pour servir de suite à ses ouvrages, et de mémoires à l'histoire de sa vie* (Geneva: [Cramer], 1771); *Vie polémique de Voltaire, ou Histoire de ses proscriptions, avec les pièces justificatives* (Paris: Dentu, 1802).

2. See O. Ferret, *La Fureur de nuire: Échanges pamphlétaires entre philosophes et antiphilosophes (1750–1770)*, SVEC, 2007:03. J. Macary has twice edited collections of the 'facéties': Voltaire, *Facéties*, Paris: Presses universitaires de France, 1973, and Paris: L'Harmattan, 1998; see also the critical study by D. Guiragossian, *Voltaire's 'Facéties'* (Geneva: Droz, 1963). I shall not consider here Voltaire's many anti-biblical works, focusing rather only on those quarrels which see Voltaire engaging directly with his enemies.

3. See C. Volpilhac-Auger (ed.), *Œuvres majeures, œuvres mineures?* (Lyon: ENS, 2004).

4. On this quarrel, see T. E. D. Braun, *Le Franc de Pompignan: Sa vie, ses œuvres, ses rapports avec Voltaire* (Paris: Lettres modernes, 1972).

5. J.-J. Lefranc de Pompignan, *Discours de réception prononcé devant l'Académie française, le 10 mars 1760* (Paris: Brunet, 1760), pp.4–5.

6. Moland, vol.24, pp.111–12.

7. J.-J. Lefranc de Pompignan, *Mémoire présenté au roi le 11 mai 1760* (n.p., 1760), p.58.

8. Moland, vol.10, pp.560–4.

9. Moland, vol.24, pp.261–4.

10. A. Morellet, *Mémoires de l'abbé Morellet, de l'Académie française, sur le dix-huitième siècle et sur la Révolution*, ed. J.-P. Guicciardi (Paris: Mercure de France, 1988), p.99. On Morellet, see R. Darnton, *The Literary Underground of the Old Regime* (Cambridge, MA: Harvard University Press, 1992), chap.2.

11. Moland, vol.10, pp.97–131.

12. Moland, vol.24, p.125.

13. Moland, vol.10, pp.567–71.

14. Voltaire's quarrel with J.-G. Lefranc de Pompignan is explicitly about religious matters. In *Les Honnêtetés littéraires*, for example, Voltaire attacks him as the author of the *Instruction pastorale . . . sur la prétendue philosophie des incrédules modernes et sur l'hérésie* (Paris: Gaubert, 1763): see *OCV*, vol.63B, p.80.

15. Moland, vol.22, pp.231–2. In *Le Pauvre Diable*, Voltaire sums up Pompignan's 'sacred canticles' ('cantiques sacrés') with the incisive line: 'Sacred they must be, for nobody touches them' ('Sacrés ils sont, car personne n'y touche', Moland, vol.10, p.105).

16. Moland, vol.25, p.138.

17. [S.-N.-H. Linguet], *Théorie du libelle, ou l'Art de calomnier avec fruit* (Amsterdam: n.p., 1775). This text, itself a kind of pamphlet, is an attack on Morellet's *Théorie du paradoxe* (Amsterdam: n.p., 1775).

18. V. Nabokov, *Despair* (London: Weidenfeld and Nicolson, 1966), p.14.

19. See, for example, the picture that Voltaire paints of Jean-Jacques Rousseau in 1767 in *La Guerre civile de Genève*, *OCV*, vol.63A.

20. See the edition of *Les Honnêtetés littéraires* by O. Ferret, *OCV*, vol. 63B, p.1–174; and also C. Lauriol, *La Beaumelle: Un protestant cévenol entre Montesquieu et Voltaire* (Geneva: Droz, 1978), J. Balcou, *Fréron contre les philosophes* (Geneva: Droz, 1975), and D. Delafarge, *La Vie et l'œuvre de Palissot, 1730–1814* (Paris: Hachette, 1912).

21. *Le Préservatif*, Moland, vol.22; *Mémoire du sieur de Voltaire*, *OCV*, vol. 20A. On Desfontaines, see T. Morris, *L'Abbé Desfontaines et son rôle dans la littérature de son temps*, *SVEC*, 19 (1961).

22. *Anecdotes sur Fréron*, *OCV*, vol.50; *L'Écossaise*, *OCV*, vol.50.

23. *OCV*, vol.66, pp.204–10. Coger, Larcher and Riballier all participate in the controversy caused in 1767 by the publication of Marmontel's *Bélisaire*: see J. Renwick, *Marmontel, Voltaire and the 'Bélisaire' affair*, *SVEC*, 121 (1974).

24. *OCV*, vol.66, pp.371–2.

25. *OCV*, vol.48, p.213.

26. Moland, vol.10, p.103.

27. [C.-M. Guyon], *L'Oracle des nouveaux philosophes pour servir de suite et d'éclaircissement aux œuvres de M. de Voltaire* (Paris: Hérissant, 1759).

28. See J. Lough, 'Did the *Philosophes* take over the Académie Française?', *SVEC*, 336 (1996), 153–94.

29. *La Vanité, par un frère de la doctrine chrétienne*, Moland, vol.10, p.118. Voltaire alludes to this episode in a letter to Thiriot of 1760 (D9449).

30. R. Barthes, 'Le dernier des écrivains heureux', in *Essais critiques* (Paris: Seuil, 1964), p.96.

31. See J.-M. Moureaux, 'Voltaire apôtre: de la parodie au mimétisme', *Poétique*, 66 (1986), 159–77.

32. See J. Sareil, *Voltaire et les grands* (Geneva: Droz, 1978).

33. *Conformez-vous aux temps*, Moland, vol.25, p.318.

34. See J. Habermas, *The Structural Transformation of the Public Sphere: An Inquiry into a Category of Bourgeois Society* (1962), trans. T. Burger and F. Lawrence (Cambridge: Polity Press, 1989), and R. Chartier, *Les Origines culturelles de la Révolution française* (Paris: Seuil, 1990).

35. This is certainly the case in those texts in which Voltaire disrupts generic categories: on these, see the articles in *Revue Voltaire*, 6 (2006).

I2

JOHN RENWICK

Voltaire and the politics of toleration

It would be an understandable mistake if, in seeking a working definition of the problem of toleration, we came to believe that it was essentially a matter for theological debate.[1] Works of reference rarely explain that, in the eighteenth century, even the Church looked upon this theological issue as being, in parallel, a practical problem with distinct political ramifications. Similarly, Voltaire's own concern with toleration – all too easily linked with his campaign against l'Infâme (dogmatic, revealed religion in all its worst manifestations) – was always deeply political. Furthermore we cannot adequately define the political nature and above all the specificity of Voltaire's views on toleration with reference to Voltaire alone. He did not evolve in a self-sufficient vacuum. For example, his celebrated Traité sur la tolérance (1763) was long presented – even by the most reputable scholars – as though it was to be understood with exclusive reference to his campaign against l'Infâme. A more appropriate reading takes account of the years 1751–62 which saw a concerted campaign for and against toleration within a particular political and economic framework where Voltaire responds belatedly to specific conservative proponents of the status quo.[2] No investigation, therefore, into Voltaire's complex views can possibly dispense with some preliminary examination of the background against which those views evolved and to which they often ultimately proved to be a response.

Persecution of the Protestants to the 1750s

The Edict of Nantes (1598), a peace treaty established between the two rival religious and political camps, Catholic and Protestant, guaranteed the latter liberty, security and civil rights. However, after the supposed success of the numerous anti-Huguenot edicts of the 1660s onwards, and the missionary zeal of the Church in reclaiming those who had erred and strayed, Louis XIV's religious advisers persuaded him to believe that the task of conversion was complete. The Edict of Nantes, now addressing a 'non-existent' problem, was therefore revoked. The sixty-five years which separated the Revocation of the Edict of Nantes (1685) from the first of the numerous exchanges of the 1750s on the Protestant 'problem' are a catalogue of disasters. Preceding, and immediately following, the Revocation there had occurred the gradual depopulation of the kingdom which had also led to the export of capital along with the exodus of professional and manufacturing skills, which went to benefit Protestant states which were already, or about to be, serious rivals to French influence in the world. In the fifteen years following the Revocation, the government – having to deal with considerable numbers of recalcitrant Protestants who now had no legal status – embarked upon a combined policy of persecution, repression and vexatious *dragonnades* (the quartering of dragoons upon Protestant households, a costly and unpleasant experience). Such cruelty led directly, in the years 1700–15 (the time of the War of Spanish Succession) to the ruinous civil strife known as the *Guerre des Camisards* which served to prove yet again that Huguenots – animated since the middle of the sixteenth century by a spirit of independence which necessarily led, through 'Republicanism', to 'sedition' – continued to be a highly dangerous element within the body politic of the nation. Necessarily, war and the deleterious conditions of existence hastened their renewed emigration. Thereafter this disturbing situation was exacerbated on three separate occasions by repressive legislation that prompted yet further departures: in 1724, the Edict of Fontainebleau distilled in draconian fashion all the anti-Huguenot legislation of the previous sixty years; in 1745 came the Ordonnance ordering the forced baptism of all Protestant children and, often, their removal from their parents for safer keeping in Catholic hands; in 1750, consecrating ten years of sporadic persecution of those Protestants who had contracted marriage vows in the presence of their pastors (thus flagrantly refusing to acknowledge Canon Law and marry according to Catholic rites), the government decreed that all people who had thereby contravened article 15 of the Edict of Fontainebleau should be prosecuted. In 1739, breaking with the usual tradition of turning a blind eye to such contraventions, Saint-Florentin, Ministre de la Maison du Roi (Minister of the King's Household), had given the *présidial de Nîmes* permission to prosecute contraveners. Immediately the Parlements of Grenoble, Toulouse and Bordeaux followed suit. Several hundred marriages were declared null and void, the men were condemned to the galleys, the women to prison, and their goods confiscated. This response (fortified by the decree of 17 January 1750) was to remain the standard response until the mid-1750s.

In sum, ever since 1685 (and in practice since well before that date), being pursued for Protestant convictions had often been a cruel experience: fines, confiscation of property, imprisonment, flogging, branding, the galleys, death. Such punishments were not applied consistently, and Protestant fortunes knew erratic ebbs and flows: some periods were calmer, more tolerable than others, and varied from province to province. Everything depended upon seemingly unconnected, even extraneous circumstances (such as foreign policy), or the modus vivendi of state and Church at any given moment, or even upon local conditions and humours. And yet, even in the case of the worst manifestations of intolerance, we are looking at what the historian might call 'l'écume des choses et des jours': that surface froth, or those superficial appearances which hide a deeper reality.

The various emerging patterns that can be discerned in the 1750s (well before Voltaire became active in 1762) show that attitudes were changing. Many influential people – statesmen and lawyers, public-spirited individuals and the educated social elite – increasingly found themselves confronted with a political, legal and moral situation which defied common sense. The state was arguably the least comfortable with this complex and apparently insoluble problem of its own making. When, in our modern world, laws become obsolete or counter-productive, governments may take steps to rescind them. No such solution was available to Louis XV. The Revocation of 1685 could not be undone since Louis XIV had stipulated that it was to be 'perpétuelle et irrévocable'. How then was the government to work with unworkable legislation, precisely at a period when – despite policies designed to ensure the contrary – Protestantism was experiencing a revival, and demonstrating a vitality which stupefied all concerned observers? What, moreover, to do when it was becoming increasingly evident that France, seriously weakened by the War of Austrian Succession (1741–8), had to find radical solutions to its mounting financial problems?

The initiative which ignited the great debate of the 1750s, and which proved that the law of the land and the needs of the land were totally at variance, occurred in this economic context.[3] In the spring of 1751, Machault, the *contrôleur général des finances*, concluded that the Huguenots, and particularly the Huguenots of the diaspora, whose aptitude for commerce was well established, should be invited to help extricate France from its mounting economic crisis. When his indulgence was discovered, the reaction of the Church was instantaneous: Gilbert de Chabannes, Bishop of Agen, set the tone for the conservative responses in favour of the status quo. In his open reply to Machault, he adopted a stance which was essentially political: time and again he stressed the fact that Protestants were factious, seditious, untrustworthy Republicans whose reintegration would be folly.[4]

Such attitudes did not go unchallenged. Protestants found an increasing number of influential allies in that most conservative of professions – the law. Lawyers were naturally predisposed to express anxiety about the anti-Huguenot legislation because the very spirit of the law of the land is not best served in being ignored or circumvented by the ad hoc responses which Versailles either itself made or allowed its representatives in the field (provincial governors, *intendants*, military commanders) to make on its behalf. But the essence of their disquiet, like that of Chabannes, was political. Lawyers were unhappy with the consequences of the Edict of Fontainebleau because it regularly caused civil disruption. More particularly they were concerned by the most frequent and enduring cause of upheaval, namely article 15 of the Edict of 1724 which stipulated that all marriages were to be celebrated in accordance with Catholic rites. Indeed the major grievance of many French Calvinists in the 1750s was not their right to freedom of worship, nor even the prospect of their reintegration into the mainstream of French political and economic life, but the validation of their marriages. Many lawyers were disturbed by the growing discrepancy between law and practice in this domain, as Protestants were contracting clandestine marriages 'in the wilderness' ('le Désert'), the biblical term adopted by Protestants after the Revocation to designate those inaccessible places in the countryside where they gathered to perform their forbidden religious duties, to solemnise their marriages and have their children baptised. Such illegal marriages rendered their children illegitimate and hence incapable of inheriting, and with increasing frequency such marriages were giving rise to lawsuits (usually brought by disgruntled collaterals) concerning legitimacy and inheritance which undermined the principles of family solidarity, parental authority and the orderly transmission of property down the generations. These marriages were also causing lawsuits as a result of the repudiation of one partner by the other on the convenient grounds that a marriage celebrated 'in the wilderness' was illegal and therefore null. But, above all, such problems were understood to signify that all the parties involved were giving explicit agreement to the contention that the marriage of all French subjects should conform to canon law. Many lawyers found such a contention to be an unreasonable demonstration of the Church's influence over human affairs and an encroachment upon fields that should rightly concern the state alone.

It was against such a background that certain lawyers (and even some of Louis XV's ministers) started to advocate a form of civil union as an answer to the problem. Such a stance also reflected a political agenda. The numerous ideological statements made by those lawyers in the *civiliste* tradition reflect their hostility to clerical (*canoniste*) control of the civil status of French subjects. These lawyers bitterly regretted the surrender of the royal prerogative (made at the time of the Council of Trent) to the *canonistes* as regards the moral obligation placed upon sovereigns to guarantee a secure family status for all their subjects irrespective of creed. That is why, in the thirty-odd contributions to this particular debate in the years 1752–65,[5] we are often witnessing subterranean, highly political confrontations between state and Church, between supporters of monarchical independence and ultramontane subservience to Rome. (Equally, the *grands commis* or high office-holders of state at Versailles, and the king's various representatives in the provinces were, by working against the views of the bishops and the General Assemblies of the Church, just as deliberately helping the monarchy to withstand the intransigent claims of the clergy and its militant traditionalist supporters.) Two other types of motivation should be mentioned because, though not political, they were not without significance. As the century progressed, and as the phenomenon known as dechristianisation or secularisation gained momentum, France experienced in tandem either religious indifference or a growing preference for religious liberalism. Secondly, there is that closely allied phenomenon which is the urbane ideal of *honnêteté* or *politesse* as embraced by the urban social elites, particularly in Paris. Those elites were, as the century progressed, looking with increasing disapproval upon the negative treatment of Protestants as being unworthy of a polite and cultured society.

Finally, the most widespread argument of all is also the simplest. Numerous champions of Protestant civil rights – encompassing lay and ordained members of both the Catholic and Protestant communities, intellectuals, liberals and compassionate deists, who were all essentially but not exclusively concerned by France's dramatic retreat from pre-eminence in the world – constantly invoked the demographic, commercial and economic stagnation of the country. It was an emotively powerful argument which had been given prominence, just after the Revocation, in *Les Soupirs de la France esclave* (1687), which had been used by Montesquieu, Prévost, Voltaire and sundry *encyclopédistes*, and which would still be figuring prominently, just before the long-awaited Edict of Toleration, in Malesherbes's two *Mémoires sur le mariage des Protestants* (1785, 1787). It was indeed an argument which, in the period 1687–1787, seemed more and more pertinent as an increasingly ailing France could only look on while Holland and England, had – thanks to their tolerant spirit – allied increasing strength with rampant prosperity. In sum, if France were to re-assert itself, one of the means available was to grant Calvinists civil status and give them the opportunity to turn their talents and their energies towards the regeneration of the state in an atmosphere conducive to genuine incorporation and reconciliation.

Although Voltaire did not play any active role in this unfolding campaign of the 1750s, there were many points of contact between his views on toleration and those of his contemporaries. Opposing the claims of the Catholic

Church to a privileged relationship to the Truth, he had been an early believer in the relativity of religious belief and a precocious proponent of toleration. It was however only in 1722 that the anti-clerical reasons for his hostility to intolerant Catholicism (which never deserted him) were copiously reinforced by socio-economic considerations of a geopolitical nature.

In the middle of the seventeenth century, most (usually English) observers of Holland had concluded that its attitude towards liberty, equality and toleration coincided perfectly with its commercial supremacy. Though Voltaire's 'holy trinity' can be found in slightly different forms (in the *Traité sur la tolérance* we can read it as 'liberty, commerce, prosperity'), this version is the one most commonly found; in *La Princesse de Babylone* (1768), for example, Amazan finds among the Batavians 'freedom, equality ... , toleration' ('la liberté, l'égalité ... , la tolérance').[6] Voltaire arrived at this conclusion after observing at first hand Holland (1722) and then England (1726–8).[7] In October 1722, he spoke for the first time with evident admiration of that great trading and tolerant city, Amsterdam (granted iconic status by Spinoza for identical reasons), and was equally enthusiastic, in the same letter (D128), about The Hague. His correspondence from London, then his *Lettres philosophiques* (1734), conveyed the same boundless enthusiasm for that kindred civilisation. Indeed for the next half century (*Essai sur les mœurs*, *Socrate*, *Réflexions pour les sots*, *Pot-pourri*, etc.), to one of his last important works, the *Prix de la justice et de l'humanité* (1766),[8] he would openly and constantly present those two great and vibrant states as inspirational examples of good practice.

The 1760s: Voltaire becomes *l'homme aux Calas*

The decade of the 1760s is marked by Voltaire's most frenetic activity on behalf of toleration and by his most famous statements in favour of its implementation. The nature of the problem of toleration in this period needs careful definition. What exactly preceded the Calas affair and what makes the 1760s different in both complexity and intensity from the earlier period? Before the 1760s, political and economic arguments in favour of toleration had co-existed in Voltaire's thought along with equally frequent meditations on toleration and humanity as a means of tempering religious fanaticism and its allied brutality. Voltaire's thoughts on these matters go back to 1716 when he had conceived the idea of *La Henriade*. In this epic poem the hero, Henri IV, is presented by the author as being neither Protestant nor Catholic, but a deist, a humanitarian, unconcerned by differences in religious dogma. His toleration, like that of his creator, was not a means towards ensuring that men of deep religious conviction would come to respect the spiritual integrity of those holding opposing confessional views, nor was it a device intended to bring about a modus vivendi between those believers. What he and Voltaire were advocating was a politically oriented toleration that set peace and concord above all else, conveying a purely pragmatic and utilitarian vision of mankind, a vision soon to be reinforced, as we know, by the tolerant practices epitomised by the economically thriving Protestant states of Holland and England.

Any examination of the years 1716–60 would show, however, that Voltaire's thoughts on toleration were what has already been characterised as 'meditations'. To the end of the 1750s his published work amply reflected his commitment to the ideal, but it was – however intensely he experienced it – an ivory-tower form of commitment. True, he did denounce divisive social, political and moral problems, and he did deal with them appropriately in writing. And that is a form of activity. It is not however the specific activity with which both his contemporaries and posterity associate the crusading *homme aux Calas*. This latter transformation occurred because his commitment became practical, inseparable from a sense of active duty towards himself and towards others, inseparable from a willingness to concern himself with the well-being of fellow-suffering human beings.[9] Literally, if belatedly, he chose to take a stand. As Raymond Naves remarked: 'There is with Voltaire a parallel need to make a success of his own life and to make the lives of others better' ('Il y a ... chez Voltaire un besoin parallèle de réussir sa vie et d'améliorer la vie des autres').[10]

The catalyst for that dramatic and heightened sense of urgency came in 1762 with the execution of Jean Calas, the Protestant merchant of Toulouse, accused of having murdered his son, Marc-Antoine, because he wished – so Catholic Toulouse claimed – to convert to Rome.[11] Voltaire was profoundly shaken by the resurgence of sectarian hatred which he perceived as having contributed to the precarious state of Calas's position, and by the dubious nature of the legal process which had moreover been contaminated by the atmosphere which had led to his condemnation, and he was moreover disgusted by the barbarity of his punishment and by the resulting destitution of the family. As a result, Voltaire made Herculean efforts over the next three years to persuade the authorities in Versailles to disavow the Parlement de Toulouse. One of the essential elements in that seemingly impossible campaign was the *Traité sur la tolérance*.

Voltaire transmits his complicated messages in this work in his usual oblique fashion: discrete enquiries and examinations with their intertextual echoes, cross-references and insinuations ultimately form a mosaic of great complexity. The relationship of reader to author is, in fact, analogous to that in the *Lettres philosophiques*: in both works the reader is tempted to form a three-dimensional picture of the narrating persona. There is no need here to examine Voltaire's treatment of the futility of doctrinal disputes and the baleful influence of religious bigotry. The *Traité* was never primarily intended to be a systematic discussion of the problem of doctrinal intolerance (even less to serve the unique purpose of showing his loathing of *l'Infâme*). It is, of course, that. But it is just as essentially a whole series of interlocking, political statements that are germane to the France of 1763. In fact, with the *Traité*, whose programme is ambitious and whose grievances are encyclopaedic, Voltaire was discreetly offering to Louis XV and his enlightened ministers (Choiseul, Praslin, Bertin, Lamoignon, Malesherbes) the opportunity to reverse French decline which had disastrously quickened during the Seven Years War (1756–63), to efface the disgraceful stain of blood left on the throne by the St Bartholomew massacre (1572), and to expunge the effects of that disastrous Protestant diaspora which had so besmirched the reputation of Louis XIV.

Few of the political and socio-political arguments used in the *Traité* are new. Voltaire reiterates his oft-repeated geopolitical lessons: wherever toleration is admitted, different faiths manage to live peaceably together. This is good. For commerce – the true barometer of the well-being of a nation – can flourish only in an atmosphere of tranquillity and self-confidence. Even the great multi-faith states (the Ottoman Empire, Russia, India, China, Japan), where enmities might have been expected, are at peace with themselves in their prosperity. Conversely, active intolerance leads to emigration, depopulation, a decline in commerce, industry and agriculture, a loss of riches, and ultimately to stagnation. Religious fanaticism leads to massacres (as, for example, in Mérindol and Cabrières); it is also exemplified in the Inquisition (leading to the expulsion of the Jews and the Moors from Spain, and at variance with Portugal's economic interests in Goa): such happenings, encouraged by the state or tolerated by it, are the totally stultifying examples of political malpractice with nefarious social and economic consequences. It is for this reason that another major idea of the *Traité* is Voltaire's equally long-standing (Erastian) conviction that there must be a necessary separation of the faith from all those activities which are useful, even vital to the state: the latter must be absolute master in its own house and not feel obliged to share it with the Church. To give some idea of Voltaire's vehemence concerning these matters, in the *Essai sur les mœurs* (1741–69), he pillories 'that foul Inquisition' ('cette infâme Inquisition', *Ode sur le fanatisme*, 1736) sixty times; in the *Dictionnaire philosophique* (1764–9), forty-six times; in the *Questions sur l'Encyclopédie* (1770–2), fifty-seven times. Between 1723 and 1776, the term occurs on more than four hundred occasions in over seventy of his works.

Belatedly joining the debate of the 1750s, and expanding its parameters very considerably, Voltaire managed therefore to transform the individual drama of Jean Calas into a matter for general human concern with political repercussions. Within those far-reaching bounds the author was constantly comparing and juxtaposing the evils of intolerance, human cruelty and stupidity, economic decline, depopulation and stagnation with the advantages of the spirit of free enquiry. There is an overarching concern as to how government can keep maleficent and reactionary forces in check, and ensure – in a compact with progressive thought – the well-being of all its charges.

It is not however entirely satisfactory to present Voltaire's views on toleration, whether religious or political, as we have done so far. If we are to grasp their role and significance, we must see them within the conceptual space of Voltaire's ideal society. That alternative world, in which one finds liberty, equality and the greatest amount of happiness for the generality of the nation, is most conveniently viewed in that work – the quintessence of his thought – which he was composing in parallel with the *Traité*, namely the *Dictionnaire philosophique*.[12]

At first sight this work may appear to be a disparate collection of articles, arranged for the sake of convenience in alphabetical order. Beware! The apparent incoherence, the seeming discontinuity of the content – from the first article ('Abbé') to the last ('Vertu') – cannot hide for long the fundamental cohesion of the authorial stance. Each separate article, different avatars of the same problem, operates in the manner of numerous, intersecting circles which ultimately coalesce to create one central overarching meaning. Voltaire himself warns us that 'everything is inter-connected' ('tout est lié'), and in the preface to the *Dictionnaire*, we are expressly invited to create the meaning of the work in tandem with the author: 'the most useful books are those that are half created by the readers themselves' ('les livres les plus utiles sont ceux dont les lecteurs font eux-mêmes la moitié'). Enlightenment is a collaborative venture. In Peter Gay's phrase, the *Dictionnaire* contains 'one theme and many variations'.[13] But once that meaning or theme is created, it constitutes what Julien Benda called 'a document of capital importance for the political and moral history of France' ('un document capital pour l'histoire politique et morale de la France').[14]

The vision that emerges from this work is that of a world in which everything is regulated strictly in accordance with reason and fair-mindedness. It is hence a world that is profoundly hostile to metaphysical speculation and obscurantism, to fanaticism however defined, to any form of mindless (and above all intolerant) partiality for tradition or authority. The *Dictionnaire philosophique* is the denunciation of any evil that makes man's precarious existence, and his precarious hold on happiness, even more insecure. It conveys with obsessive insistence an all-inclusive vision of liberty: personal liberty, civil liberty, liberty of conscience in matters of faith, and, by extension, the liberty to speak and write.

It is in relation to freedom of speech that the notion of toleration assumes its full political significance. For years Voltaire (in the *Lettres philosophiques*, for example) had seen no distinction between matters of religious and civil concern, and hence had claimed a natural right to free enquiry. For years he had been suggesting, and would tirelessly repeat until his death in 1778, that a compact between progressive thinkers and the seat of power could produce spectacular results for the collective well-being of the nation. For a full six years (1762–8), Voltaire's campaign for toleration – to which the Calas case had given decisive impetus – was to loom large among his most urgent political priorities. First, overlapping with the *Dictionnaire* and with Calas, had come the Sirven affair. This latter event, forced to mark time because of the paramount needs of Calas and subsequently because of the sheer complexity of the case itself, bore witness to the selfsame evils of intolerance and deficiencies in a system of criminal justice which Voltaire could now see was hideously imperfect.[15] Second, prompted largely by the shock that the Calas case had administered to his susceptibility, there came Jean-François Marmontel's *Bélisaire* (1767). In this philosophical novel of sixteen chapters, which set out to indicate to Louis XV the politico-moral means of reversing French decline and of governing the country to better effect, the question of toleration (raised in chapter 15) is both religious and, above all, political – as Voltaire had long recognised. This gave rise to the *Bélisaire* affair (1767–8), which achieved notoriety precisely because Voltaire leapt to the defence both of the author and of the thesis which were being vigorously attacked by the Sorbonne.[16] Finally, hard upon the heels of this affair, Voltaire decided to administer the *coup de grâce* to intolerance and fanaticism with his tragedy *Les Guèbres ou la tolérance* (1768–9).

In these repeated interventions we may detect three underlying arguments, all of them political. The first concerns the efficacy of the campaigns of the 1750s, which had been crowned and crystallised by the Calas affair, and seemingly brought to a satisfactory conclusion by the *Bélisaire* affair. Henceforth the situation in which Protestants found themselves was much more tolerable. The actions of the government (for example, its disavowal, at the close of the *Bélisaire* affair, of the Sorbonne and theologically inspired demands for extirpation of the Huguenot heresy) showed that it was finding its own legislation increasingly repugnant, and that it was intent on seeking an accommodation with Protestants quite independently of the Church. That did not however signify that the battle had been won. Anti-Huguenot legislation was still the law of the land. It still had powerful and increasingly insistent champions, and in parallel with these liberally inspired campaigns, the General Assemblies of the French clergy were, with increasing frequency (1762, 1765, 1770, 1772, 1775), pressing the king for the vigorous enforcement of the Edict of 1724. There was nothing in 1767–8 to suggest that the relative toleration, so recently obtained, might not as quickly be lost again. Voltaire was adamant that history teaches us that the human condition, politics, governmental stances, are all subject to constant change.[17] *Les Guèbres* was an illustration of Voltaire's belief that one could not afford to rest upon laurels that had still to be won in the political and legal senses.

The second reason concerns the fairly striking parallels that Voltaire must surely have discerned between Protestants and *philosophes*. Neither represented a threat to the state. On the contrary, both could be defended as potentially useful contributors to its well-being. And yet both were subject to legislation which could vacillate between the draconian and the lax, both vulnerable to active persecution alternating with relative toleration.

The final reason is again intimately associated with the current laws of the land, whose vagaries offended Voltaire's susceptibility. By increasingly common consent, it was evident that the anti-Huguenot legislation was unworthy of a civilised country. But that offence was compounded by the totally ad hoc manner in which it was enforced. The outside world was clearly being invited to see French justice as a grotesque travesty. This was to be one of Malesherbes's objections to the legislation operational in the period 1752–74.[18] The Calas case highlighted further serious deficiencies in the criminal law of the land, and these shortcomings were henceforth to figure prominently in Voltaire's campaigns (Sirven, Lally, La Barre) over the next fourteen years. One now begins to sense what was an insistent affront to Voltaire's patriotism.[19] From 1758 onwards it was being constantly tested by the mindless stupidity, the lamentable lack of vision, the sheer inability on the part of so many people, at so many different levels, to appreciate how best to defend the common interests of the generality of the nation. Voltaire's patriotism must not, however, be confused with its nineteenth- and twentieth-century versions. It has nothing to do with vulgar, jingoistic navel-gazing. It has much more to do – since Enlightenment patriotism is highly cosmopolitan – with what each nation can do for the general well-being of humanity. That is why Voltaire's concerns must be placed firmly against a European background. Given what he saw as the patchy nature of French commitment to its own best interests, his patriotism – highly political – is both a lament for France's lost cultural and intellectual hegemony, and the expression of the fervent hope that the ruling elite, recognising its responsibilities, would so order the governance and the policies of the state that France would 'rejoin' the commonwealth of truly civilised nations.

The extent of Voltaire's anger and dismay of the 1760s (when he is constantly faced with France's retreat on so many fronts, and with its 'barbaric' practices conducted in full view of Europe) is eloquently typified in this outburst of 1762 to d'Argental (D10404): 'we are the utter shite of the human race' ('nous sommes la chiasse du genre humain').

It is tempting to think that after 1768–9 Voltaire relegated toleration as a subject for pugnacious argument to the background. The *Bélisaire* affair seemed to have exhausted the Sorbonne, silenced militant Catholics, neutralised the conservative Establishment, and swung its progressive wing behind the *philosophes*; whereas, on the other hand, the sheer amount of nervous energy that Voltaire had (fruitlessly) expended in trying to arrange the staging of *Les Guèbres* had momentarily drained him of determination.[20] Voltaire, it might appear, was now giving pride of place to problems associated with biblical exegesis and, above all, with the maladministration of criminal law and the unsatisfactory nature of the legal establishment.[21] But this notion that Voltaire was becoming less committed to toleration is false. In fact Voltaire remained fully engaged in that campaign because these issues were all interchangeable components of one and the same problem: how to create the alternative society and so ameliorate the human condition?

NOTES

1. See *Encyclopaedia of Religion and Ethics* (Edinburgh, T. & T. Clark 1908–26), vol.12 (1921), pp.360–5; *Chambers' Encyclopaedia* (Oxford, Pergamon Press 1967), vol.13, pp.682–4; *New Catholic Encyclopaedia* (New York, McGraw Hill 1967), vol.14, pp.192–3; *New Encyclopaedia Britannica* (New York, Encyclopaedia Britannica Inc. 1974), Micropaedia, vol.10, pp.31–2; *Collier's Encyclopaedia* (New York, Macmillan Educational Corporation, 1983), vol.22, pp.355–6.
2. See my edition, *OCV*, vol.56C, pp.71–81.
3. For comprehensive bibliographies, see A. Lods, 'Les partisans et les adversaires de l'édit de tolérance', *Bulletin de la Société de l'Histoire du Protestantisme Français*, 36 (1887), 551–65, and 619–23, and J. Poujol, 'Aux sources de l'Édit de 1787: une étude bibliographique', *Bulletin de la Société de l'Histoire du Protestantisme Français*, 133 (1987), 343–84.
4. *Lettre de M. l'évêque d'Agen à Mr le Contrôleur Général contre la tolérance des Huguenots dans le royaume* (Agen, 1 May 1751), pp.2–21.
5. See Poujol, 'Aux sources de l'Édit de 1787', pp.360–8.
6. *OCV*, vol.66, p.149.
7. See J. Vercruysse, *Voltaire et la Hollande*, *SVEC*, 46 (1966), particularly pp.131–40, 159–70; and A.-M. Rousseau, *Voltaire et l'Angleterre*, *SVEC* 145–7 (1976). For the period following Voltaire's return from London, see C. Dédéyan, *Le Retour de Salente ou Voltaire et l'Angleterre* (Paris: Nizet, 1988), particularly p.115–42. As time passed, he added to these two exemplary tolerant states Prussia and Russia, and also mentioned approvingly Venice, Hamburg and Danzig.
8. Moland, vol.30, p.566.

9. On the (partly political) reasons for this transformation, see J. Renwick, 'Theory Becomes Action: Toleration from Calas (1762) to *Les Guèbres* (1768)', in *Voltaire et ses combats*, ed. U. Kölving and C. Mervaud (Oxford: Voltaire Foundation, 1997), vol.1, pp.581–91.

10. *Voltaire: L'homme et l'œuvre* (Paris: Boivin, 1942), p.157.

11. For background material concerning the case and Voltaire's involvement, see my edition of the *Traité*, OCV, vol.56C, pp.43–81.

12. See OCV, vol.35, Introduction by C. Mervaud, pp.3–227; T. Besterman, *Voltaire* (Oxford: Blackwell, 1969), chap.35; and C. Todd, *Voltaire: Dictionnaire philosophique* (London: Grant & Cutler, 1980).

13. P. Gay, *Voltaire's Politics: The Poet as Realist*, 2nd edn (New Haven, CT: Yale University Press, 1988), p.209.

14. Quoted from his edition of the text (1935).

15. On Sirven, see VST, vol.2, pp.237–41, 341–4.

16. See J. Renwick, *Marmontel, Voltaire and the 'Bélisaire' Affair (1767)*, SVEC, 121 (1974), and my critical editions of the Voltairean interventions of the year 1767: OCV, vol.63A, pp.155–88, 191–208, 211–22, 223–30.

17. See, for example, my edition of the *Histoire du parlement de Paris*, OCV, vol.68, pp.65–72. As late as 1785, La Fayette was presenting the same problem in different words when he wrote to George Washington: 'Les protestants sont soumis à un intolérable despotisme. Bien qu'il n'y ait pas à présent de persécution ouverte, ils dépendent du caprice du roi, de la reine, du parlement ou d'un ministre' (letter of 11 May 1785, in La Fayette, *Mémoires*, ed. F. de Corcelle, Paris. H. Fournier, 1837–8, vol.2, p.121).

18. *Mémoire* of 1785, p.87.

19. On this general problem, see E. Dziembowski, *Un Nouveau Patriotisme français (1750–1770): La France face à la puissance anglaise à l'époque de la guerre de Sept Ans*, SVEC, 365 (1998), particularly pp.20–34, 113–19, 132–40, 150–4.

20. On the latter, see my edition of the text, OCV, vol.66, Introduction, pp.429–74.

21. See, for example, *Histoire du parlement de Paris*, Introduction, pp.1–136; the *Procès de Claustre* (Moland, vol.28, pp.77–90); *Voltaire's Political Pamphlets of 1771*, ed. D. Echeverria, OCV, vol.73, pp.193–290; my various editions: *La Méprise d'Arras*, OCV, vol.73, pp.351–85; *Essai sur les probabilités en fait de justice*, OCV, vol.74A, pp.243–384; the *Nouvelles Probabilités en fait de justice*, vol.74A, pp.385–414; and my *Voltaire et Morangiés 1772–1773*, SVEC, 202 (1982).

13

GRAHAM GARGETT

Voltaire and the Bible

It was long thought, or at least claimed, that Voltaire's knowledge of the Bible was superficial, even derisory, and that in consequence his biblical criticism was negative, partisan and worthless. This view was not only held by contemporaries such as Claude-François Nonnotte, Antoine Guénée and Louis-Mayeul, Dom Chaudon; J. Steinman still thought so in 1956.[1] Yet research carried out over recent years has demonstrated that few in the eighteenth century knew the Bible better than he: comments on, and quotations from, the scriptures not only occupy a prominent place in the litany of Voltaire's self-proclaimed anti-Christian texts (books, pamphlets, dialogues of all types), perhaps even more significantly they permeate his other works, including those having no apparent connection with religion, and even his thousands of letters. Furthermore, almost despite himself, Voltaire sometimes responded positively to the Bible and was capable of insightful judgements beyond the received wisdom of his times as to its composition, context and background.

How did Voltaire's attitude to the Bible develop?

Bertram Eugene Schwarzbach underlines the rather surprising fact that, apart from the article 'Juifs' (1756), 'Voltaire did not publish any serious [biblical] criticism until the *Sermon des cinquante* in 1761.'[2] This may however have been read aloud or even preached as a mock-sermon while Voltaire was at the court of Frederick the Great in Berlin in 1752. And Voltaire's interest in the Bible goes back much further than that, no doubt to his childhood. The fairly rigorous religious observance of his family was balanced by a quite different influence during his schooling at the famous Jesuit college of Louis-le-Grand. The 'enlightened' Catholicism taught there already went some way to rationalising the Christian religion, as witness one of the textbooks, the Protestant pastor Jacques Abbadie's *Traité de la vérité de la religion chrétienne* (1684).[3] In addition, one of Voltaire's teachers, Père

Tournemine, was suspected by some of being a closet atheist and he certainly tried to explain certain biblical passages in naturalistic terms. Although Voltaire's first literary success was the pious *Ode sur sainte Geneviève* (1710), he doubtless became a sceptic at an early age. His godfather, the Abbé de Châteauneuf, introduced him to *libertinage*, encouraging him to read *La Moïsade*, a subversive poem implying that, like other religious patriarchs, Moses had cynically used religion to control the masses.[4] Later, Voltaire's travels acquainted him with numerous religious sects, often divided by their interpretation of the Bible. He became familiar with clandestine anti-biblical tracts and with the work of the so-called 'English' deists: Anthony Collins, Thomas Woolston, Matthew Tindal, Thomas Chubb, Conyers Middleton, Peter Annet and John Toland.[5] Biblical allusions feature prominently in the first two letters (on the Quakers) of the *Lettres philosophiques*, Voltaire's great work about English culture and society, published in 1733–4, some six years after his return from exile in England. The ensuing scandal, and another caused by *Le Mondain*, in which Voltaire refers dismissively to Adam and Eve, led to years of semi-exile at Cirey, where Voltaire and his mistress clearly spent considerable time studying the Bible. Indeed, Mme Du Châtelet appears to have composed the manuscript *Examen de la Bible*, a systematic critique of biblical contradictions.

A few months after Mme Du Châtelet's death in 1749, in the overtly antireligious atmosphere of Frederick the Great's court and surrounded by fellow *philosophes* such as Julien Offroy de La Mettrie and the Marquis d'Argens, Voltaire almost certainly sketched preliminary versions of articles on biblical subjects that would appear in the *Dictionnaire philosophique* some dozen years later. During his wanderings after his break with Frederick, Voltaire spent three weeks in Lorraine at the Abbey of Senones, whose abbot, Dom Calmet, was the most distinguished biblical commentator of the age (see below). Finally settling near Geneva in late 1754, Voltaire cultivated the friendship of Jacob Vernes and Paul Moultou, 'liberal' Calvinist pastors whose expertise in early Church history would certainly influence his own ideas. In addition, such crucial events as the Lisbon earthquake, the Seven Years War, and the Calas case crystallised Voltaire's attitude to *l'Infâme* (dogmatic religious orthodoxy and its tendency to persecute) and galvanised his attack against it. Above all, *l'Infâme*, most characteristically – though not uniquely – symbolised by the Catholic Church, drew its authority and intellectual underpinning from the Bible. Indeed the Christian Church as a whole based its transcendental claims on the Scriptures, the New Testament being portrayed not only as the successor of the Old Testament but also as its fulfilment. Persistently, tenaciously, perhaps obsessively, Voltaire set out to undermine and discredit both parts of the Bible.

Voltaire's anti-biblical works

Despite its late appearance, the *Sermon des cinquante* signalled a veritable deluge of biblical criticism which continued for the next sixteen years and whose diversity is intriguing, since as well as outright attack and bitter invective one sometimes finds more moderate, even conciliatory pieces, with material relative to the Bible also figuring in the *contes Histoire de Jenni* (1775), *Pot-pourri* (1765) and *Le Taureau blanc* (1773–4), and some historical works. This enormous production cannot be listed here,[6] but in the resolutely hostile category come the *Catéchisme de l'honnête homme* (1763), the *Examen important de milord Bolingbroke* (1766), the *Dîner du comte de Boulainvilliers*, *Questions de Zapata* and *Lettres à Mgr le prince* of 1767, and *Dieu et les hommes* (1769), whereas the apparently more moderate class includes the *Traité sur la tolérance* (1763), the *Homélies prononcées à Londres* (1767), the *Sermon de Josias Rosette* and *Instructions à Antoine-Jacques Rustan* (1768). No clear chronological development emerges, but Voltaire now and then acknowledges that the uneducated need some form of organised religion, hence an occasional difference in emphasis. Both the *Dictionnaire philosophique* (1764) and *Questions sur l'Encyclopédie* (1770–2) contain a huge amount of biblical material. Above all, two late books illustrate Voltaire's dual preoccupation: a continuing determination to attack the Bible and a desire to understand and explain it in non-transcendental, purely human, terms. *La Bible enfin expliquée* (1776) is an extraordinary work consisting of some three hundred pages of biblical text translated or summarised into French by Voltaire, accompanied by a wealth of footnotes repeating, summing up, sometimes deepening and completing his previous speculation. Finally comes the *Histoire de l'établissement du christianisme* of 1777, Voltaire's most systematic attempt to show how a new religion became established upon the contradictory and fragmented materials represented by the New Testament.

Voltaire's sources

The catalogue of Voltaire's library and the marginal comments in his books allow us to appreciate his breadth of documentation and knowledge in the area of biblical criticism.[7] Along with several versions of the Bible itself, Voltaire's collection contained works by the Fathers of the Church, St Augustine, St Cyprian and St Cyril, among others. The spectrum of material available to him surprisingly lacked Spinoza's notorious *Tractatus* though it did include other sources of potentially anti-biblical documentation, for example, Pierre Bayle, Anton Van Dale, Johann Christoph Wagenseil (for rabbinical opinions hostile to Christ), the English deists Woolston and Collins, and the seventeenth-century biblical scholar Richard Simon, a convinced Catholic but one whose oriental studies had persuaded him that traditional versions of the biblical text often needed substantial correction or revision and who, in his own times, had been extremely suspect to the ecclesiastical authorities.[8] Voltaire's library was also well furnished with orthodox publications, both Catholic and Protestant. Above all we must point to the works of the Benedictine scholar Dom Calmet, often mocked by Voltaire – he is mentioned as early as *Le Mondain* (1736), and *Le Taureau blanc* is ironically presented as 'translated from Syriac by dom Calmet'. But his *Commentaire littéral sur tous les livres de l'Ancien et du Nouveau Testament* (1707–16) was Voltaire's single most important source, and he also owned Calmet's other principal works.

The Old Testament

Voltaire has often been accused of anti-Semitism, and admittedly he says many things about the Jews, commonplaces in their day, which would nowadays be considered unpardonable. However, Voltaire was writing long before the horrors of modern Nazism, at a time when such excesses were literally unthinkable. Indeed, he was extremely indignant about massacres related in the Bible, but these were massacres carried out by the Jews themselves against neighbouring peoples. It seems inconceivable that Voltaire wanted to punish modern Jews for the crimes of their forefathers, let alone have them massacred in their thousands; and in a letter to Isaac Pinto, Voltaire went so far as to admit that some of what he had written about the Jews was 'violent and unjust' (D10600). In the *Catéchisme de l'honnête homme*, for example, he dwells on the paradox of Christians persecuting Jews, asking: 'If God is the God of Abraham, why do you burn the children of Abraham? And if you burn them, why do you recite their prayers, even while you are burning them? Why do you, who adore the book of their law, put them to death for having followed their law?' ('Si Dieu est le Dieu d'Abraham, pourquoi brûlez-vous les enfants d'Abraham? Et si vous les brûlez, pourquoi récitez-vous leurs prières, même en les brûlant? Comment, vous qui adorez le livre de leur loi, les faites-vous mourir pour avoir suivi leur loi?').[9] Voltaire's distaste is simple to explain. What he regarded as the primitive and often barbaric mythology of the Jews was lionised by Christians as sacred history, as a text providing moral precepts and, worst of all, a justification for the power, continuing pretensions and overweening arrogance of the Christian Church. If the Old Testament could be comprehensively discredited and the 'Chosen People' exposed as a horde of robbers and bandits, if the miraculous events portrayed there could be explained away or destroyed through mockery, then Christianity would be based on nothing but sand.

This ambitious attack was carried out on several levels and used many different approaches. Obvious targets in Genesis were the Creation, the Fall, Noah's flood and Abraham. The Creation raises all kinds of awkward questions. Why are there apparently two different accounts of the creation of woman?[10] What language did Adam use when he named all the animals? Where was the Garden of Eden, and how does it correspond with contemporary geography, since the four rivers mentioned as running round it are nowadays far distant from each other?[11] Above all, could a creation from nothing actually happen, especially when the biblical text states clearly that *something* existed already when God began his six days' labour?[12] The Fall of Man, a doctrine synonymous for the orthodox with the disobedience of Adam, causes even more awkward questions. How could God forbid his new creature to eat of the fruit which gave knowledge of good and evil? Should he not have done the exact opposite? In any case, what was this mysterious fruit, which appears to have completely disappeared from the face of the earth? Voltaire asks these questions in the most forceful way, preserving his apparent orthodoxy with the briefest of pirouettes: 'It seems to our poor reason that God should have ordered a lot of this fruit to be eaten; but we must submit our reason' ('Il semble à notre pauvre raison que Dieu devait ordonner de manger beaucoup de ce fruit; mais il faut soumettre sa raison').[13] Yet perhaps an even worse contradiction follows, since eating the fruit does not cause the death of Adam and Eve, as God has threatened. What it does do is yet more scandalous and incomprehensible, since Adam and his posterity are punished eternally for this original sin. As the *honnête homme* observes in his *Catéchisme*: 'One sees with a little surprise that God . . . condemned Adam to death, and all his posterity to hell for an apple' ('On voit avec un peu de surprise que Dieu . . . ait condamné Adam à la mort, et toute sa postérité à l'enfer pour une pomme').[14] Visibly, in all these and many other such passages, Voltaire heightens his critique by the liberal use of ridicule and *reductio ad absurdum*. Yet, as Schwarzbach demonstrates, he does nothing that had not been already done, or at least suggested, by various biblical critics who had preceded him.[15]

The rest of Genesis is subjected to the same incredulous scorn, tempered with fake submission. Rarely can Voltaire's irony have had a more promising target than the flood and Noah's ark. Even assuming that a man aged 600 and his family could build such a vessel, how could they have assembled so many animals, birds and insects in it, fed and watered them, and finally prevented the carnivorous species from devouring the rest? And, if they succeeded in this, what nourishment could they provide for the flesh-eaters? Considerations of physics also arise, since Voltaire argues that there was not enough water in the oceans to cover the highest mountains, as the Bible claims. But, even assuming that all the events in the biblical account actually occurred, Voltaire – like other contemporaries – was left to wonder how a man aged by now 601, the few other members of his family, and their descendants, were not only able to re-people the earth with such startling rapidity but also to create the various different races found there, from China to South America.[16] The Tower of Babel, 'ten times higher than the pyramids of Egypt' ('dix fois plus élevée que les pyramides d'Égypte'), similarly leads Voltaire to muse on the extraordinary technical progress that necessarily must have occurred so soon after the flood (he calculates 117 years) for such a building to be constructed. His conclusion? 'We must ... regard this adventure as a prodigy, just like that of the universal flood' ('Il faut ... regarder cette aventure comme un prodige, ainsi que celle du déluge universel').[17] Clearly, as the reader is left to infer, this is all the most arrant nonsense.

The list of immoral, ignorant, unscientific, farcical and fabulous Old Testament incidents ridiculed by Voltaire is long indeed. Jacob's willingness to sacrifice his only son Isaac to God (which prompts Voltaire to speculate that human sacrifice had been an established Jewish practice);[18] the attempts of Sodom's inhabitants to commit mass buggery on two visiting angels; the linguistic accomplishments of Balaam's ass; the conduct of Jonah's obedient whale (or *poisson*): these are a few characteristic targets. And although generalisation is dangerous, it is largely the naïve, unscientific and legendary aspect of the Old Testament's early books that catches Voltaire's attention. Reversing the technique of orthodox seventeenth-century scholars such as Pierre-Daniel Huet, who tried to prove that the pagans systematically borrowed their deities from figures in the Old Testament, Voltaire portrays Moses as a legendary figure, most likely an imitation of Bacchus. From Genesis onwards, though particularly in the historical books, Voltaire is appalled by the violence and immorality depicted in scripture. For example, he frequently mocks Abraham, venerable patriarch and founder of the Jewish nation, for passing off his wife Sarah as his sister so that she may seduce the pharaoh and Abimelech, king of Gerar.[19] David, the so-called 'man after God's heart',[20] type and ancestor of Jesus Christ, is for Voltaire, like Bayle and Annet before him, a liar, adulterer and murderer.[21] The prophetic books provide further scope for mock-horrified ridicule. For example, Voltaire gloats over the 'too naïve depictions' ('des peintures trop naïves') of the *libertinage* shown by two sisters Oholah and Oholibah, 'of which it is difficult to speak in front of ladies' ('dont il est difficile de parler devant les dames').[22] And God's command to the prophet Ezekiel, 'You are to eat your bread baked like barley cakes, using human dung as fuel'[23] conjures up an image which the satirist finds irresistible, translating it as: 'You will eat it, you will cover it with the shit which comes out of the body of man' ('Tu le mangeras, tu le couvriras de la merde qui sort du corps de l'homme').[24] Shorthand references to Ezekiel's unpalatable 'breakfast' abound in Voltaire's anti-biblical sorties.

In commenting on the Old Testament, indeed on the Bible as a whole, Voltaire not only takes every chance to emphasise physical and other scientific errors; in a more general way he seeks to discredit miraculous events, which are as far as possible explained away naturalistically. Typical examples include the burning bush, Lot's wife, and the crossing of the Jordan by Moses. Even more radically, Voltaire contests the very idea of a miracle, which he considers as contrary to the general laws established by God to enable nature to function: seen in this light, a miracle would be tantamount to God contradicting himself. But Voltaire's most indignant criticisms of Old Testament miracles concern their alleged immorality, as for example with Joshua 10, 12–14, where God lengthens the day to give the Israelites more time to kill the Amorites. Voltaire exclaims in disgust: 'it is in favour of these monsters that the sun and the moon were halted at midday' ('c'est en faveur de ces monstres qu'on fait arrêter le soleil et la lune au plein midi').[25] Indeed what incenses him most is the fact that the massacre is presented as being committed in God's name and by God's express command. For Voltaire, such fanaticism has echoed through the ages, all too often justified by biblical models. In *La Bible enfin expliquée* he recalls 'the war of the Cévennes fanatics' ('la guerre des fanatiques des Cévennes'), and in particular 'a prophetess called *great Mary*' ('une prophétesse nommée *la grande Marie*') who, 'once the spirit had spoken to her, condemned to death the captives taken in the war' ('dès que l'esprit lui avait parlé, condamnait à la mort les captifs faits à la guerre'). There follows a veritable outburst:

> It is characteristic of fanatics who read the holy scriptures to tell themselves: God killed, so I must kill; Abraham lied, Jacob deceived, Rachel stole: so I must steal, deceive, lie. But, wretch, you are neither Rachel, nor Jacob, nor Abraham, nor God; you are just a mad fool, and the popes who forbade the reading of the Bible were extremely wise.
>
> (C'est le propre des fanatiques qui lisent l'Écriture sainte de se dire à eux-mêmes: Dieu a tué, donc il faut que je tue; Abraham a menti, Jacob a trompé, Rachel a volé: donc je dois voler, tromper, mentir. Mais, malheureux, tu n'es ni Rachel, ni Jacob, ni Abraham, ni Dieu: tu n'es qu'un fou furieux, et les papes qui défendirent la lecture de la *Bible* furent très-sages.)[26]

Nonetheless, there is a more positive side. Almost despite himself, Voltaire sometimes, indeed more frequently than one might expect, reacts positively to the poetry of the Bible. Although knowing no Hebrew, he often castigates the language for its characteristic 'oriental' tendency to hyperbole and exaggeration, yet he is not always deaf to its attraction. Voltaire composed both a *Précis de l'Ecclésiaste* and a *Précis du Cantique des cantiques* and clearly responded to the depiction in Ecclesiastes of the transitory nature of human life. He was also moved by the account of Jacob reunited with his brothers in Egypt. *La Bible enfin expliquée* comments simply: 'This story has always been regarded as one of the most beautiful in Antiquity' ('Ce morceau d'histoire a toujours passé pour un des plus beaux de l'antiquité').[27] The Book of Ruth, 'written with naïve and touching simplicity' ('écrite avec une simplicité naïve et touchante') also finds favour.[28] Moreover, as Schwarzbach perceptively remarks, 'with its innocent population and lush vegetation', El Dorado (in *Candide*) is far more like the Garden of Eden than 'Periclean Athens or republican Rome'.[29]

At a deeper level, Voltaire has real knowledge of the biblical text. Rather than merely attacking it, he tries to understand it and its relation to the society in which it was written. The special position of Moses's brother Aaron who, far from being punished for casting the golden calf is confirmed in his priestly functions, leads Voltaire to suspect that a self-interested scribe had been at work to protect the interests of his cast.[30] The fact that, in the Book of Judges, 'Micah and his mother make gods, sculpted idols ... without the God of Israel paying the slightest attention to them' ('Michas et sa mère font des dieux, des idoles sculptées ... sans que le Dieu d'Israël y fasse la moindre attention') means that this passage could predate Genesis and Exodus.[31] Following William Warburton, Voltaire insists that the Old Testament says nothing about the immortality of the soul. Above all, he attacks the orthodox belief that Moses composed Genesis, Exodus, Leviticus, Numbers and Deuteronomy, because 'none of the books of the Pentateuch is referred to by name, and ... not a single verse or law is quoted'.[32] For Voltaire, these first books of the Old Testament were most likely written after the return from exile in Babylon, possibly by Edras. Such speculation is generally derivative, but sometimes Voltaire had personal intuitions that foreshadow the so-called 'high criticism' of the nineteenth century. Though clearly an enemy of the Old Testament and the Chosen People, Voltaire is a surprisingly well-informed one, and on occasion even betrays a reluctant admiration for the Scriptures he so often castigates.

The New Testament

Voltaire's works contain many attacks on the New Testament. In the first place, he questions the Christian canon and the way it was selected. For him the four Gospels are not the most ancient texts of Christian tradition and their key role reveals much about the struggles and disputes of the different early Christian groups. In 1769 he even published a *Collection d'anciens évangiles*,[33] and he emphasised that documents such as the Gospels according to James and Nicodemus are quoted as authoritative by certain early Church Fathers.[34] The beginning of the Christian era was characterised by such struggles, as the disagreements between Peter and Paul well illustrate. Voltaire distrusts early Christian traditions, exemplified by 'pious frauds',[35] and he questions whether Peter actually ever visited Rome.[36] St Paul is treated even more harshly: for Voltaire this classic religious leader, dogmatic, domineering, intolerant, only became a Christian because his former master Gamaliel (a member of the Jewish Sanhedrin) refused him his daughter in marriage.[37] Christianity's instinctive tendency to persecute is also manifest in the insane disputes over the Trinity and associated doctrines. For Voltaire the acme of this madness was reached in the division of Eastern and Western Christianity over one Latin word, *que* ('and'), the Eastern churches refusing to believe that the Holy Spirit proceeded from the Son (*filioque*) as well as from the Father.[38]

The connection (or rather lack of connection) between such suicidal quibbling and the New Testament is obvious: nowhere in Scripture are theological terms such as 'trinity' or 'consubstantiality' even mentioned.[39] Jesus Christ is a simple man, the son of a carpenter. The idea that he was somehow the Divine Word, the Second Person of the Trinity, is – in Voltaire's opinion – a late importation from Neo-Platonism. Voltaire is at pains to demonstrate that the term 'Son of God', used in connection with Jesus in the New Testament, was also applied to many other people, without this having any divine overtones. Part of the special association in the case of Jesus comes – at least indirectly – from his role as an alleged miracle worker, and many passages in Voltaire's works ridicule these alleged events. The miracle at Cana in Galilee is a shameful trick, one moreover which is designed to please a company already drunk.[40] Other 'miracles' seem even less admirable. Why did Jesus blast a fig tree which could not in any case be in fruit, since figs were out of season? Why did he send a company of demons into a herd of pigs, which promptly rushed off to drown themselves, killing many innocent beasts and bankrupting their owner? Even more suspect are those miracles involving the healing of the sick or the raising of the dead, notably Christ's own resurrection. Here Voltaire, like Woolston before him, sees only the most blatant imposture. Particularly revealing is the fact that the end of the world predicted by Christ in his generation did not occur.[41]

Criticisms such as these are accompanied by systematic doubt as to the alleged connection between New Testament events and the prophecies of the

Old Testament. A characteristic example concerns the prophecy that 'A virgin shall conceive': Voltaire claims, rightly as it turns out, that the word *alma* does not necessarily mean 'virgin',[42] thereby chipping away at one block of the traditional Christian edifice. Using the *Toldos Jeschut* and other rabbinical texts and arguments, Voltaire further suggests that the birth and childhood of Jesus were perfectly explicable in natural terms. The clumsiness of early attempts to prove his divine status are evident in the discrepancies between the New Testament genealogies of Jesus. Perhaps worst of all, non-Christian sources such as Josephus are virtually silent about Christ, his life, death and resurrection.[43]

The third of the *Lettres philosophiques* implied that George Fox, the founder of the Quaker movement, and his followers, bore a close resemblance to Jesus Christ and his disciples. Fox was the 'son to a silk-weaver', who 'took it into his head to preach . . . with all the requisites of a true apostle, that is, without being able either to read or write'. To ignorance was added fanaticism, 'and as enthusiasm is an epidemical distemper, many were persuaded, and those who scourg'd him became his first disciples'.[44] By implication, Jesus was thus an ignorant, though well-meaning, fanatic. This hostility is present in many Voltairean attacks, and often the well-meaning motivation is absent, replaced by duplicity and the will to gain power by founding a new sect. Yet Voltaire's attitude to the New Testament and to Jesus showed some tendency to evolve favourably in his later years. This did not mean any change in his basic hostility to the doctrinal aspects of Christianity; however, as Marie-Hélène Cotoni shows, he became increasingly prepared to enlist a non-dogmatic Jesus in the cause of reasonable and tolerant deism.[45]

This change is best shown in the remarkable 'Section seconde' of the article 'Religion' (1771) published in the *Questions sur l'Encyclopédie*.[46] Allegedly transported by an archangel to 'la désolation', Voltaire sees a man with a simple and humane face, and a compassionate air, whose wounds leave little doubt as to his identity. Jesus says that he was killed by hypocrites, and explains his beliefs and teaching in a most appealing way. But Voltaire is not satisfied. Did Jesus not teach that he had come to bring not peace but a sword? No, comes the reply. That was a copyist's error. In fact, Jesus had said the exact opposite. Thus, in his last years, worried by the progress of atheism, Voltaire is prepared to enlist Jesus as a spokesman for theism and toleration, though this must be on his own terms.

All the same, this extraordinary dialogue surely illustrates the importance of the Bible for Voltaire. He fought it, attacked it, ridiculed it. Yet, in the last analysis, he felt its power and even the attraction of Jesus. This meeting of apparent opposites is intriguing, and so is Voltaire's overall encounter with the Bible.

NOTES

1. J. Steinman, See *La Critique devant la Bible*, quoted in M.-H. Cotoni, *L'Exégèse du Nouveau Testament dans la philosophie française du dix-huitième siècle*, *SVEC*, 220 (1984), p.357. This chapter is indebted to many studies, in particular: B. E. Schwarzbach, *Voltaire's Old Testament Criticism* (Geneva: Droz, 1971); Cotoni, *Exégèse du Nouveau Testament*, esp. pp.306–63; and F. Bessire, *La Bible dans la correspondance de Voltaire*, *SVEC*, 367 (1999).

2. Schwarzbach, *Voltaire's Old Testament Criticism*, p.11.

3. R. Pomeau, *La Religion de Voltaire*, new edn (Paris: Nizet, 1969), p.51.

4. *VST*, vol.1, p.35; Pomeau, *La Religion de Voltaire*, pp.30–2.

5. See N. L. Torrey, *Voltaire and the English Deists* (New Haven, CT: Yale University Press, 1930).

6. For fuller analysis, see Cotoni, *Exégèse du Nouveau Testament*, pp.334–8.

7. For detailed information, see the specialist studies already referred to, especially Cotoni, *Exégèse du Nouveau Testament*, pp.322–32.

8. See Cotoni, *Exégèse du Nouveau Testament*, pp.14–30.

9. *Mél.*, p.949.

10. A characteristic example occurs in *La Bible enfin expliquée* (Moland, vol.30, p.6, note 1).

11. See 'Genèse', *Dictionnaire philosophique*, *OCV*, vol.36, pp.155–6.

12. 'Genèse', p.157.

13. 'Genèse', p.157.

14. *Mél.*, p. 653.

15. As well as those listed earlier, Schwarzbach mentions Sa'adiah (*Voltaire's Old Testament Criticism*, pp.34, 97–8), Da Costa (p.30), Shor (p.136) and Ibn Ezra (pp.61–4).

16. See *La Philosophie de l'histoire*, *OCV*, vol.59, pp.172–3; and M.-S. Seguin, *Science et religion dans la pensée française du XVIIIe siècle: Le mythe du Déluge universel* (Paris: Champion, 2001).

17. *La Bible enfin expliquée* (Moland, vol.30, p.20, note 4).

18. *La Bible enfin expliquée*, pp.34–5; another example is Jephtha's daughter ('Jephté', *Dictionnaire philosophique*, *OCV*, vol.36, pp.240–2).

19. See *Catéchisme de l'honnête homme* (*Mél.*, p.952).

20. See *Les Questions de Zapata* (*Mél.*, p.958).

21. See H. T. Mason, *Pierre Bayle and Voltaire* (Oxford: Oxford University Press, 1963), pp.29–30; and Voltaire's 'David' (*Dictionnaire philosophique*, *OCV*, vol.36, pp.1–8).

22. *Traité sur la tolérance*, *OCV*, vol.56C, p.212; *Le Dîner du comte de Boulainvilliers*, *OCV*, vol.63A, p.367. See Ezekiel, chap.23, which is, however, clearly referring to the 'prostitution' of Israel and Judah.

23. Ezekiel, chap.4, verse 12 (translation from *The New English Bible*).

24. *Instruction à Frère Pédiculoso* (1768), *Mél.*, p.1269.

25. *Examen important de Milord Bolingbroke* (*Mél.*, pp.1033–4).

26. Moland, vol.30, p.136, note 1.

27. Moland, vol.30, p.63, note 2.

28. Moland, vol.30, p.155, note 1.

29. Schwarzbach, *Voltaire's Old Testament Criticism*, p.169.
30. See *La Bible enfin expliquée*, Moland, vol.30, p.89, note 2.
31. Moland, vol.30, p.147, note 1.
32. Schwarzbach, *Voltaire's Old Testament Criticism*, p.78. According to the *Traité sur la tolérance*, 'Aben-Hezrah' (Ibn Ezra) claimed that six passages mentioning things that happened after Moses cannot be by Moses (OCV, 56C, p.195, note g).
33. OCV, vol.69, pp.1–245.
34. Cotoni, *Exégèse du Nouveau Testament*, p.347. As might be expected, Voltaire always regarded the Book of Revelation as an example of complete fanaticism.
35. See *Dieu et les hommes*, OCV, vol.69, pp.440–9.
36. See *Les Questions de Zapata*, Mél, p.964.
37. 'Paul', *Dictionnaire philosophique*, OCV, vol.36, p.417. Note 8 shows that Epiphanius says exactly what Voltaire claims. For Paul, see also *Examen important de Milord Bolingbroke* (Mél., pp.1048–52).
38. See *EM*, vol.1, pp.415–21.
39. See *Homélie sur la superstition*, Mél., p.1155.
40. See *Examen important de Milord Bolingbroke*, Mél., p.1045; and *Les Questions de Zapata*, Mél., p.962.
41. See *Dieu et les hommes*, OCV, vol.69, p.450.
42. Schwarzbach, *Voltaire's Old Testament Criticism*, p.49, note 65.
43. See *Catéchisme de l'honnête homme*, Mél., p.657.
44. *Letters*, pp.17–18.
45. Cotoni, *Exégèse du Nouveau Testament*, pp.353–7.
46. Moland, vol.20, pp.342–8.

14

DANIEL BREWER

The Voltaire effect

In a media-infused society, the cultural significance of writers may seem limited to glittery fame, if not mere notoriety. Yet the case of Voltaire refutes this sceptical view of the writer's importance in society and of literature's value more generally. In his own time Voltaire enjoyed a literary significance that extended well beyond fame, both in France and among Europe's lettered elite. The best-known writer of the eighteenth century, 'the patriarch of Ferney', lived on during the next two centuries as a deeply haunting presence in France's collective cultural memory. Repeatedly, Voltaire was pressed into service in the pitched battles over the contested meaning of France's past and the direction of its future. Referred to more often than read, acquiring a cultural significance that was often decoupled from the *philosophe*'s works themselves, 'Voltaire' became a token or signifier, a telegraphic way of staking claims, phrasing values and intervening in the political arena. The case of Voltaire, understood less as influence than as legacy, as afterlife or 'the Voltaire effect', reveals a good deal about engaged, liberal, reformist writing in the eighteenth century. The story of how 'the Voltaire effect' comes about also illustrates how an author is constructed as a culturally iconic object in order to advance or slow down that reform, or to effect change in some other way.

Voltaire's fame mixes literary celebrity, social critique and political controversy. Early in his career his public skirmishes with Church and government led to brief imprisonment in the Bastille and periods of exile from Paris, notably in England (1726–8). His *Lettres philosophiques* (1734) grew out of that experience, presenting an oblique yet critical view of France by praising England's promotion of religious tolerance, commerce, science and personal freedom. Official response to the *Lettres philosophiques* was swift and tempestuous: the book's publisher was imprisoned and an arrest warrant was issued for its author, who prudently fled Paris for a time. (The book continued to be brought out in pirate editions, a highly successful yet risky enterprise; although it soon disappeared from the market under that title, it was read throughout the century in partial, camouflaged versions.) Voltaire was allowed to return to Paris the following year, and with the protection of the powerful, including the *favorite* of Louis XV, Mme de Pompadour, he negotiated a successful re-entry into court life. His poetry earned him critical acclaim and comparison to Virgil, perhaps in part because of its celebration of French military exploits. But his poetry could also be sharply topical, as was the epic poem *La Henriade*, which celebrated Henri IV and his efforts to end the wars of religion. Voltaire's neo-classical dramatic writing was immensely successful, with his twenty-seven tragedies and twelve comedies earning more for the Comédie-Française than the plays of Corneille and Racine combined. Voltaire was also known as the author of historical works, including histories of the courts of Louis XIV and of Charles XII of Sweden. Such was hardly the kind of writing that would lead to fame in the eighteenth century, when history-writing was considered little more than fables written for royal patrons. It was rather for his acts of social engagement that Voltaire would become especially well known – or notorious. He mounted several highly public letter-writing campaigns to obtain justice for victims of religious intolerance, such as the Calas family, and he wrote several works harshly critical of intolerance, including the *Traité sur la tolérance* (1763) and the *Dictionnaire philosophique* (1764).

In promoting the cause of reform, Voltaire was as indefatigable as he was canny. *Écrasez l'infâme*, the phrase he began appending to his letters in the early 1760s, encapsulated the Enlightenment project of rooting out error, superstition and intolerance by means of reasoned argument, common sense and often a healthy dose of biting irony. Quickly becoming a battle cry, penned in condensed, symbolic form as 'ÉCRLINF', the phrase had preserved all its caustic energy when, a century later, Friedrich Nietzsche inserted it throughout his *Ecce Homo*. But in addition to all Voltaire did to advance reform (and to promote himself in order to promote reform all the more effectively), he had the good fortune to have history on his side. He represented the idealised, utopian figure of the writer-intellectual that numerous eighteenth-century writers were imagining and aiming to become, a figure described in his *Encyclopédie* article 'Gens de lettres' as a more independent, freethinking and socially useful individual, whose writing should be protected and promoted because it contributes to civilising society. Voltaire's substantial wealth granted him freedom from the patronage system and a certain distance from court life. He could enjoy the pleasures of civilised society without having to confront the disillusion, compromise and alienation of materialist, bourgeois culture that the nineteenth-century writer would experience. He also embodied the engaged, sociable and useful writer that liberal, reformist elements of French society were arguing was so necessary to France. During the reign of Louis XIV the 'great men' praised in state funeral orations, academic paintings and official sculptures were kings and nobles. Voltaire criticised this official prestige-granting, just as he reproached Jacques-Bénigne Bossuet for having praised only the aristocratic great of the reign of Louis XIV and not Jean-Baptiste Colbert, the king's invaluable finance minister. During the eighteenth century, as the bour-geoisie became more central to state administration, they claimed due rec-ognition for their services, arguing that other 'great men' should be accorded a place of honour in cultural memory for having served their nation by serving the state. 'O memory! O names of the handful of men who served the state well' ('Ô mémoire! ô noms du petit nombre d'hommes qui ont bien servi l'État'), exclaims Voltaire in his encomium for the officers who died in 1741 in the War of Austrian Succession.[1]

It is one of literary history's ironies that Voltaire too would be made into a writer who served the state well. During the following centuries his fame acquired a useful plasticity during the 'hot' moments of French history, these grand clashes of ideas and ideologies. But his fame was invoked during quieter moments as well, in micro-cultural practices such as the designing of school curricula and the erection of city monuments. Voltaire was overtaken by history almost as he entered it, made usable and put to use, just as elements of the past in general are taken in hand to forge a present (or surge up in a present trying to forget them). Voltaire remains 'a man and his works', a truly great writer who merits careful reading. But he surely also became an effect, a product of his readers (or his would-be readers). 'The Voltaire effect' resides in the relation between his texts and the cultural practices that gave meaning to them, acts such as reading, teaching or commemoration that recover Voltaire's texts and thus establish (their) meaning in and for the present moment.

Constructing an afterlife

In 1778, at the age of 84, Voltaire made a triumphant return to Paris from his estate at Ferney near the Swiss border. His brief stay in the capital before his death was a moment of celebration, an apotheosis that helped fix in cultural memory the image of the *philosophe* that would endure as syn-onymous with the Enlightenment. For some twenty years, the home of 'the patriarch of Ferney' was a destination point for grand tourists, and the 'visit to Voltaire' had become a literary sub-genre, exemplified by such writers as Casanova and Edward Gibbon. These visits were not without their theatrical side, and Voltaire cleverly staged his appearance before his guests to heighten the dramatic effect of the experience. (The ritual of a theatricalised visit to Ferney continues today, through to the guided tour, 'Impression-Voltaire', offered by the local tourist bureau.)

Champion of tolerance, witty and acerbic polemicist, wise philosopher-hero portrayed most iconically in the seated marble statue Jean-Antoine Houdon exhibited in the 1781 Salon, Voltaire by the time of his death had become both a catalyst for liberal reform and a lightning rod for its opponents. He could play this role in no small measure because of the attention he paid to the publication and diffusion of his writings. It was the production, circulation and reception of the Voltairean text – first poetry and theatre, then letters followed by edited works – that produced the idea of Voltaire as a writer-author, and not just another person who wrote. His personal letters and his works were diffused throughout Europe. Written in an age known for its great letter-writers, in numbers alone the Voltairean correspondence remains staggering: some 15,300 letters still exist, from a correspondence that included over 1,500 readers. Across this vast epistolary network, Voltaire's letters were copied, circulated and discussed, producing an identity known throughout Europe.

The enterprise of writing resulted in creating a 'life' for Voltaire, who through his writing worked to achieve a cultural afterlife as well. He closely oversaw the production of various 'miscellanies', 'collections' and 'complete works of M. Voltaire'. During his last years he helped prepare what would be the most complete edition of his works to date. Published across the Rhine from Strasbourg between 1783 and 1790, the posthumous edition had as its prime movers (in both an intellectual and a financial sense) Pierre de Beaumarchais and the Marquis de Condorcet. The edition reached a remarkable seventy volumes in octavo format. Illustrating how material factors can contribute to an author's impact, the octavo edition acquired a far wider readership than did the larger, more 'aristocratic' quarto volumes. The edition was even more popularly affordable and easier to read and transport in the smaller duodecimo format, which ran to ninety-two volumes.

From the moment of his death, the construction of Voltaire's legacy by others began in earnest. Hostage to the process, his remains took on a powerfully symbolic significance. Fearing he could not obtain a proper burial and would end up in a pauper's grave, Voltaire had made a partial retraction of his writings, an act the Church nonetheless deemed insufficient. Those close to Voltaire had arranged to transfer his remains to Ferney, resorting one last time to the well-tested strategy of flight from the capital. Voltaire's family had other plans, and his remains were buried in an abbey near Paris where Voltaire's nephew served as Abbé. This compromise between religion and freethinking philosophy was short-lived, however, for Voltaire's remains would soon play a role of national significance. In 1791,

Fig. 5 *Translation de Voltaire au Panthéon français*, engraving, 1791 (private collection)

calling on Voltaire on behalf of the nation, the revolutionary Constituent Assembly decreed that his remains should be interred in the newly nationalised and secularised Panthéon (fig. 5). Built to replace the ruined church of the Abbey Sainte-Geneviève, the neo-classical edifice designed by Jacques Soufflot and named in honour of the patron saint of Paris had been commissioned by Louis XV in 1744. The church was to rival St Peter's in Rome, providing a symbolic demonstration of France's long-standing affirmation of Gallican liberties, the principle of independence that French kings had claimed with respect to Rome. Announcing on its pediment France's gratitude to her great men, 'the fatherland is grateful to its great men' ('Aux grands hommes, la patrie reconnaissante'), the building became the site where the French state continuously performed its history by expressing the idea of a grateful nation, as well as of a national subject, produced in the gesture of national recognition.

Voltaire's 'pantheonisation' continued the symbolic work of the edifice, work that was not without political consequences. For in claiming Voltaire as one of its own, the Revolution celebrated itself through him, aiming to legitimise itself and its policies. Voltaire might have been somewhat amused by his revolutionary apotheosis. In his *Dictionnaire philosophique* he took great pleasure in revealing how institutions re-write their history as it suits them, and he had constantly exposed the unreliability of religious documents and practices designed to promote self-interested individuals. He might have understood less well the notion of revolution espoused by the revolutionaries who appropriated him, as he tended to use the term to designate a slow and extensive process rather than a sudden and violent event. This instance of a difference between Voltaire's thought and the use to which the writer was put highlights a constant feature of the Voltaire Effect, the act of cultural appropriation in which Voltaire becomes a text referred to more often than read. As if to signal this transformation from writer to works, and from text to effect, on the hearse bearing Voltaire's coffin in the interment ceremony were placed several volumes of the Kehl edition, including the one containing Condorcet's *Vie de Voltaire*. The coffin itself had three inscriptions: one proclaimed his efforts in numerous causes célèbres to root out intolerance; the second praised him as poet, philosopher and historian who had prepared the way for freedom; the third celebrated his fight against atheists and fanatics, and his struggle to reclaim the rights of man against serfdom and feudalism. Thus, already in 1791 Voltaire had become a collage, the collection of *idées reçues* that Gustave Flaubert ironically represents a half-century later in *Madame Bovary* through the character of the village pharmacist, the posturing, anti-clerical M. Homais.

Voltaire's revolutionary appropriation was one of numerous attempts to tell the story of the new republic, to script a narrative of national unity that would heal deep wounds in political culture. The republic itself, the revolutionaries claimed, would unite the men and women of France, transforming monarchical subjects into republican citizens. Although the republican calendar began with Year One, symbolically making 1792 the dawn of a new political age, the republic's incorporation of Voltaire demonstrated how republican political culture could conjoin past and present, thereby seeking to overcome the profound break represented by 1789. A similar fate of appropriation befell Jean-Jacques Rousseau, who had died in the same year as Voltaire and whose entry into the Panthéon was decreed by the National Convention in 1794. The act brought together two figures who, in eighteenth-century prints and popular thinking, were viewed as irreconcilable enemies – Voltaire the representative of rationalism and group tolerance, and Rousseau the champion of lyric sensibility and the individual. But the reconciliation the revolutionary leaders hoped to achieve both symbolically and politically was not so easily realised. Joined symbolically in the Panthéon, the two writers continued to signal a profound and enduring tension in French political culture. The political history of nineteenth-century France, at least until the establishment of the Third Republic in 1870, when secular republicanism won out over religious monarchism, can be written as the struggle between these positions, a struggle that crystallised in the debate over the cause of the cataclysmic, traumatic events of the

French Revolution. Was the Revolution 'Voltaire's fault or Rousseau's?' ('la faute à Voltaire ou la faute à Rousseau?'). So went the ditty sung by Gavroche, street urchin and son of Paris, as he died in a hail of bullets on the barricades in Victor Hugo's *Les Misérables* (1862). So long as 'Voltaire' or Voltaireanism meant an intransigent anti-clerical liberalism, and 'Rousseau' signified an uncompromising socialising populism, any political reconciliation between these positions was impossible. Hugo would associate them in the overarching emancipatory work of the Revolution, declaring in the oration he delivered in 1878 on the hundredth anniversary of Voltaire's death that in railing against the oppressors of the weak, the poor and the downtrodden, Voltaire was waging 'Christ's war', and doing so better than the Church. If this union beneath the revolutionary banner was rhetorically possible for Hugo, the republican synthesis was still too fragile a solution to the vexing and long-standing problem of political differences in 1878, when it was prudently decided to hold the centennial commemoration of the death of Voltaire and Rousseau separately.

This commemoration of the Revolution and its republican heritage would help fix a largely positive image of Voltaire in cultural memory. Yet throughout the nineteenth century, he had been a prime target for monarchists, Catholics and conservatives. Prior to 1848, all threats to social order and the status quo were viewed with alarm by those in power, whether the power in question was that of the Napoleonic state or the Bourbon Restoration that followed Napoleon's removal in 1814. Eighteenth-century philosophy was just such a threat, for it was seen as promoting atheism, materialism and a resurgence of the popular violence that contributed to revolutionary excesses. This nineteenth-century anti-terrorist discourse had its own strategic ends. By denouncing the bloody excesses that had occurred during the reign of Robespierre and the Jacobin party, which ended with the Revolution of Thermidor in 1794, an argument could be made indirectly, yet no less effectively, for maintaining the status quo. Within this anti-terrorist discourse, the names of the *philosophes* were interchangeable. Diderot, Rousseau, Voltaire, D'Alembert – these authors represented a philosophical 'sect' whose sole aim was overturning established order and whose works could remain unread, covered over and silenced beneath slogans. In the highly charged atmosphere of nineteenth-century politics, no reference to the eighteenth century remained politically neutral. Politicising the previous century was often the aim of political discourse, rather than an unavoidable outcome.

But even in literary historical terms, assuming they can be kept separate from political intent, Voltaire did not fare well in the early nineteenth century. He was equated with the pleasure-seeking superficiality of the *ancien régime*, and his writing, like that of the eighteenth century more generally, was not considered to be great literature. Held up as model instead was the literature of the seventeenth century, the *grand siècle* that was appropriately aristocratic, monarchical and Catholic. In comparison, the writing of the eighteenth century seemed frivolous, mannered and artificial – no more than light entertainment. Moreover, Voltaire represented the century of wit, analysis and rationalism, in other words all that the Romantics saw as being hostile to religious and poetic sentiment, stifling creativity and preventing genius from producing great poetry. Charles-Augustin Sainte-Beuve, whose literary portraits would mark literary history for the rest of the century, was categorical: 'As an artist, Voltaire excels in mockery alone, that is, in a genre that by definition is anti-poetic' ('Voltaire, comme artiste, ne triomphe plus que dans la moquerie, c'est-à-dire dans un genre qui est antipoétique par excellence'). Gustave Flaubert put the opposition between wit and poetic genius most succinctly: 'Who was wittier than Voltaire and who was less a poet?' ('Qui eut plus d'esprit que Voltaire et qui a été moins poète?'). Octave, the alienated young hero of Alfred de Musset's *Confessions d'un enfant du siècle*, expresses the period's anti-philosophical hostility to eighteenth-century rationalism. 'Poisoned as a youth by all that was written in the last century, early on I was nursed on the sterile milk of impiousness' ('Empoisonné dès l'adolescence de tous les écrits du dernier siècle, j'y avais sucé de bonne heure le lait stérile de l'impiété').[2] For Musset's 'child of the century', the sour milk of eighteenth-century atheist materialism expresses Romantic aspirations negatively, by referring to all that the previous age supposedly lacked and the legacy it had failed to provide. In literary discourse as in political discourse, Voltaire and the eighteenth century mediated a sense of present and past, signifying a dissatisfaction with the present, experienced as a vague sense of loss. If Voltaire's writing was devalorised for being either too witty and frivolous or too rational and critical, it was so that nineteenth-century literary innovation appeared all the more striking. A cut-out figure, the image of Voltaire served as floating signifier, a foil expressing nineteenth-century writers' and critics' sense of their own plight, caught in a moment they experienced as being hostile to all forms of creative genius. At times, nineteenth-century cultural imagination will attempt to recover that lost past, as do Jules and Edmond de Goncourt in their resuscitation of a delicate, feminine and pleasure-loving eighteenth-century salon culture. With the return of the aristocratic émigrés, a bygone world is invoked that existed prior to revolution and exile, a recreated world that provides an antithesis to the pale and conflict-ridden present. In clothing, hairstyles, Louis XV furniture, and pastiches of the nostalgic *fêtes galantes* paintings of Jean-Antoine Watteau and Nicolas Lancret, eighteenth-century salon culture returns as the ghost-like model of harmless aesthetic production and disengaged cultural life. Yet even in this depoliticised, aestheticised version of the eighteenth century, Voltaire cannot be presented in a positive light. The Catholic right cannot forgive him his anti-clericalism, the populist left cannot accept his praise of luxury and commerce, the nationalists take him for a cosmopolitan, believers see him as an atheist, and materialist non-believers reject his deism. The witty deftness of Voltaire's style will receive universal praise, but only because style can be appreciated without embracing the ideas it conveys.

The state of memory

In the current view of the eighteenth century, the *philosophes* are now seen as having had less influence on the French Revolution than earlier generations of scholars accorded them. An intellectual history of political ideas is being rewritten as a cultural history of material practices, a revision that makes it possible to examine all the more closely how and why the *philosophes* were read – or not – by subsequent generations. This shift of perspective has resulted in reading the *philosophes'* writings otherwise than through the deforming lens of the Revolution, which for a century or more shaped interpretations of the *philosophes* and the pre-Revolutionary period in general. Besides reading the *philosophes'* texts more carefully, literary and cultural historians are subjecting to critical scrutiny the view of the eighteenth century that was produced by the myth-making imperative of nineteenth-century republican culture. Successful precisely because it could overcome political fractiousness in the name of the Republic, rewriting socio-economic particularisms through the script of national unity, republicanism did not – and probably could not – expose its own need for myths. Increasingly, the question is asked whether those same myths are wearing out. Can national unity still be achieved by appealing to French history as a long march to republicanism, the solution designed to overcome intense social conflict by uniting individuals as citizens in a republican society? Has republicanism become too closely associated with nationalism? Or can republicanism become something other than a myth, founded on another finality besides the unspoken rewriting of its cultural past? Such questions could not be posed during the nineteenth century, so long as the outcome of the struggle to impose republicanism was still uncertain.

That political struggle took place symbolically as well, through the diffusion of books, in the development of educational curricula and in forms of public commemoration. In the case of Voltaire, some thirty-two editions representing 1 million volumes were published between 1830 and 1848. Later in the century the Moland edition of Voltaire's complete works appeared between 1877 and 1885, the time of the centennial of the Revolution. A less scholarly 1,000-page edition was also prepared for the centennial celebration. The Catholic, monarchical right had always viewed this increased availability of Voltaire's text with alarm. With one quarter of the popular centennial edition given over to texts on religion, Mgr Dupanloup, the firebrand anti-Voltairean Bishop of Orléans, decried the edition, claiming that it would empty the churches and contribute to fomenting social unrest. But Voltaire could be read selectively and strategically, in support of either progressive or conservative positions. His widespread popularisation throughout the nineteenth century reflected the attempt to transform France's past into a shared cultural heritage. Schools and universities played a crucial role in making that heritage accessible to a greater number of citizens. The past became a national narrative, designed to bridge conflicts by inculcating moral and civic values – both religious and republican – that remained socially conservative.

A new discipline in nineteenth-century curricula, the teaching of history became that place where the past was conserved and where cultural memory was created and maintained, sometimes at the cost of being re-written. Literature was pressed into service in this enterprise, as the great texts of the past were taught as examples of a national heritage. An entire apparatus of anthologies and literary histories had to be produced to teach the new national history, forms of instructional texts that mediated access to the literary text and thus made it easier to promote certain values and marginalise others. Voltaire fared far better than other eighteenth-century writers in these anthologies and literary histories, but he received much less space than did such writers of the 'great century' as Corneille, Fénelon, and Bossuet. The publishing house Hachette began bringing out its 'Great French Writers' series in 1887, but only in 1896 did the national education ministry suggest that the term 'classic' may be used to refer to any other than seventeenth-century writers. After 1880, the education reforms put through by Jules Ferry contributed to secularising education, and as a result Voltaire occupied a much more prominent place in the curriculum and state examinations. Gustave Lanson's work in the late nineteenth century assured Voltaire's entry into scholarly sanctioned research topics, an incorporation into the academy guaranteed by the 1905 law officially separating Church and state. But once again, the crucial question is which Voltaire, the writer of brilliantly crafted verse or the *engagé* polemicist? Ironically, either Voltaire could be brought into the national pantheon. Eugène Geruzez, author of several uninspired nineteenth-century literary histories, observed that in his poetry, 'Voltaire . . . sums up and improves upon all the qualities of French *esprit*: naturalness, clarity, witticisms, finesse, and good sense' ('Voltaire . . . résume et embellit toutes les qualités de l'esprit français: le naturel, la netteté, la saillie, la finesse et le bon sens').[3] A century and a half later, a website maintained by the French Ministry of Foreign Affairs calls Voltaire 'one of the great symbols of our cultural memory, along with the Louvre and the *Marseillaise* . . . Among national writers he is probably the one who best defines French identity' ('un des grands symboles de notre mémoire culturelle, au même titre que le Louvre ou *La Marseillaise* . . . Il est sans doute parmi les écrivains nationaux celui qui définit au mieux l'identité française').[4]

No writer was as vigorously commemorated during the nineteenth century as Voltaire. A form of cultural memory, commemoration involves forgetting as well as remembering, as the story of Voltaire's statues suggests. The Houdon and Jean-Baptiste Pigalle sculptures having never received widespread public display in Paris, a campaign was launched in 1867 by the anti-clerical daily *Le Siècle* to erect an open-air statue of the writer, who had been linked once again to national imperatives in 1864, when his heart had been presented to Emperor Louis-Napoléon on behalf of the nation. The Emperor had already begun this symbolic linkage in 1852, with an architectural project joining the Louvre and the Tuileries and that included Voltaire among the eighty-six statues of France's great. Later, on the rebuilt Hôtel de Ville, burnt during the Commune uprising of 1871, a statue of Voltaire would be placed next to one of Molière, thereby joining two centuries that many political scripts had placed into opposition. The open-air statue of Voltaire was finally installed in 1870, a week after the Prussian army declared a state of siege on Paris (see fig. 6). After the establishment of the Third Republic, the statue was still too strongly associated with Louis-Napoléon and the Second Empire. Removed from its public location in the Place Voltaire (now renamed the Place Léon-Blum) in the eleventh arrondissement, then a militant, working-class area of Paris, it was reinstalled in the Rue Monge, a quiet academic neighbourhood in the bourgeois fifth arrondissement. Voltaire was inscribed on the urban toponymy, but in a way that amounted symbolically to a contained depoliticisation.

The Third Republic was only eight years old in 1878 on the eve of the centennial of the French Revolution. The period was marked by fierce political and ideological battles, whose outcome involved control of the state, the role of education and the Church, and resolution of 'the social question', that is, achieving economic progress despite the condition of the working classes. The Universal Exhibition was held in the same year, designed to demonstrate France's revival from the Franco-Prussian wars of 1870 and the bloody civil strife of the Commune by displaying advances in the area of technology, as well as French colonial expansion. Commemorations of Voltaire's death were planned in 1878 throughout the nation and indeed

Fig. 6 F. T. Lix, *The Guillotine Burned in Front of the Town Hall of the Eleventh Arrondissement*, woodblock engraving published in *L'Illustration*, 15 April 1871 (private collection)

beyond, and staunchly anti-Voltairean events also took place, with expiation masses and the placing of wreaths at the statue of Joan of Arc. A century later, in 1978, bicentennial commemoration took the more restrained form of conferences organised by scholarly specialists, with special emphasis accorded to Voltaire the champion of tolerance and human rights. The aim, it would seem, was to rescue him from the fate of personifying witty irreverence to which much of twentieth-century literary history had consigned him.

Before Émile Zola and his 'J'accuse' launched against anti-Semitism in the nineteenth century, or Jean-Paul Sartre's unflagging social activism in the twentieth, Voltaire first characterised the modern intellectual. Exasperated by Voltaire's tenacious criticism, Louis XV was supposed to have asked, 'Can't that man be kept quiet?' Two centuries later, when deciding how to deal with Jean-Paul Sartre and his association with a public manifesto denouncing the French government's Algeria policy, Charles de Gaulle remarked, 'let the intellectuals do what they want . . . one doesn't arrest Voltaire'. The modern intellectual has consistently been defined through reference to Voltaire, be it to embrace that legacy, to resist it or to bemoan its eclipse. Thus Paul Valéry, in a speech given at the Sorbonne in late 1944 following the liberation of Paris, praised Voltaire's campaign to denounce 'crimes against humanity' and his ability to remake his century 'with the sole power of the pen, by *esprit* alone'. Yet Valéry also asked in a more sombrely historical sense whether the Voltaires of the present were destined to fail to realise their legacy in 1944, at a time when Voltaire's name had been recently invoked to promote anti-Semitism and when victims of *l'Infâme* numbered not a handful but in the millions. A half-century later, 'Voltaire' still marks the space of a problematic ethical imperative: 'Can one still ask the question, "What is tolerance?" as Voltaire did in the first sentence of his article on the subject in the *Dictionnaire philosophique*? How would this article be written today? Who would write it, with and without Voltaire?'[5] Voltaire can no longer be used as he was in the nineteenth century by partisans of one fundamentalism or another. We cannot afford to forget Voltaire, or indeed the past in general. As Jean-Marie Goulemot has cautioned, commemorative memory should not erase the antagonisms that define the cultural field, producing the illusory image of a unified cultural past.[6] Instead critical commemoration must involve a reflection upon how Voltaire, and the past in general, are introduced in and through the institutions and the discourses that shape the cultural community.

NOTES

1. OCV, vol.30C, p.222.
2. Quoted in C. Thomas, *Le Mythe du XVIIIe siècle au XIXe siècle, 1830–1860* (Paris: Champion, 2003), pp.69–77.
3. Quoted in S. Bird, *Reinventing Voltaire: The Politics of Commemoration in Nineteenth-Century France*, SVEC, 2000:09, p.171.
4. See www.adpf.asso.fr/adpf-publi/folio/voltaire/voltaire01.html.
5. J. Derrida, in G. Borradori, *Philosophy in a Time of Terror: Dialogues with Jürgen Habermas and Jacques Derrida* (Chicago, IL: University of Chicago Press, 2003), p.125.
6. See J.-M. Goulemot, *Adieu les philosophes: Que reste-t-il des Lumières?* (Paris: Seuil, 2001).

FURTHER READING

Translations into English

Candide and Other Stories, trans. R. Pearson, Oxford World's Classics (Oxford University Press, 1990; new edition, 2006).

Letters Concerning the English Nation, ed. N. Cronk, Oxford World's Classics (Oxford University Press, 1994; revised, 2005) [not a translation, but the 1733 English edition which preceded the publication of the *Lettres philosophiques*].

Micromégas and Other Short Fictions, trans. T. Cuffe, Penguin Classics (London: Penguin, 2002).

Philosophical Dictionary, trans. T. Besterman, Penguin Classics (London: Penguin, 1972).

Political Writings, trans. D. Williams, Cambridge Texts in the History of Political Thought (Cambridge University Press, 1994).

Select Letters of Voltaire, trans. T. Besterman (London: Nelson, 1963).

Treatise on Tolerance and Other Writings, trans. S. Harvey and B. Masters, Cambridge Texts in the History of Political Thought (Cambridge University Press, 2000).

Studies in English

Aldridge, A. O., *Voltaire and the Century of Light* (Princeton University Press, 1975).

Barber, W. H., *Leibniz in France from Arnauld to Voltaire: A Study in French Reactions to Leibnizianism, 1670–1760* (Oxford: Clarendon Press, 1955).

'Voltaire and Quakerism: Enlightenment and the Inner Light', *SVEC*, 24 (1963), 81–109.

'Voltaire at Cirey: Art and Thought', in *Studies in Eighteenth-Century French Literature Presented to Robert Niklaus*, ed. J. H. Fox, M. H. Waddicor and D. A. Watts (University of Exeter, 1975), pp.1–13.

'Voltaire and Samuel Clarke', *SVEC*, 179 (1979), 47–61.

'Voltaire: Art, Thought, and Action', *Modern Language Review*, 88 (1993), xxv–xxxvi.

Besterman, T., *Voltaire* (Oxford: Blackwell, 1969).

Bien, D. D., *The Calas Affair* (Princeton University Press, 1960).

Bird, S., *Reinventing Voltaire: The Politics of Commemoration in Nineteenth-Century France*, *SVEC*, 2000:09.

Bottiglia, W. F., *Voltaire's 'Candide': Analysis of a Classic*, *SVEC*, 7 (1959).

Brewer, D., *The Enlightenment Past: Reconstructing Eighteenth-Century French Thought* (Cambridge University Press, 2008).
Brumfitt, J. H., *Voltaire Historian* (Oxford University Press, 1958).
Conlon, P. M., *Voltaire's Literary Career from 1728 to 1750*, SVEC, 14 (1961).
Cronk, N., 'The Epicurean Spirit: Champagne and the Defence of Poetry in Voltaire's *Le Mondain*', SVEC, 371 (1999), 53–80.
'Voltaire, Lucian, and the Philosophical Traveller', in *L'Invitation au voyage: Studies in Honour of Peter France*, ed. J. Renwick (Oxford: Voltaire Foundation, 2000), pp. 75–84.
'The *Letters Concerning the English Nation* as an English Work: Reconsidering the Harcourt Brown Thesis', SVEC, 2001:10, 226–39.
'Inventing Voltaire', in *The Eighteenth Century Now: Boundaries and Perspectives*, ed. J. Mallinson, SVEC, 2005:10, 13–23.
Davidson, I., *Voltaire in Exile* (London: Atlantic, 2004).
Dawson, D., *Voltaire's Correspondence: An Epistolary Novel* (New York: Peter Lang, 1994).
De Beer, G., and A. -M. Rousseau, *Voltaire's British Visitors*, SVEC, 49 (1967).
Fargher, R., 'The Retreat from Voltairianism, 1800–1815', in *The French Mind: Studies in Honour of Gustave Rudler*, ed. W. Moore, R. Sutherland and E. Starkie (Oxford: Clarendon Press, 1952), pp.220–37.
Gay, P., *Voltaire's Politics: The Poet as Realist*, 2nd edn (New Haven, CT: Yale University Press, 1988) [first edn 1959].
Gossman, L., 'Voltaire's Heavenly City', *Eighteenth-Century Studies*, 3 (1969–1970), 67–82.
Goulbourne, R., *Voltaire Comic Dramatist*, SVEC, 2006:03.
Gray, J., *Voltaire: Voltaire and Enlightenment* (London: Phoenix, 1998).
Guiragossian, D., *Voltaire's 'Facéties'* (Geneva: Droz, 1963).
Howells, R., *Disabled Powers: A Reading of Voltaire's 'Contes'* (Amsterdam: Rodopi, 1993).
Israel, J. I., *Enlightenment Contested: Philosophy, Modernity, and the Emancipation of Man, 1670–1752* (Oxford University Press, 2006) [chapter 29 treats 'Voltaire's Enlightenment'].
James, E. D., 'Voltaire on the Nature of the Soul', *French Studies*, 32 (1978), 20–33.
'Voltaire and Malebranche: from Sensationalism to "tout en Dieu"', *Modern Language Review*, 75 (1980), 282–90.
'Voltaire and the *Ethics* of Spinoza', SVEC, 228 (1984), 67–87.
'Voltaire on Free Will', SVEC, 249 (1987), 1–18.
Lee, J. P., 'The Unexamined Premise: Voltaire, John Lockman and the Myth of the *English Letters*', SVEC, 2001:10, 240–70.
'The Apocryphal Voltaire: Problems in the Voltairean Canon', in *The Enterprise of Enlightenment: A Tribute to David Williams from his Friends*, ed. T. Pratt and D. McCallam (Berne, 2004), pp.265–73.
Leigh, J., *Voltaire: A Sense of History*, SVEC, 2004:05.
Mason, H., *Pierre Bayle and Voltaire* (Oxford University Press, 1963).
Voltaire: A Biography (London: Granada, 1981).
Mylne, V., 'Literary Techniques and Methods in Voltaire's *Contes Philosophiques*', SVEC, 57 (1967), 1055–80.

Pearson, R., *The Fables of Reason: A Study of Voltaire's 'Contes Philosophiques'* (Oxford: Clarendon Press, 1993).

Voltaire Almighty: A Life in the Pursuit of Freedom (London: Bloomsbury, 2005).

Renwick, J., *Marmontel, Voltaire and the Bélisaire Affair (1767)*, SVEC, 121 (1974).

Ridgway, R. S., *Voltaire and Sensibility* (Montreal: McGill-Queen's University Press, 1975).

Schwarzbach, B. E., *Voltaire's Old Testament Criticism* (Geneva: Droz, 1971).

Spitzer, L., 'Explication de Texte Applied to Voltaire', in *A Method of Interpreting Literature* (Northampton, MA: Smith College, 1949), pp.64–101.

Stewart, P., 'Holding the Mirror up to Fiction: Generic Parody in *Candide*', *French Studies*, 33 (1979), 411–19.

Taylor, S. S. B., 'Voltaire's Humour', SVEC, 179 (1979), 101–16.

Todd, C., *Voltaire: Dictionnaire philosophique* (London: Grant & Cutler, 1980).

Undank, J., 'The Status of Fiction in Voltaire's *Contes*', *Degré second*, 6 (1982), 65–88.

Wade, I. O., *Voltaire and 'Candide': A Study in the Fusion of History, Art, and Philosophy* (Princeton University Press, 1959).

Weightman, J. G., 'The Quality of *Candide*', in *Essays Presented to C. M. Girdlestone*, ed. E. T. Dubois *et al.* (Newcastle-upon-Tyne: King's College, University of Durham, 1960), pp.335–47.

Williams, D., *Voltaire: Literary Critic*, SVEC, 48 (1966).

Voltaire: Candide (London: Grant & Cutler, 1997).

Studies in languages other than English

Apgar, G., ' "Sage comme une image": trois siècles d'iconographie voltairienne', *Nouvelles de l'estampe*, 135 (1994), 4–44.

Artigas-Menant, G., *Du secret des clandestins à la propagande voltairienne* (Paris: Champion, 2001).

Barr, M.-M. H., *A Bibliography of Writings on Voltaire: 1825–1925* (New York: Institute of French Studies, 1929).

Quarante années d'études voltairiennes: Bibliographie analytique des livres et articles sur Voltaire, 1926–1965 (Paris: Armand Colin, 1968).

Belaval, Y., 'L'esprit de Voltaire', SVEC, 24 (1963), 139–54.

Bessire, F., *La Bible dans la correspondance de Voltaire*, SVEC, 367 (1999).

Bibliothèque de Voltaire: Catalogue des livres (Moscow, Leningrad: Academy of Sciences of USSR, 1961).

Billaz, A., *Les Écrivains romantiques et Voltaire: Essai sur Voltaire et le romantisme en France, 1795–1830* (Paris: Champion, 1974).

Brockmeier, P., R. Desné and J. Voss (eds), *Voltaire und Deutschland* (Stuttgart: J. B. Metzler, 1979).

Cambou, P., *Le Traitement voltairien du conte* (Paris: Champion, 2000).

Cotoni, M.-H., *L'Exégèse du Nouveau Testament dans la philosophie française du dix-huitième siècle*, SVEC, 220 (1984).

Cronk, N. (ed.), *Études sur le 'Traité sur la tolérance' de Voltaire* (Oxford, Voltaire Foundation, 2000).

(ed., with Christiane Mervaud) *Les Notes de Voltaire: Une écriture polyphonique*, SVEC, 2003:03.

De Gandt, F. (ed.), *Cirey dans la vie intellectuelle: La réception de Newton en France*, SVEC, 2001:11.

Delattre, A., *Voltaire l'impétueux* (Paris: Mercure de France, 1957).

Deloffre, F., *Genèse de 'Candide': Étude de la création des personnages et de l'élaboration du roman*, SVEC, 2006:06.

Delon, M., and C. Seth (eds), *Voltaire en Europe: Hommage à Christiane Mervaud* (Oxford: Voltaire Foundation, 2000).

Diaz, F., *Voltaire storico* (Turin: Einaudi, 1958).

Dictionnaire général de Voltaire, ed. R. Trousson and J. Vercruysse (Paris: Champion, 2003).

Ferret, O., *La Fureur de nuire: Échanges pamphlétaires entre philosophes et antiphilosophes (1750–1770)*, SVEC, 2007:03.

Fontius, M., *Voltaire in Berlin* (Berlin: Rütten & Loening, 1966).

Ginzburg, Carlo, 'Tolleranza e commercio: Auerbach legge Voltaire', *Quaderni storici*, 109 (2002), 259–83.

Goldzink, J., *Voltaire: La légende de Saint Arouet* (Paris: Gallimard, 1989).

Goulemot, J.-M., and E. Walter, 'Les centenaires de Voltaire et de Rousseau', in *Les Lieux de mémoire*, vol.1 (Paris: Gallimard, 1984), pp.381–420.

Haroche-Bouzinac, G., *Voltaire dans ses lettres de jeunesse (1711–1733): La formation d'un épistolier au XVIIIᵉ siècle* (Paris: Klincksieck, 1992).

Inventaire Voltaire, ed. J. Goulemot, A. Magnan and D. Masseau (Paris: Gallimard, 1995).

Iotti, G., *Virtù e identità nella tragedia di Voltaire* (Paris: Champion, 1995).
   'Voltaire et l'histoire par la fiction', *Rivista di letterature moderne e comparate*, 55 (2002), 149–62.

Kölving, U., and C. Mervaud, *Voltaire et ses combats*, 2 vols (Oxford: Voltaire Foundation, 1997).

Magnan, A., 'Dossier en Prusse (1750–1753)', SVEC, 144 (1986).
   Voltaire: Candide ou l'Optimisme (Paris: Presses Universitaires de France, 1987).

Maiello, G., *Voltaire, narratore fantastico* (Naples: Liguori, 1985).

Martin-Haag, É., *Voltaire: Du cartésianisme aux Lumières* (Paris: Vrin, 2002).

Menant, S., *L'Esthétique de Voltaire* (Paris: SEDES, 1995).

Mervaud, C., *Voltaire et Frédéric II: Une dramaturgie des Lumières*, SVEC, 234 (1985).
   Le 'Dictionnaire philosophique' de Voltaire (Oxford: Voltaire Foundation, 1994).
   Voltaire à table (Paris: Desjonquères, 1998).
   Bestiaires de Voltaire, SVEC, 2006:06.

Mervaud, C., and S. Menant (eds), *Le Siècle de Voltaire: Hommage à René Pomeau*, 2 vols (Oxford: Voltaire Foundation, 1987).

Milza, P., *Voltaire* (Paris: Perrin, 2007).

Moureaux, J.-M., 'Voltaire apôtre: de la parodie au mimétisme', *Poétique*, 66 (1986), 159–77.
   'Race et altérité dans l'anthropologie voltairienne', in *L'Idée de 'race' dans les sciences humaines et la littérature (XVIIIᵉ–XIXᵉ siècles)*, ed. S. Moussa (Paris: L'Harmattan, 2003), pp.41–53.

Naves, R., *Le Goût de Voltaire* (Paris: Garnier, 1937).
   Voltaire: L'homme et l'œuvre. (Paris: Boivin, 1942).

Orlando, F., *Illuminismo, barocco e retorica freudiana* (Turin: Einaudi, 1997).

Pomeau, R., *La Religion de Voltaire*, new edn (Paris: Nizet, 1969) [first edn 1956].

Pomeau, R., *et al.*, *Voltaire en son temps*, new edn, 2 vols (Paris: Fayard, 1995).

Porset, C., 'La "philosophie" de Voltaire', *Europe*, 781 (1994), 53–62.

Renwick, J., *Voltaire et Morangiés 1772–1773*, SVEC, 202 (1982).

Rousseau, A.-M., *Voltaire et l'Angleterre*, 3 vols, SVEC, 145–7 (1976).

Sareil, J., *Essai sur 'Candide'* (Geneva: Droz, 1967).

Voltaire et les grands (Geneva: Droz, 1978).

'Voltaire polémiste ou l'art dans la mauvaise foi', *Dix-Huitième Siècle*, 15 (1983), 343–56.

Spear, F. A., *Bibliographie analytique des écrits relatifs à Voltaire: 1966–1990* (Oxford: Voltaire Foundation, 1992).

Spitzer, L., 'Quelques interprétations de Voltaire', in *Études de style*, ed. J. Starobinski (Paris: Gallimard, 1970), pp.336–66 ['Einige Voltaire-Interpretationen', first published 1931].

Starobinski, J., 'Le fusil à deux coups de Voltaire', *Revue de métaphysique et de morale*, 71 (1966), 277–91; reprinted in *Le Remède dans le mal* (Paris: Gallimard, 1989), pp.144–63.

'Sur le style philosophique de *Candide*', *Comparative Literature*, 28 (1976), 193–200; reprinted in *Le Remède dans le mal* (Paris: Gallimard, 1989), pp.123–44.

'*Candide* et la question de l'autorité', in *Essays on the Age of Enlightenment in honor of Ira O. Wade*, ed. J. Macary (Geneva: Droz, 1977), pp.305–12.

'Voltaire et le malheur des hommes', *Genève-Lettres*, 6 (1978), 13–32.

Thomas, C., *Le Mythe du XVIIIe siècle au XIXe siècle, 1830–1860* (Paris: Champion, 2003).

Trousson, R., *Visages de Voltaire (XVIIIe–XIXe siècles)* (Paris: Champion, 2001).

Van den Heuvel, J., *Voltaire dans ses contes* (Paris: Armand Colin, 1967).

Vercruysse, J., *Voltaire et la Hollande*, SVEC, 46 (1966).

INDEX

Cambridge Companions to ...

AUTHORS

Edward Albee edited by Stephen J. Bottoms

Margaret Atwood edited by Coral Ann Howells

W. H. Auden edited by Stan Smith

Jane Austen edited by Edward Copeland and Juliet McMaster

Beckett edited by John Pilling

Aphra Behn edited by Derek Hughes and Janet Todd

Walter Benjamin edited by David S. Ferris

William Blake edited by Morris Eaves

Brecht edited by Peter Thomson and Glendyr Sacks (second edition)

The Brontës edited by Heather Glen

Frances Burney edited by Peter Sabor

Byron edited by Drummond Bone

Albert Camus edited by Edward J. Hughes

Willa Cather edited by Marilee Lindemann

Cervantes edited by Anthony J. Cascardi

Chaucer, second edition edited by Piero Boitani and Jill Mann

Chekhov edited by Vera Gottlieb and Paul Allain

Kate Chopin edited by Janet Beer

Coleridge edited by Lucy Newlyn

Wilkie Collins edited by Jenny Bourne Taylor

Joseph Conrad edited by J. H. Stape

Dante edited by Rachel Jacoff (second edition)

Don DeLillo edited by John N. Duvall

Charles Dickens edited by John O. Jordan

Emily Dickinson edited by Wendy Martin

John Donne edited by Achsah Guibbory

Dostoevskii edited by W. J. Leatherbarrow

Theodore Dreiser edited by Leonard Cassuto and Claire Virginia Eby

John Dryden edited by Steven N. Zwicker

W. E. B. Du Bois edited by Shamoon Zamir

George Eliot edited by George Levine

T. S. Eliot edited by A. David Moody

Ralph Ellison edited by Ross Posnock

Ralph Waldo Emerson edited by Joel Porte and Saundra Morris

William Faulkner edited by Philip M. Weinstein

Henry Fielding edited by Claude Rawson

F. Scott Fitzgerald edited by Ruth Prigozy

Flaubert edited by Timothy Unwin

E. M. Forster edited by David Bradshaw

Benjamin Franklin edited by Carla Mulford

Brian Friel edited by Anthony Roche

Robert Frost edited by Robert Faggen

Elizabeth Gaskell edited by Jill L. Matus

Goethe edited by Lesley Sharpe

Thomas Hardy edited by Dale Kramer

David Hare edited by Richard Boon

Nathaniel Hawthorne edited by Richard Millington

Ernest Hemingway edited by Scott Donaldson

Homer edited by Robert Fowler

Ibsen edited by James McFarlane

Henry James edited by Jonathan Freedman

Samuel Johnson edited by Greg Clingham

Ben Jonson edited by Richard Harp and Stanley Stewart

James Joyce edited by Derek Attridge (second edition)

Kafka edited by Julian Preece

Keats edited by Susan J. Wolfson

Lacan edited by Jean-Michel Rabaté

D. H. Lawrence edited by Anne Fernihough

Primo Levi edited by Robert Gordon

Lucretius edited by Stuart Gillespie and Philip Hardie

David Mamet edited by Christopher Bigsby

Thomas Mann edited by Ritchie Robertson

Christopher Marlowe edited by Patrick Cheney

Herman Melville edited by Robert S. Levine

Arthur Miller edited by Christopher Bigsby

Milton edited by Dennis Danielson (second edition)

Molière edited by David Bradby and Andrew Calder

Toni Morrison edited by Justine Tally

Nabokov edited by Julian W. Connolly

Eugene O'Neill edited by Michael Manheim

George Orwell edited by John Rodden

Ovid edited by Philip Hardie

Harold Pinter edited by Peter Raby

Sylvia Plath edited by Jo Gill

Edgar Allan Poe edited by Kevin J. Hayes

TOPICS